The **Intext** Series in PSYCHOLOGICAL ASSESSMENT

Series Editor: HAROLD J. VETTER
Loyola University of New Orleans

Individual Mental Testing

Part I   History and Theories

Individual Mental Testing

Part I   History and Theories

ALLEN J. EDWARDS
University of Missouri at Columbia

INTEXT EDUCATIONAL PUBLISHERS
College Division of Intext
Scranton   San Francisco   Toronto   London

ISBN 0-7002-2358-4

Library of Congress Catalog Card Number 77-166124

Copyright ©, 1971, International Textbook Company

Preface

The use of individual tests to estimate the ability of children and adults has continued and expanded since the publication of the 1905 Binet-Simon Scale. Information gained about the individual through such measures has played an essential correlative role in decision making in all kinds of academic and clinical settings. In recent years, questions about such tests and their use have increased; hence the psychometrician must possess more complete knowledge than traditional training in administration and scoring has provided.

The series of three books (of which this is the first) is intended to assist in the normal training of psychometrists, with added roles as well. This first of these volumes discusses the history of the intelligence-testing movement and the events leading to our current measures, assumptions, and score expressions. An individual-historical approach is used, allowing for the inclusion of theoretical concepts and models where relevant. Such knowledge helps the psychometrist by providing the basis for relating present strengths and limitations of tests to their development. Similarities and dissimilarities among tests are seen more easily when the psychometrist has such a background. Although it is easy to become involved in the immediate test and test situation, this diversion limits most efficient use of a scale.

The author wishes to thank the writers and publishers who have cooperated so generously in releasing materials for quotation. To the editors associated with this series, Hal Vetter and John L. Dugan, Jr., appreciation is extended as well. Mrs. Mary Wiles and Miss Vicki Prather performed yeoman duties in obtaining clearances and in other tasks essential to successful completion. Most of all, my wife has given moral support and has worked through the several drafts in a manner well beyond the call of duty. To all of these persons, whatever strengths the book possesses are largely due.

A.J.E.

June, 1971

Contents

Individual Mental Testing

Part I History and Theories

1

What is "Intelligence"?

Probably no phenomenon in human society creates the interest that is generated over intelligence. Though what the term means might vary from person to person, there is common agreement that we observe the effects of intelligence in ourselves and others. Beyond this general point, there is inconsistency. On the one hand, there is rather common acceptance that some trait of intelligence exists and has its effects on behavior. On the other hand, there is disagreement about attempts to measure such a trait.

Most educators consider it impractical if not impossible to teach youngsters (that is, to have them learn materials of a certain level of complexity) unless the children have reached a certain level of intelligence. There is an assumption, then, of a positive relationship between intellectual development and attainment of success in schools. Consistently with this assumed relationship, some youngsters are observed to learn more quickly and efficiently than others; and educators operate on the basis that this difference is due, in some measure, to differences in intelligence. In addition, the inference is drawn that, since such differences exist, they are measurable. By measuring the intellectual abilities of pupils, fairly accurate predictions may be made about learning rates and special curricular needs. A basic assumption is made in this argument: There are differential intellectual growth rates in children, these are directly correlated with academic achievement, and differences between children in intellectual growth may be measured and quantified.

Such assumptions are based upon test scores. The *source* of such intellectual differences as are observed and measured by tests remains a matter of some debate.

In recent years, increasing emphasis has been placed on environmental determinants of intellectual differences. In this view, a child reared in a relatively impoverished background will reflect deficiencies in behaviors tested by intelligence measures. The argument may be presented that such a child scores low on the test because of poor environment, not because of low intelligence *per se*. By contrast, a child raised in a rich experiential background will appear much brighter on the intelligence test. The test must measure environmental differences, not true intellectual differences. Accordingly, the importance of environment is such that attempts to improve and expand experiences of children from relatively impoverished homes must begin, must be continued, and must be expanded. Most research results (e.g. Skeels, 1938; Skodak, 1939; Spitz, 1945; Bloom, 1964; Hunt, 1961; Strodtbeck, 1965) imply strongly that such changes must take place early in the life of the individual (beginning in the first year) and must be massive in effect, including all members of the family and all aspects of the home. That environmental manipulation can have large behavioral effects has been demonstrated in several animal studies (e.g. Rosenzweig, 1964; Melzack, 1964; Krech, 1969), and it would seem reasonable that at least some such effects may be found in humans. Implicit within the argument is the view that environmental effects are reflected in the content and subsequent scores of so-called intelligence tests. If the test scores are thus reflective, the school program and curriculum must equally reflect such environmental bias. Experiential change should bring change in scores and subsequent increases in school achievement.

So far, the discussion of intelligence and its measurement has been restricted to the academic setting. Formal learning situations, however, are not the only ones where the concept is important. The layman, through his conversation, implies the importance of intelligence and its effects on the ability of the individual to perform adequately both socially and vocationally. It is not unusual to hear such terms as "bright," "dumbbell," "genius," "stupid," "sharp," and "idiotic" in everyday speech.

Nor is the mundane world of daily conversation the only nonschool setting where intelligence assumes importance. Traditionally, ability level influences occupations sought and successfully held (Super and Crites, 1962). The surveys of ability levels in various occupational groups indicate that there is overlap in ability for members of selected occupations (see, for example, Stewart, 1947). Ability, as such, is not then the sole determiner of the job selected by the individual. Nevertheless, marked differences in average measured ability are found between occupational groups.

Level of intelligence, at least to some minimum degree, even enters such specific and behaviorally important settings as counseling success. White (1956) maintains that sub-normal ability bars psychotherapy completely, and concludes there is doubt that even dull-normal ability persons with emotional upsets are apt clients for therapeutic setting. In I.Q. terms, probably those with I.Q.'s below 90 will be intellectually too limited for the counseling relationship to be beneficial. With children, Kanner (1955) points to the use of high ability by paranoid patients to control verbally-threatening aspects of the environment. There is evidence to indicate that higher level of intelligence is one factor leading to continuation in therapy beyond a few preliminary sessions (Streper and Wiener, 1965).

In the contexts discussed, various expressions of intelligence are observed, and the problem becomes one of describing systematically the degrees of relationship between measures and behaviors. Such an approach will disclose deficiencies and limitations in test scores and thereby clarify strengths. The history of intelligence testing has to a large degree followed such a course.

In very recent years, however, a more strident note has recurred with increasing intensity. Many persons have expressed increasing doubt about the validity of the measures. Such a viewpoint taken to an extreme would maintain that there are no intellectual differences of any consequence from one person to another. Under appropriate circumstances, all children will act and be intelligent enough to achieve at any reasonable task. Children from impoverished backgrounds perform poorly in school, yet adapt well in their environments. The discrepancy in performance between settings must be due to some lack in the tests and the school curriculum, not to intellectual deficiency in the child. There is consequent pressure for schools to drop the use of any such tests. The reason for removing intelligence test scores from classroom data is the belief that scores bias teacher judgments of a child and lead to educational expectations by both teacher and child which produce lowered achievement. With the publication of studies concerning the so-called "self-fulfilling prophecy" (see Rosenthal and Jacobson, 1968), the movement to abolish intelligence testing has acquired added impetus. The popular press has reflected the arguments against tests and has apparently increased the acceptance of the criticism, since both New York City and Los Angeles public schools have discontinued certain aspects of intelligence-testing programs. Though conclusions drawn about the self-fulfilling prophecy are doubtful from data actually available (Thorndike, 1968), the defenses of intelligence testing have been publicized only within the limited press of professional societies and have had little influence, evidently, on the attitude of the general public. In any event, those who advocate abolishing tests apparently presume that students will be able to perform better in school if ability scores are not available to teachers or, more precisely, if expectations of teachers are set at a higher level than a given ability score would predict.

The purpose of all this discussion is to indicate some features that are significant to a construct called *intelligence*. For many, this construct is a practical necessity and not the whim of a few persons in the "testing business." The importance of the question is undoubted, regardless of the position taken. The accuracy and efficiency of measurement, however, are not well established. This text takes the position that intelligence tests offer sources of data for decision-making too important to ignore. Though test scores have limitations which must be recognized and included in decisions, they remain superior to subjective efforts, which induce attitudinal sets at variance with behavioral realities.

The Nature of the Problem

Regardless of what it measures or of its applicability, intelligence is a concept that is widely used. The concept implies that we have answers to two crucial questions: (a) What is intelligence? and (b) How do we measure intelligence? From the quantity of tests available, one might assume that both questions are answered. But the great quantity of tests raises another question: *If* we really know what intelligence is, why is it necessary to have so many different tests? The answer must lie in one of two directions. Either intelligence is much too complex to be measured by any one instrument, or else we do not know what intelligence is. Among psychologists, proponents may be found for either extreme, but the large majority probably would subscribe to both explanations at the same time. That is, most psychologists would say that our study of this phenomenon has shown it to be much more complex than the construct originally conceived, and they would agree that at the present time we do not "know" what intelligence is. As a result, we may need many instruments which measure certain things in common but also seem to measure somewhat different things. In this way, we may acquire a more accurate picture of the individual's general and specific abilities. There is, of course, an assumption that whatever measures of whatever qualities are achieved are systematically related to behaviors directly allowed by "intelligence."

There are, then, many tests available. Without exception, these are objective measures of something. The test constructor and publisher state that the test measures intelligence, either of a general nature or of some specific types. How true is such a statement? To answer this question, it is necessary to return to the first of the two crucial questions posed: What is intelligence?

This is not a new question. Answers have been sought in a variety of directions for many years. Particularly have persons tried to determine the quality of intelligence since it could lead to control (e.g., Galton, 1914). However, intelligence has proved an elusive trait; just as a worker believes he has identified its nature, exceptions occur.

Many behaviors which should result from the extent of intelligence possessed by the individual can be logically and systematically defined and described. How much of the trait is necessary to expression is not so described, nor can direct correlates be determined. Either intelligence is a myth, or it is of some nature that is not amenable to direct measurement at the present time. Included within the latter possibility are all the chemical-electrical-protein suggestions about the brain currently under investigation. Though rigorous answers are not possible yet, the construct is too important to ignore. Hence we must explore the problem without them.

Intelligence as a Construct

Since hard data are lacking on the true nature of intelligence, we must deal with it as a construct. To do so requires that we observe behaviors of individuals and make inferences about the type, or degree, or level of intelligence leading to the behavior. Whatever knowledge we gain about the construct is dependent on descriptions of behavior.

One problem in such a procedure lies in evaluating the adequacy of the construct. There are certain useful, though arbitrary, criteria which may be used.

1. *Consistency.* One means of assessing the acceptability of a construct is to determine the degree of agreement among observers, particularly among acknowledged experts. The content of this book reflects a set of statements about the nature and measurement of intelligence. Though the psychologists cited do not agree on the nature or the best means of measurement, they all implicitly reflect an acceptance of the construct itself. Such consistency does not prove the construct, but it provides a basis for agreeing that such a quality does exist though it can be expressed only in construct form.

2. *Congruent and concurrent relationships.* A construct assumes added validity if it can be demonstrated to be related to other constructs already accepted as valid. To achieve such a relationship requires having measures of the constructs, or an agreement among experts, again, about the

presumed relationships among constructs. Certainly, the more restricted and limited the construct, the less acceptance and use it will find. Yet the very criterion cited is circular, since only constructs showing relationships to other constructs achieve much merit and this limits the possibility of expansion of the constructional matrix.

3. *Quantification.* To some degree, quantification seems necessary for a construct to achieve acceptance. Only when quantified, for example, can the kinds of relationships cited above be found. There is less importance to the numerical system than to the fact that quantification allows computation of score limitations (reliabilities and measurement errors) and empirical relationships (primarily correlational). Given some estimate of limitations to the construct, the strengths of the construct may then be determined.

Taken singly or in combination, the three above criteria for evaluating a construct are unimpressive. Left only to these criteria, most of our most usable constructs (including intelligence) would be meretricious. Some other criterion must be available in combination with the above three to give merit to the use of the construct.

4. *Prediction.* This latter condition, the cement that holds all the others together to give strength to constructs, is utility for prediction. Ultimately, only those constructs which predict human behavior best will be retained. And the best predictors have been those utilizing the other three criteria as an undergirding for predictive efficiency. No matter how logical, reasonable, convincing the construct, predictability is the ultimate criterion. The chief reason why intelligence has held such dominance in the field of constructs is that it is one of the best predictors of selected behaviors. We do not know *why*, we do not know whether some third quality other than the predictor-criterion relationship is responsible, we do not know whether we are measuring an imagined quality, but we do know from much experience that the construct "intelligence" meets the predictive criterion. For that reason, it is maintained and used.

The Purpose of This Book

This volume deals in part with proposed theories about the construct, and in part with a historical survey of efforts to determine and measure "intelligence." Theories assume importance because they state some general conditions which may be used to generate specific hypotheses. The nature of the theory of intelligence adopted by a man, then, will determine to some degree the means he will follow to evaluate expressions of intelligence. To understand the tests we use, it is helpful to understand the theory of the individual devising the test. Additionally, an historical perspective of the writings about intelligence will give us better understanding of our current knowledge and position.

In this book, several of the major theories of intelligence are surveyed, though some of them have not led to specific instruments for measurement. Perhaps in this survey we may achieve some reasonable answer to the question: What is intelligence?

References

Bloom, B., *Stability and Change in Human Characteristics*. New York: Wiley, 1964.

Galton, F., *Hereditary Genius: An Inquiry into Its Laws and Consequences*. New York: Macmillan, 1914.

Hunt, J. McV., *Intelligence and Experience*. New York: Ronald, 1961.

Kanner, L., *Child Psychiatry*. Springfield, Ill.: Charles C Thomas, 1955.

Krech, D., "The Chemistry of Learning," *SRIS Quarterly*, 1969, 2, no. 2, 1–5.

Melzack, R., "Influence of Early Experience on the Cue-Arousal Effects of Stimulation," in A. J. Edwards and J. F. Cawley (eds.), University of Kansas *Symposium, Physiological Determinates of Behavior: Implications for Mental Retardation*. Lawrence: University of Kansas Press, 1964.

Rosenthal, R., and Jacobson, Lenore, *Pygmalion in the Classroom: Teacher Expectation and Pupils' Intellectual Development*. New York: Holt, Rinehart and Winston, 1968.

Rosenzweig, M., "Effects of Heredity and Environment on Basic Chemistry, Brain Anatomy, and Learning Ability in the Rat," in A. J. Edwards and J. F. Cawley (eds.), University of Kansas *Symposium, Physiological Determinates of Behavior: Implications for Mental Retardation*. Lawrence: University of Kansas Press, 1964.

Skeels, H. J., "Mental Development of Children in Foster Homes," *Journal of Consulting Psychology*, 1938, 2, 33–43.

Skodak, Marie, "Children in Foster Homes: A Study of Mental Development," University of Iowa *Studies in Child Welfare*, 1939, 16, no. 1.

Spitz, R. A., "Hospitalism. An Inquiry into the Genesis of Psychiatric Conditions in Early Childhood," *Psychoanalytic Studies of Children*, 1945, 1, 53–74, 113–117.

Stewart, N., "A.G.C.T. Scores of Army Personnel Grouped by Occupations," *Occupations*, 1947, 26, 5–41.

Streper, D., and Wiener, D., *Dimensions of Psychotherapy*, Chicago: Aldine, 1965.

Strodtbeck, F. L., "The Hidden Curriculum in the Middle-Class Home," Chapter 4 in J. D. Krumboltz (ed.), *Learning and the Educational Process*. Chicago: Rand McNally, 1965.

Super, D. E., and Crites, J. O., *Appraising Vocational Fitness.* New York: Harper, 1962.

Thorndike, R. L., "Review of *Pygmalion in the Classroom.*" *American Educational Research Journal,* 1968, 5, 708–711.

White, R. H., *The Abnormal Personality.* New York: Ronald, 1956.

2

Alfred Binet: The Early Work
(1895-1905)*

At a time when most psychologists were using sensorimotor tasks to measure individual differences (Galton, 1894; 1907; 1914), interest in another direction of potential measurement was developing in France.

In 1892 Binet joined the staff of the psychological laboratory at the Sorbonne, and in 1894 became director. From this time until his death in 1911, he devoted his major efforts to the study of individual differences, the understanding of the nature of intelligence, and the development of scales to measure intellectual level. Regardless of one's agreement or disagreement with the assumptions of the Binet scales and the conclusions drawn by him from empirical work, he is the departure point of every major development in theories and measures of intelligence since 1895.

Individual Psychology

Though several articles already published contained the essence of the approach Binet was to emphasize (e.g., Binet, 1886; Binet, 1894; Binet and Henri 1894a; Binet and Henri, 1894b), the role of an article published under the title *"La Psychologie Individuelle"* (Binet and Henri, 1896) became the basis for explicit development of a method to measure expressions of intellectual competence. The article began with a review

*Though original sources and translations form a major part of this and the subsequent chapter, Joseph Peterson's *Early Conceptions and Tests of Intelligence* (1925) proved an invaluable source for organizational and suggestive purposes. I acknowledge a great debt to this text.—A. J. E.

of research and methods currently in vogue, and rejected these as emphasizing sensorimotor behavior for determining important individual differences. One of the consequences of using sensory data is the assumption that discrimination in this dimension reflects intellectual differences. Galton had been willing to make such an assumption, based upon his observations of severely deficient persons. Binet and Henri, also on the basis of empirical observation, concluded that the assumption is false. Their argument was that an individual may be slow in reaction time relative to discrete sensory stimulation, yet not be slow in other forms of behavior. Instead of the use of sensory tests that offer precision but may not be generalizable to other, more general forms of behavior, some other measurement basis is needed.

For this purpose, one must ask the question: What kinds of functions will most discriminate between two individuals in intellectual behavior? Sensorimotor functions probably will not do so, but complex mental functions certainly will do so. Admittedly, there are problems with such an approach. For one thing, the "complex processes" are not so available to measurement as are sensory reactions; but Binet and Henri believed that imprecision is negated by the great differences between individuals in such complex processes. Thus was made an assumption of crucial importance to determining intellectual differences, an assumption that still underlies most of our testing procedures. Are, in fact, differences in complex mental faculties so large *between* individuals that crude, gross measurements of their effects *adequately and accurately* reflect such differences? The assumption apparently has been accepted, at least in the sense that the methodological procedures and item content suggested by Binet and Henri have been used extensively.

There is an outgrowth of this assumption that is of considerable importance. If one is going to use some result of superior, complex mental functions to reflect individual differences intellectually, how many such functions are there? If there are many of these, which ones should be measured? This problem was avoided by Binet and Henri. At this point, they suggest that testing of *all* functions (even superior ones) in which individuals differ is not necessary. Instead, select several which are representative and significant of the differences between persons. They mention several possible functions (presented and discussed below); the basis for the ones chosen is not clear. Indeed, they recognize problems by advocating the need for substitutions, changes, and expansions in the suggested list. Essentially, then, the problem was to be met in a pragmatic fashion. Determine which functions best reflect the extent of individual differences by empirical trial-and-error. There is no model presented, no structure which will guide the efforts to determine the best possible combination. There is a strong hint here already of some combination of tests which reflect *general* ability without regard to the specific abilities contained in the total test.

Yet another problem pointed out by Binet and Henri concerned the individuals with whom such tests should appropriately be used. The "content" of complex mental functions would differ for persons of different backgrounds and intellectual level. They advocated then that different tests would be needed to reflect accurately and appropriately such differences. Either this must mean a battery of tests of different types and content to be used according to characteristics of the specific persons to be tested, or a variety of items ranging from simple to complex and reflecting a relatively large number of mental processes within the same test. The development of the scales which follows in the next decade reflects this latter viewpoint.

Specific suggestions are made as to functions which might be tested, and items reflecting each function. Whatever items reflecting these functions are used, they should be simple in nature, they say, easy to administer and take, and so objective that results among different examiners may be fairly compared. Some ten "mental functions" are suggested.

1. *Memory.* Binet and Henri had taken the position, in their 1896 article, that memory is a complex function, having expression in a large number of "partial memories." Indeed, work done by Charcot and others had demonstrated that memories of certain kinds were lost in cases of abnormality, while other types of memory were kept intact. Binet and Henri reasoned from this that memory function must have a number of reflections. Any test of memory function, then, must sample as many types of memories as possible.

Binet and Henri believed that a memory test reflected more than some ability for short-term retention. Such a test, they asserted, yields information of a more general nature. For one thing, the performance on a memory task gives information about the general nature of acquisition for the individual. In addition to this general acquisition feature, some more specific mental behaviors are reflected in memory test scores, Binet and Henri believed. One aspect of what a person remembers is what he chooses to allow to enter a storage mechanism. Certain stimuli will be screened out, and the person's memory storage reflects to some degree selective perception of stimuli. In this sense, what is demonstrated as output contains some degree of this stimulus selectivity. Binet and Henri reflected this position by assuming that an individual's memory store is affected by his voluntary concentration of attention. Perhaps as some subset of this concentration feature is the particular nature of memories present to the individual. Binet and Henri advocated that the person's tastes and tendencies are reflected in his particular and special memories.

As the individual functions with his vast store of memories, he tends to make errors. Even on a short term memory task, certain substitutions or omissions occur. Binet and Henri stated that the examiner may use the errors made as a basis for judging the general mental disposition of the examinee.

Above all, memory tests are a source of significant information about the power of comprehension of the individual. The general intellectual level of the person is reflected in this power of comprehension. The level of intellect must affect the memory function of the examinee. The lower the intellectual level of the examinee the less competent the memory function.

2. *Imagery.* A logical argument can be presented that mental content contains some clear and distinct images, at least as reported by the person experiencing them. Extending this logical argument, it would seem reasonable that the kinds, extent, and possible clarity of images is a function of intelligence. Some measurement of imagery would constitute one function of the complex mental faculties proposed for study by Binet and Henri. Now one is faced with a problem: What constitues an image, and what item content might require differential amounts and types of imagery? The attention afforded this matter by Binet and Henri is disappointing in some degree. Binet does however, return to this matter in a significant later study and concludes that imagery is a relatively insignificant function (Binet, 1903).

3. *Imagination.* Just as in the case of imagery, a logical argument may be offered that differences in imagination should accompany differences in other mental abilities. The quality of imagination, particularly, should differ among individuals of different intellectual levels. What constitutes imagination then becomes the issue. Binet and Henri apparently assumed that it was some unique, individual use of experience.

In this context, Binet and Henri propose tasks to sample two qualities of the imaginative function. The first of these would reflect imagination of an involuntary type and would use tasks such as the inkblot test. The purpose of such a task was not to draw inferences about the personality structure of the individual, but to reflect a type of mental content, not wholly under control of the person, which reflects one aspect of a complex mental faculty.

The second type of imagination, voluntary in nature, is called creative imagination by Binet and Henri. The quality of invention reflects this function at work, and they adovcated measurement by verbal tasks.

4. *Attention.* The factor of attention still engages the efforts of psychologists, and a large measure of the problem in its study was realized by Binet and Henri. They pointed out that the essential nature of attention, though widely studied, was unknown. But the importance of attention in intelligent behavior was too great to ignore. Its inclusion in

their article signifies that Binet and Henri considered it one of the mental faculties, rather than some motivational state dependent upon organismic and environmental conditions.

5. *Comprehension.* Binet and Henri state that this is a complex function, utilizing several forms of expression, and requires complex tasks for its manifestation. The authors' most usable tasks employ verbal behavior. They claimed that such tasks lead to the expression of individual differences, because they apparently tap some complex mental functions, either because of method or through their verbal nature or by a combination of both.

6. *Suggestibility.* Binet had early concluded that suggestibility was a trait which would differentiate intellectual level with some degree of accuracy. He believed, from his observations, that young children (and intellectually dull older ones) could be rather easily persuaded to take positions at variance with reality. Suggestibility is used here as a means of reflecting complex functions, and Binet conducted further experimentation on its behavior. So persistent is this belief that a suggestibility test is included in the scales developed later.

Binet and Henri point out that illusion should not be used. Instead, the task should be presented in such a way that the alternative chosen by the child, and reflecting his suggestible nature, really seems like a reasonable alternative to him.

7. *Aesthetic appreciation.* Seemingly, one of the behaviors which superior intelligence in man should allow is the development of an artistic expression and temperament. At least, throughout man's history there have been attempts at expression which transcend the directly experiential. Logically, then, one might reason that some differences in artistic appreciation might accompany intellectual differences. From such a position, apparently, Binet and Henri suggest this area for possible testing.

8. *Moral sentiments.* The use of terminology like "moral sentiments" signifies a measurement area difficult both to define and defend. Indeed, the task suggested by Binet and Henri would yield data only tangentially inferential to "moral sentiments." Items are used which will be interesting to the examinee, and all reference to "test" as such is avoided. The child may select whatever objects he chooses and spend as much time as he wishes with each. Notation is made of the objects selected, their order, and the time spent with each.

9. *Muscular force (will power).* A test of muscular force would seem to measure motor skills, and in essence this task does that. However, it includes an aspect beyond the motor performance itself. Binet and Henri state that the datum to be used is the individual's duration of effort. Does he persist in the task even when it becomes increasingly uncomfortable (noted by muscle trembling, respiratory changes, the lowering of the

hand, and the like)? Such a task may be used, they believe, to obtain an accurate measure of the will power of the individual. Again, the relation of this "will power" to intellectual status is not clear.

10. *Motor skill.* This suggested area does indeed enter the realm of sensori-motor tasks commonly used in other countries. One task stated by Binet and Henri is taken from the work of the American psychologist Bryan (Bryan, 1892). This is the *tapping test,* still used in some performance scales. A second kind of task included under this general area is titled judgment of visual space.

One might be quite critical, in some respects, of the suggestions made by Binet and Henri. Such criticisms, however, are not completely fair. We must remember that these men are proposing measurement in an area (complex mental faculties) not defined previously and of a type inconsistent and at variance with those employed by recognized, competent psychologists in the field. Under these conditions, the "sense and sensibility" of the suggestions in the light of subsequent events is astounding. Hebb (1958, pp. 246–250) has made the point that Binet set out to measure something without any real notion of what he was measuring. His success has been amply demonstrated ever since.

There is the further consideration that the suggestions *are* suggestions, and in only restricted instances based upon empirical data. Binet was an empiricist of the first order. During the remainder of his life, he experimented with tasks and results to a degree seldom approached by those in the business of building tests. Of course, one might say that he had to, since he didn't know quite what he was doing. Perhaps so, but no conclusion was plausible to him unless it could be demonstrated. His openness to criticism, particularly when substantiated by data, was one of the traits which make him appealing.

In any event, Binet and Henri recognized the limitations inherent in their suggestions, and advocated study by all persons interested in individual psychology. To them, individual psychology was synonymous with intelligence and its measurement, and restricted to this trait. They propose that the field of individual psychology must direct its attention to two problems: (1) What is the extent and nature of variations in intelligence from one person to another? and (2) What interrelationships exist among the various complex mental processes of the individual? From the tone of their famous article, their interest lies more in answering the first question than the second. Subsequent events confirm this position. It was not a matter of general versus specific intelligences, then, but a matter of direction. To Binet, the question becomes: How do the faculties, whatever their number and discrete nature, combine to influence the general forms of behavior of the individual? The kinds of items presented and discussed by them in that article should offer evidence about the *general* level of differences among individuals. At the same time, development of tasks to determine the possible processes of the faculties and their relative importance to individual forms of behavior is left open for others to investigate.

Measurement in Individual Psychology

Having made suggestions about possible content, the problem of how to measure becomes paramount. This matter Binet (1898) faced in terms not only of problems but also of specific methodology. Though we may have to use rough, imprecise measures, he says, some kind of measurement is essential to the scientific endeavor in studying intelligence, just as it is for more exact sciences. Certainly scientific accuracy is more attainable with measures of sensory acuity and discrimination. But this does not lessen the need for measurement in the field of individual psychology.

There is a problem of precise definition, necessary in exact measurement, when we consider the functions of the mind to include judgment, ingenuity, and inspiration. No final statement could be proposed at that time, Binet said, since the work had hardly begun. With the experience he already had, Binet suggested two possible measurement procedures depending upon task characteristics.

1. *Measurement with task constancy.* In this approach, degrees of adequacy in the response made by the examinee determine the credit to be given.

2. *Measurement with test gradation.* The second measurement possibility involves increases in difficulty of sub-parts of items. Such a procedure is intentional, not arbitrary; and it is dependent upon demonstrated gradation of discriminable difficulty from sub-item one through whatever number of items are used.

Binet points out that neither of these methods yields a measure that is truly precise in the sense of physical measurement. Though in physical measurement we may demonstrate differences that are absolute, psychological measurement is not so precise. Suppose we have three examinees. On a digit span test, one has a score of 5, one of 7, and one of 9. It is not possible to say that the difference in memory between the first and the second examinee is the same as between the second and the third, even though in each instance there are two units of measured difference. Binet explains that this is because we do not know zero in psychological measurement. Since we do not know the point from which we begin measuring, we are unable to make comparisons in the truly numerical sense. Thus, in the example given, the difference in psychological meaning of scores from 5 to 7 may be less, the same, or more than the difference between 7 and 9. Though this restriction does limit remarks we may make about the nature of the measured differences, we still can use the obtained values in a meaningful way. For example, we may use the information obtained as a predictive source of behavior in other situations. In a task requiring functions of the type measured by the digit span test, what can the person who obtains a score of 9 do which the person who obtains a score of 5 cannot do? This type of functional utility is unaffected by lack of knowledge about an absolute zero point in the scale. Attempts to establish a psychological measuring scale with a true zero have never been successful, though several have tried since Binet made his point.

A second point, relative to psychological measurement, made by Binet deals with individual qualitative differences. Interests, emotional states, needs, and so on, will affect behavior and consequent score expressions. One task of individual psychology, Binet says, is to determine what qualities exist and influence individual production. Differences are not by degree only, then, but in quality as well. Wechsler (1950) has made the same point in discussing sources of variation in test scores.

Method of Item Selection

By 1900, Binet had settled on a procedure for deciding what tests to use in a scale intended to reflect individual differences (Binet, 1900). Though the article reported results on attention and adaptation by the child, this content will not be discussed. Instead, emphasis will be placed on method.

Binet had a teacher and the school's director select, in a class of 32 pupils, the 5 judged most intelligent and the 5 believed to be least intelligent. Thus, clearly discriminable differences in behavior should be identified. The mean age of the bright group was 10.7 years; for the dull group, it was 11.25 years. To the children in each group, a large number of tasks were administered. If a task gave about the same results for the groups, it was thrown out, since it would not fit the conception of behavioral effects of intelligence accepted by Binet. In turn, those tasks which differentiated best between the two groups, favoring the children selected as most intelligent, were kept as adequate measures of the desired trait. Of course, results which favored the least intelligent would have been thrown out.

Given sufficient tasks, Binet could now determine which tasks discriminate and which do not. Given the assumption that the tasks reflect intelligence at work, the conclusion may be drawn as to which items to include in a test designed to measure intellectual differences. Variety in tasks is necessary if one is to generalize to other, more general behavioral situations. In this study, the tasks reflected a fairly narrow range; but it is the method that is important for this discussion anyway. In point of fact, each task that was used showed a clear discrimination favoring the more intelligent group.

Given two groups of widely different "intelligence," selected as described above, the results should reflect certain characteristics and not others. The tasks which discriminate are probably related more closely to school educability than any other factor. The predictive efficiency of the tasks will be greatest for this setting. Though performance on the tasks may also predict for other situations, it would not be surprising that the prediction will be less accurate. The degree of predictive precision will be affected by the utilization of mental faculties necessary to success in school more than in other settings. In other words, the predictive measure achieves high accuracy only as it reflects directly the behaviors involved. Though we might devise a measure so general that it would predict in many, many situations, the chances are excellent that the predictive correlation coefficient for any one situation would be low. We are caught on the horns of a dilemma, then: the more specific the measure, the more limited the predictive situations; the more general the measure, the less accuracy in the prediction for any given situation.

In any event, with the procedure employed by Binet, greatest prediction from test scores should apply to school achievement. We can, of course, devise measures to predict other situations just as well. It is perhaps unfortunate that the general label "intelligence" was applied to such tasks. Maybe it would be better if we called such tests "school-ability tests," as some people have suggested. But the label is not the villain; nor are the test content, purpose, and outcome. The psychometrist who is knowledgeable about the construction and content of a given test will also acquaint himself with predictive correlation coefficients and know the situations in which the test may be best used. Application for other kinds of prediction will increase error; and this the psychometrist will take into account as well.

The Experimental Study of Intelligence

A landmark demonstrating the care followed by Binet in his method of studying individual differences was *The Experimental Study of Intelligence* (Binet, 1903). The principal subjects were his adolescent daughters, and the major outcome was a delineation of personality differences between them. These differences were based upon a number of tasks, largely verbal, each administered a number of times so that the responses could be examined extensively.

One purpose of the study was to demonstrate the effectiveness of verbal material as a stimulus. The psychological laboratories of Germany and the United States continued to use methodology from physiology, so that what represented the nature of a stimulus depended upon a source usable with the afferent system. Binet believed that this procedure unnecessarily restricted the concept of "stimulus," and advocated its extension to any source which controlled the behavior of the subject. Such a viewpoint, of course, allows the use of verbal instructions, questions, and materials as stimuli. Any form of language must operate as an effective, if subtle, stimulus in this context.

Further, the effect of a stimulus of whatever nature is complex in terms of the reactions created, and the stimulating effects may continue to affect behavior after the stimulus is removed. The effect, then, generalizes to facets of the individual beyond those directly affected. To Binet, it was as necessary to study these generalized effects as the direct ones. No new techniques were necessary, he thought, only the patience to pursue the group of reactions which might follow from the stimulus. Using words for study, for example, then required determining immediate and present responses, and subtle relationships not directly represented in the responses, with preferences, feelings, other words, and so on. Such study should offer information on the complex nature of the individual's mind and its content.

In this context, Binet studied his two daughters with some twenty tasks. He began with an investigation of twenty words, expanding this to suggestions the words had for the girls, moving then to phrases, and the development of a theme. He had the girls describe objects and an event, and perform on a letter-cancellation test. Digit repetition, copying, and reaction time followed. Memory was tested specifically for poetry, words, objects, a story, and a drawing. Finally, there were two instances of reproduction tasks. These were the kinds of tasks already advocated by Binet in previous writings.

Periods of time during some three years were given to the experiment; the elder girl, Marguerite, was fourteen and one-half and the younger, Armande, thirteen at the conclusion of the experiment. Over this period, as Binet notes, the number of investigations were extremely numerous and, one might add, exhaustive of their type.

Initially, a fairly simple verbal task was presented. He instructed his subjects to list twenty words, any words which occurred to them. He timed them for rapidity of responding. Once the list was completed, Binet studied each word listed, and went over the list word by word with the subject, inquiring about the significance of the word. He asked the subjects to introspect about the thought processes at the time the word was listed. Following this, he examined the list for distinguishable characteristics: how many words are external, what memories seem to be involved in the words chosen, what wishes are implicit in the kinds of words listed. He continued his analysis by examining the lists for evidence of the quality of imagination, or the lack of it. What associations may be noted from one word to the next, signifying something about mental processes? Is there some theme running through the list? This procedure was followed not just once, but day after day, through some sixteen such lists. By this time, Binet felt he had achieved considerable stability. Certainly the procedure illustrates the painstaking care and patience he had.

Binet examined the lists to determine vocabulary differences. He reports marked differences, with the younger sister showing greater knowledge than the elder, despite eighteen months of difference in age. The nature of the vocabulary depends upon the intellectual nature of the individual. In fact, Binet comments that, though the girls have been schooled in the same environment, they do not speak the same language. This difference Binet ascribes to the fact that some factor of intelligence intervenes in experience to determine vocabulary. Some internal influence, a psychological individuality, modifies external similarities. Though Binet was aware of environmental influences, and investigated them in terms of performance on later scales, he apparently believed that some inherent factors would lead to individual differences even under ideal circumstances. Binet follows this study of words with a study of sentences, then on to the other tasks used. In his conclusions to the volume, Binet comments on some issues of procedure and testing, as well as summarizing his conclusions on personality differences between Marguerite and Armande.

For one thing, Binet criticizes procedures followed by American writers. Large numbers of subjects are used in their studies, and as a result, Binet believes their conclusions are misleading. With a large sample, one must measure quickly and with imprecision. Mental testing deserved a more intensive study, he believed, and his attentive study of his two daughters over a three-year period should yield more usable results about mental processes than some mental test applied hastily to virtual strangers. Not only care is needed, then, but extensive knowledge of the character and experiences of the persons studied, so that results may be interpreted against this background. He believed that psychology had not advanced to a stage of knowledge where any source of information could be ignored.

An additional factor, arising in part from the above suggestions, concerns the mental disposition of the subject. Binet says that, if we wish to understand the meaning of responses, we must know the spirit in which they are given: seriously or foolishly, in a passive, constrained or critical attitude. He calls such conditions a part of the "mental adaptation" of the individual, and insists that the examiner must describe it with care if the psychological state of the person is to be known.

Binet advocated the repetition of a task a large number of times on the same subject, as was done in this study. This procedure is not sufficient, however. It is necessary to include an analysis of other, slightly different experiences which add information about the original task. With only a single type of task, results may be equivocal. The total of several parallel studies of the same function should render a more exact interpretation.

As mentioned earlier, Binet employed an introspective procedure which might be directive of efforts. He comments, however, that he never lost sight of the heart of the scientific method: control. He maintained control through his objectivity, and did not direct the responses of his subjects by any suggestion or hint. He calls suggestion a grave source of error, pointing out that one simple word said by an experimenter can change completely the mental disposition of the subject. Despite the abstract nature of the trait he wished to study, Binet tried to remain the scientist in all his efforts. This combination of objectivity with concern about the individual was a trait uniquely French at that time, and of a most enviable type. Only in such an atmosphere could such intensive study of two subjects of some emotional attachment to the experimenter be trusted.

Binet proposed several alternatives to explain mental organization and change in the individual, but he pointed out that these are speculative. Whether it is mental or physical in nature he does not know, he says, but he is certain that there is some kind of mental continuity among the various mental properties investigated by him with his daughters. This continuity seemed to him the important issue, since it represents the reflection of intelligence at work. Attempts to determine the mental continuity in the individual had been hindered by certain methods of study in psychology, including statistical presentation of results on unpublished tests, used with a sample of, say, a hundred persons. The statistics look good, but Binet doubts their validity for demonstrating much about "mental continuity."

There is a potentially more fruitful approach advocated by Binet. To him, if a mental test is to have value, one must understand its significance. When a test is used with a fairly large sample of persons, the results are useful and interesting only if one groups the relation between the character and the mode of responding of the subjects. Conversely, to use twenty tests with a single individual yields information only if the test results bear some logical pattern. Admittedly, he did not find this latter procedure totally successful in some instances. There was some incoherence in the results, because the tasks were either poorly chosen, poorly administered, or poorly interpreted. In this study of his daughters, however, he exerted special effort and believed he was successful. He found a bond among the several tests for each subject, a relationship discovered only with great patience and work. These relationships are summarized for each girl.

Since each test was administered several times, rather than merely once, Binet believed that he had a stability of results that demonstrated clearly individual differences in thought. In fact, he was more interested in the effectiveness of the method than the differences disclosed. He does not talk about actual differences in intelligence in a quantitative sense, then, but in differences in mental processes peculiar to two sisters raised in essentially the same setting. And though there are differences *between* the girls, there is harmony in the processes *within* each girl.

Whether or not the description of mental processes of each daughter is accurate is probably less important than the demonstration of an effective method of disclosing behavioral differences between individuals. This method, the "Binet method," offers an opportunity for measurement not previously possible. It becomes the heart of individual testing, regardless of whether the test is of the Binet type or some other. Essentially, Wechsler, for example, may disagree about the need for the mental age concept and consequent measurement of *level* of functioning, but he uses the method of Binet in a context which essentially differs only in score expression. This statement is true, not only for Wechsler, but also for other originators of individual tests whatever their theoretical persuasion. Probably no higher tribute could be paid to Binet's work.

What is the reason for this conformity? The major reason lies in the ability to gain information beyond quantification, important as that may be. The insistence on observation, and some interpretation of that observation, reflects the methodology used and advocated by Binet. Admittedly, three years of repeated testing with a carefully-selected variety of tests is not practical or possible. Yet the individual testing situation is intended as a microcosm of the procedures followed in this experimental study of intelligence. Unfortunately, Binet's great objectivity is not always as well represented in the test setting.

Diagnosis in Retardation

In 1904, the Minister of Public Instruction established a commission to determine instructional procedures necessary for mentally defective children. Binet and Simon (1905) then published a paper dealing with problems in deciding which children should receive whatever special educational methods were decided upon.

The commission concerned itself largely with administrative matters:

types of facilities, admission qualifications, teacher qualifications and numbers, teaching methods. As a part of the admission procedures, the commission decided that every child must be screened with an educational and medical examination to make sure that the child could not benefit from regular class instruction. Such a procedure should ensure that the special classes would not become depositories for problem children who were not mentally defective. Though in agreement with the principle of selection, Binet and Simon point out that the commission specified nothing about the nature and extent of the examination. To this deficiency, Binet and Simon direct their article.

In the absence of definite guidelines, they indicate that decisions are apt to be haphazard, subjective and uncontrolled. Though some such decisions may turn out to be just and correct, just as often they will be merely capricious. Children deserve a better fate, particularly if they are to be assigned to a special educational facility. Binet and Simon point out that membership in a class for the mentally deficient can never be a mark of distinction, and considerable care should be exercised to assure that those who should not be members are excluded. One way to avoid inaccurate assignment is to use scientific precision in the decision. Frequently, such precision will be possible. And they urge that since too little scientific objectivity has been applied in educational endeavors, on principle alone it should now be employed.

There was an immediate problem as to the definition of mental deficiency. Historically, there had been great discrepancies in decisions about mental subnormality, leading to imprecision in terminology. Most often, several grades of subnormality were recognized, commonly leading to three levels. *Idiocy* was a term used for the lowest grade, *imbecility* for some intermediate degree, and *moronity* for the level of subnormality closest to a normal state. Even where these terms were common to different users, however, the *behavior* exemplifying each state was differently described. An example of this was in the divergent medical diagnoses on a patient by several physicians, with all examinations occurring in the space of a few days.

One of the drawbacks recognized by Binet and Simon in this lack of agreement was in comparative statistics from place to place and country to country. If there is such disagreement in medical diagnosis, how may incidence figures for deficiency be compared from country to country? What will be the meaning of school records where children have widely divergent terminology applied to essentially the same condition? Since questions like these could not be answered, no answers were possible to more important questions about relative effectiveness of educational methods and amelioration of a condition.

They comment on the use of graded questions as a means of accurately differentiating degrees of intellectual competence. Attempts had already been made in this direction by others, but the instruments had some deficiencies for the purposes desired. A more precise procedure is possible, they state, allowing accurate differentiation of normality and subnormality, as well as degrees of subnormality. This procedure is explicated as the Binet-Simon scale, the first workable measure of intelligence emanating from complex mental faculties.

The First Scale

From a considerable background of method and research, the 1905 Scale was formulated (see, for example, Binet 1894a, 1894b, 1894c; Binet and Henri, 1896; Binet and Henri, 1895a, 1895b; Jacobs, 1887). Binet and Simon (1905b) began by restating the need for such a test. Under certain conditions, it is necessary to determine whether or not a child is retarded or normal in intelligence. Under such conditions, a reasonably exact measure of the intellectual level of the child must be available as a basis for the decision. The current intellectual functioning of the child should be the sole determinant, they say; his past history (and future, for that matter), and consequently the etiology of his functioning is unimportant. Deficiency should be considered in its present scope and form, without attempts to define it as acquired or congenital. Brain pathology, its determination and extent, is not a matter of concern in an examination with the measure advocated by them. Personality abnormalities were not suitable for such testings, and persons suffering from these should not be included. As with historical antecedents, prognosis also must be ignored. Curability or amelioration of a deficiency disclosed by test performance is neither wise nor possible, they felt. A practical purpose was basic to the scale construction: some means to give a current estimate of the intellectual status of a school-age child, such that his educability can be determined.

There is the possibility of a number of aptitudes operating in the expression of intelligence, each of which might reflect a superior mental faculty. Despite the importance of determining what these aptitudes might be, Binet and Simon point out that this problem is left for later work. In the current scale, they are concerned with some combination of faculties that may be called "general intelligence." The term "general" signifies only a form of total test performance not directly traced to any particular abilities. Specifically, differences in amount of general ability among mentally defective individuals is the source of this work. If they can evaluate and quantify differences among defectives, the work will have been a success. Essentially, they say, the scale should indicate the intellectual level at which the child currently functions. Given this level, comparisons may be made with the level of normal children of the same chronological age, or with children of the same level of various ages. Though not explicitly stated, the mental-age concept is reflected here and is employed in the later scales.

In such a scheme, then, comparisons may be drawn between a child of say, six, and one of twelve, if the latter is sufficiently retarded to behave intellectually like the former. Binet and Simon, however, caution about overgeneralizing from the behavioral data. They point out that despite similarities which can be demonstrated, there are also differences in other behavioral aspects, some evident and some not. Binet and Simon considered the deficient person one who has had an arrest in the development of certain functions. Other functions may have developed more normally. They point out that certain special aptitudes, such as music or calculation, can develop normally. The mental-age concept must be restricted to those behaviors and faculties directly concerned. In other words, prediction must be restricted to relevant criteria. Since the scale is designed to assess educability of school children, this is the setting in which intellectual differences must be reflected and measured. Obvious as this may seem, subsequent events and interpretations make it necessary to stress again and again the original purpose and limitations of tests which have been retained to the present day.

The method of measurement to be employed is the next issue discussed by Binet and Simon. Medical diagnosis had proved poor, largely because physicians had concerned themselves with parental statements and spent little time questioning the child. Parental attitudes are seldom to be trusted, because parents will be swayed by their desires and needs of the moment rather than by what is best for the child. Binet and Simon suggest that a decision about mental subnormality be based upon three criteria. The first of these should be medical, with the emphasis upon physical and psychological signs. Second, an educational criterion should be employed, yielding an assessment of the academic achievement of the child to the time of the examination. Last is a psychological criterion, employing tasks designed to observe directly and to measure the degree of intelligence possessed by the child. This psychological method stresses comprehension, judgment, reasoning, and invention on the part of the child. In combination, the three criteria should yield a satisfactory basis for a diagnosis of mental deficiency.

The particular method employed in the psychological scale required a graded series of tasks, beginning with the lowest possible intellectual level which might be measured, and continuing to the level of normal intelligence. There is a different mental level reflected in each series. One problem, of course, lies in the proper determination of "normal-intelligence level" in the case of each age group. Since what is normal for three-year-olds is less than that for six-year-olds, which is less than that for twelve-year-olds, at what point does the scale end?

There is the further point made by Binet and Simon that such a scale does not measure directly the quality of intelligence. Intellectual qualities may not be placed on a metrical scale in the way that physical qualities can. Instead, what is obtained is a type of classification: performance on the tasks may be placed in a hierarchy of performances. In essence, this classification is close enough to direct measurement for practical purposes, they believed. Having administered the tasks to two individuals and having determined the performance level of each, comparisons may be made with each other and with others of normal and sub-normal ability. Today, we would think of percentile ranks, or some such ranking procedure, but Binet and Simon had only the specific score units available for such a comparison. Even so, they felt it possible to determine not only retardation, but its degree as well.

Judgment has become such an important concept now to Binet that he takes a strong position against memory as the chief reflection of intellgence. Memory, he now says, is independent of judgment. Illustrative of this fact are the many cases of the *idiots savants,* cited frequently from history. An individual so ill-equipped that he cannot function in society may develop fantastic feats of memory. Such a "wise idiot" is a curiosity, not a mental giant. Conversely, Binet and Simon say, one may have excellent judgment but have a poor memory.

As a result, the then-current emphasis was on judgment. Of particular importance in this approach are the absurd errors that a child may make in a situation calling for good judgment. Indeed, they say opportunities are provided in the scale for absurd responses to be made. However, since some "floor" is necessary to the test, not all items reflected judgment. Memory items, particularly, were placed in the lower end of the scale along with tests of coordination and of attention.

The Content of the 1905 Scale

Whipple (1910, pp. 473–489) has presented all the tasks (thirty in number) that were included in the 1905 scale. The specific tasks included are:

1. Visual coordination.
2. Prehension provoked tactually.
3. Prehension provoked visually.
4. Cognizance of food.
5. Seeking food under difficulty.
6. Execution of simple orders.

7. Cognizing objects by name.
8. Cognizing pictured objects by name.
9. Naming objects designated in a picture.
10. Comparison of supraliminally different lines.
11. Auditory memory for three digits.
12. Comparison of supraliminally different weights.
13. Suggestibility.
14. Definitions of familiar objects.
15. Memory for sentences.
16. Differences between familiar objects recalled in memory.
17. Memory for pictures.
18. Drawing from memory.
19. Auditory memory for more than three digits.
20. Resemblances between familiar objects recalled in memory.
21. Discrimination of lines.
22. Arrangement of five weights.
23. Detection of the missing weight.
24. Rhymes.
25. Missing words.
26. Sentence-building.
27. Replies to problem questions.
28. Interchange of the clock hands.
29. Drawing from a design cut in a quarto-folded paper.
30. Distinction between abstract terms.

Scale Utilization

Normative and interpretative data were reported by Binet and Simon in an article in *L'Année Psychologique* following the presentation of the scale (Binet and Simon, 1905c). First, they felt the scale was arranged in an order of increasing difficulty, and an inspection of the items does give that appearance. They had used, as a standardizing sample, children selected by their teachers as normal in intelligence. Their ages were the equivalent of grade placement, so that "normality" here includes a heavy emphasis on average school achievement. The actual norms were based on a sample of only 50 children at these age levels: 3, 5, 7, 9, and 11. Binet and Simon report that the first nine items were passed by all members of the three-year-old group. There would then appear to be an adequate floor in the scale for school age children. The five-year-old group passed items 10 through 12, and item 14, though lack of attention unless urged was evident on item 10, and some help was needed on item 12. Both of these young age groups demonstrated their suggestibility by their performances on item 13. A clear separation between the five- and seven-year-olds was found with item 16. Distinctions between age groups above year seven are based on differential types of answers given to parts of items, or by differential qualities in responses to certain items.

Some twelve items specifically discussed by Binet and Henri were found to differentiate among normal students of ages 7, 9, and 11. These items are: No. 15, Memory for Sentences; No. 17, Memory for Pictures; No. 18, Drawing from Memory; No. 21, Discrimination of Lines; No. 22, Arrangement of Five Weights; No. 23, Detection of a Missing Weight; No. 24, Rhymes; No. 25, Missing Words; No. 26, Sentence-building; No. 27, Replies to Problem Questions; No. 29, Drawing from a Design; and No. 30, Distinction between Abstract Terms. In addition, the suggestibility task (No. 13) added information helpful in making a distinction in some cases.

Peterson (1925) makes a pertinent comment about the kinds of tasks found best for such discriminative purposes.

> The reader may be surprised, knowing Binet's depreciation of the factors of intelligence involved, to see that the majority of these thirteen tests are tests of memory or sensation. However, in tests of this kind, attention is paid by the experimenter to details which may indicate the degree of judgment possessed by the subject. Thus for verbal memory for sentences, the number of absurdities committed is held to be just as significant as the total number of sentences repeated correctly, and in this, as in the language tests particularly, the number of absurdities figures in the norms given. In test 19 the child was to indicate after each repetition of a series of digits whether or not he was satisfied with his response. Satisfaction with a repetition involving several grave errors was considered indicative of low intelligence. In the arrangement of weights, the method adopted, or the lack of method, was held to be very important. This test, together with Test 29, is classed by Binet as a sensory judgment and reasoning test. Moreover, the authors attach importance to the sensory tests because of the fact that "they will certainly be very useful in the analysis of the aptitudes of defective persons" (Peterson, 1925, pp. 176–177).

Binet and Simon present an argument, then, that what counts is not the control of items *per se* but what faculties must operate in performance. If the item performance is insufficient to the task, then added information must be gathered, as in the case of questioning the child about his satisfaction with his performance on digit repetition.

Degrees of Retardation

Despite sample limitations, Binet and Simon gathered enough data to feel that a reasonable and objective classification of degrees of retardation was feasible.

1. *Idiocy.* The lowest grade of mental deficiency they labeled "idiocy," and assigned its significance to the absence of language. In effect, the child who is to be diagnosed as idiot, regardless of age, must show an absence of vocabulary, or not use language. This nonuse of language is in the sense of using abstract terms for objects not physically present. Thus, the idiot may "parrot" certain sounds, but he cannot use these sounds to communicate meaningfully with another person. In test terms, the idiot will succeed through item 6 (execution of simple orders and imitation of gestures). However, items 7 (cognizing real objects by name) and 8 (cognizing objects in a picture by name) will not be passed by such a child. The idiot resembles in performance the normal child of two years or less. For the child of, say, age eight, to be diagnosed "idiot" would require a functional behavior in which language was absent.

2. *Imbecility.* The child to be designated an imbecile would succeed not only with tests 1 through 6, but with verbal material up through item 16 (differences between familiar objects recalled in memory). The imbecile also is most readily distinguished from morons by performance on task 22 (arrangement of five weights) and the portion of task 19 (auditory memory for more than three digits) where six or more digits comprise the sequence. It is to be noted that the distinction between imbeciles and morons is not so clear and precise as that between idiots and imbeciles. Apparently on some memory tasks, particularly, the differences between the former are too small to be conclusive (No. 17, Memory for Pictures; No. 18, Drawing from Memory; No. 21, Discrimination of Lines). Hence either the tasks are not correctly ordered, or the behavior sampled by the items is not clearly perceptible with the item content, or both. In any event, the imbecile shows some degree of verbal functioning, and overall corresponds to the normal child between the ages of two and five.

3. *Moronity.* If the distinction between imbecility and moronity was not clear, that between moronity and normality was positively muddy. Since this distinction is the one desired for the scale, some limitations and defects must be recognized and corrected. One factor to be considered in evaluating the adequacy of the scale is the procedure followed to determine cut-off points. The children whose behaviors were explicitly denoted to define idiocy and imbecility were in a state institution. But the children to be labeled "moron" were studied in the locus where the tests were to be used: the schools. Already, difficulties in discriminating between the normal child (i.e. the one who can be reasonably successful in a regular academic program) and the moron (i.e. the one who could not be successful in the formal program and needed special instructional modes) were apparent. The purpose of the scale was to make an objective and precise distinction. The method used by Binet and Simon to distinguish the one type of child from the other is important to evaluation of

the test as well as to future scale development.

The first step taken was to establish a pool of "retarded" children of different ages so that appropriate norms might be set up. A list of children between ages 8 and 13 was used to define the subgroup to be studied. School marks of each child were compared to its age, so that the oldest children in any class with the lowest marks were singled out. This was the essential method of identifying "morons." It is an operational definition of extreme consequence not only to the immediate use of the scale but to future use as well. The point cannot be overemphasized: the Binet method was employed for predicting academic achievement. The children identified by this procedure were included among a group of normal children, and the examiners were not told which were which. The test must distinguish the two levels of intellect.

The results indicated that the test indeed distinguished between the academically successful child and the academically slow one. The tasks which distinguished best were those employing abstract, verbal abilities. Binet and Simon concluded that the moron probably does not develop beyond the level of the average child of twelve. This statement applies only to those less than fourteen years of age, however, since they assume that adult morons would have had sufficient experience to perform on abstractions like children above the age of twelve. In fact, this matter of "ceiling" for morons appears to be guesswork rather than empiricism. Peterson (1925, p. 180) reports that Binet and Simon assumed the limits imposed either from data with eleven-year-olds, or from data simply not reported.

The importance of age comparisons in the use of the scale is undoubted. Binet and Simon report that no evidence of mental retardation is possible without consideration of age. Thus, the nine-year-old child shows his deficiency by behavior similar to that of a normal child of a younger age. Implicitly, the degree of retardation depends upon the difference between his chronological age and the chronological age of the normal child whom he most resembles. The procedure followed involves scaling tests over several ages, the placement dependent upon responses of normal children, then finding the age level attainable by any given child. Whether he is above-average, average, or below-average is determined by comparing his actual age with the age obtained on the test. Of course, the 1905 Scale did not provide this possibility; but the suggestion here by Binet and Simon is implemented in the 1908 Scale. The logical outcome is the mental age concept. The essential steps are taken now, and consequent events allow their development. Use of the 1905 Scale illustrates some of its limitations, including inaccurate placement of items, and Binet and Simon use criticisms (e.g. see Decroly and Degand, 1906) in preparing the refinement that is published in 1908.

Summary

The work of Binet from 1895 to 1905 reflected the development of procedures designed to reflect complex mental processes in intellectual behavior. Empirical methods were followed to determine differences among individuals in these complex processes, and only a pragmatic criterion was accepted. As a result, changes in attitude and philosophy are evident in Binet's writing even within this ten year period.

An essential step was the development of the "Binet method," based upon intensive measurement of an individual with a variety of tasks relevant to the behavior to be predicted.

The first scale, a landmark in the measurement of ability, was published in 1905. Despite its marked limitations, this scale influences the testing movement both immediately and to the present day.

References

Binet, A., *La Psychologie du Raisonnement.* 1886.

———, "La Mémoire des Joueurs d'Echecs Qui Jouent sans Voir, *"Revue Philosophique*, 1894a, 37, 222–240.

———, *Psychologie des Grands Calculateurs et Joueurs d'Echecs*, 1894b.

———, *Introduction à la Psychologie Expérimentale*, 1894c.

———, "Description d'un Objet," *L'Année Psychologique*, 1897, 3, 296–332.

———, "La Mesure en Psychologie Individuelle," *Revue Philosophique*, 1898, 46, 113–123.

———, "Attention et Adaptation," *L'Année Psychologique*, 1900, 6, 248–404.

———, *L'Étude Expérimentale de l'Intelligence.* Paris: Schleicher Frères et Cie, 1903.

———, and Henri, V., "Le Développement de la Memoire Visuelle chez les Enfants," *Revue Philosophique*, 1894a, 37, 348–350.

———, and Henri, V., "De la Suggestibilité Naturelle chez les Enfants," *Revue Philosophique*, 1894b, 38, 337–347.

———, and Henri, V., "La Mémoire des Mots." *L'Année Psychologique*, 1895a, 1, 1–23.

———, and Henri, V., "La Mémoire des Phrases," *L'Année Psychologique*, 1895b, 1, 24–49.

———, and Henri, V., "La Psychologie Individuelle," *L'Année Psychologique*, 1896, 2, 411–465.

———, and Passey, J., "La Psychologie des Auteurs Dramatiques," *Revue Philosophique*, 1894, 37, 240.

———, and Passey, J., "Études de Psychologie sur les Auteurs Dramatiques," *L'Année Psychologique*, 1895, 1, 60–118.

————, and Simon Th., "Sur la Necessité d'Établir un Diagnostic Scientifique des États Inferieurs de l'Intelligence," *L'Année Psychologique*, 1905a, 11, 163–190.

————, and Simon, Th., "Méthodes Nouvelles pour le Diagnostic du Niveau Intellectuel des Anormaux," *L'Année Psychologique*, 1905b, 11, 191–244.

————, and Simon, Th., "Application des Méthodes Nouvelles au Diagnostic du Niveau Intellectuel chez les Enfants Normaux et Anormaux d'Hospice et d'École Primarie," *L'Année Psychologique*, 1905c, 11, 245–366.

————, and Simon, Th., *Les Enfants Anormaux*. Paris: Librairie Armand Colin. 1907.

Bryan, W. L., "On the Development of Voluntary Motor Ability," *American Journal of Psychology*, 1892, 5, 125–204.

Decroly, O., and Degand, J., "Les Tests de Binet et Simon pour le Mesure de l'Intelligence: Contribution Critique," *Archives de Psychologie*, 1906, 6, 27–130.

Ebbinghaus, H., *Memory*. Translated by H. A. Ruger and C. E. Bussenius. New York: Teachers College, Columbia University, 1913.

Galton, F., *Natural Inheritance*. New York: Macmillan, 1894.

————, *Inquiries into Human Faculty and Its Development*. London: J. M. Dent, 1907.

————, *Hereditary Genius: An Inquiry into Its Laws and Consequences*. New York: Macmillan, 1914.

Goddard, H. H., "The Binet and Simon Tests of Intellectual Capacity," *The Training School*, 1908, 5, 3–9.

Hebb, D. O., *A Textbook of Psychology*. Philadelphia: Saunders, 1958.

Jacobs, J., "Experiments on Prehension'," *Mind*, 1887, 12, 75–79.

Peterson, J., *Early Conceptions and Tests of Intelligence*. Yonkers-on-Hudson, N.Y.: World Book, 1925.

Wechsler, D., "Cognitive, Conative, and Non-Intellective Intelligence," *American Psychologist*, 1950. 5, 78–83.

Whipple, G. M., *Manual of Mental and Physical Tests*. Baltimore: Warwick and York, 1910.

————, *Manual of Mental and Physical Tests. Part II: Complex Processes*. Baltimore: Warwick and York, 1915.

3

Alfred Binet: The Final Years (1906-1911)

While Binet and Simon continued refinement of the work begun with the 1905 Scale, the method found only minor implementation in other countries. In France, however important work on the procedure for the problems of estimating school educability did not diminish. It led to beginnings of acceptance elsewhere (e.g. Decroly and Degand, 1906; Goddard, 1908; Terman, 1906).

The 1908 Scale

Limitations in the 1905 Scale, both as evident to Binet in his work and as reported by Decroly and Degand (1906), led to the refinement which was published in 1908 (Binet and Simon, 1908). In the prefatory discussion to the actual test content, Binet and Simon comment on several developments and criticisms important to the testing movement.

They begin by defending an empirical approach to measuring intelligence. Some writers of the time had accused them of neglecting theory for the sake of an *a priori* method only. This they believe to be unfair. Though final decisions are based on experimentation, theory precedes experimentation to direct its efforts, they say. And this is the usual scientific method: speculation on events or conditions, followed by controlled research to determine the validity of speculation. Binet and Simon do admit that they reject quite strongly theoretical considerations that are beginning and end; i.e. those which are not followed by experimental verification or rejection. For those who use theoretical discussion to replace factual exploration or for those who use authoritative sources which are not empirically verified, they have little sympathy. To them, the scientific method is a combination of theory and experiment. The decisions made must be based upon demonstrated fact, not on opinion or wishes.

The work to date reported by them, including the 1905 Scale, was based upon this scientific method. However, the new scale was necessary because the underlying theory had not been as well conceived as it should be. Essentially, the central use of the measure is still to be in the schools, with both normal and abnormal intellectual development the point of concern. There were two purposes for the work reported in this paper: (1) the determination of the "law" of intellectual development in children through the use of a means for measuring intelligence, and (2) the study of variability in intellectual aptitudes.

The first of these purposes is concerned with determining the nature of mental growth and would require representative age groups. Since there is little discussion of standardization procedures, it is doubtful that anything approaching "lawfulness" is exemplified by the work. Binet and Simon report using Parisian school children within two months of their birthdays from ages three through twelve. Since the total sample was about 300, this plan would mean an average of 30 children per age group. How the sample was selected was not specified. As a consequence, the latter part of the first purpose, a means for measuring intelligence, is suspect also. Certainly, the scale would "measure" something; but under the circumstances the pragmatic position of performance differences allied to school achievement would be most safe. This position is reinforced by certain "check" procedures employed by Binet and Simon, and reported later.

The second purpose they admit they do not reach. A major reason for this shortcoming is that the entire problem has turned out to be more complex than they had conceived. By 1908, they have learned the essential lesson of investigation and maturity: in initial efforts, we tend to oversimplify. Now, they realize that they will do well to restrict themselves to the task of learning how to measure the child's intelligence. Admittedly, they say, the job is not complete with the 1908 Scale; but they believe the procedure is correct and usable. As a by-product, the work to this time had persuaded them that a child differs from the adult intellectually, not only in degree and quantity but in quality also. This qualitative difference they cannot now specify; they turn to this problem in later work.

To measure intelligence, they have designed a scale consisting of a series of tests graded by years. The youngest age level tested is three; the oldest, thirteen years. To be accurately placed, items at any given age level should be representative for that age and should be passed by the intellectually average child of that age. In practice, such an outcome is impossible; hence some approximations are necessary. In the 1908 Scale, Binet and Simon describe item placement in terms of observed behaviors of children of the various ages for whom the test is intended. In this description the importance of theoretical considerations is clear. It is seen in their decision as to where to try items and what kinds of items to try in empirical work. For example, they introduce the task of "showing nose, eyes and mouth" at age three by saying: "one of the clearest signs of intellectual alertness in young children is the comprehension of spoken language. For some time the young child understands only our gestures and responds only to the intonation of our words. Idiots remain at this level all their lives and do not communicate with their equals through language. The first step in possession of languages is comprehension; one comprehends the expressed thoughts of others, having become capable of expressing himself properly. As a consequence, what we demand of the child in the first test of our examination is that he demonstrate that he understands the sense of words in common language . . ." (Binet and Simon, 1908, pp. 3–4). There follows then a description of the task and performances of children of various levels of ability. The theoretical assumptions must be borne out by actual performance, and upon demonstration with the appropriate sample the task is assumed to be appropriately placed. Though the procedure is excellent, some problems of item placement are later disclosed. This may be due primarily to sample inadequacies and nonrepresentativeness.

The instructions to use in task administration are made explicit by Binet and Simon, in the hope that anyone trying the test will be able to administer it capably. Each item at each age level is described with the necessary detail as to rationale, performance differences, and administrative procedures. Whipple (1910, pp. 494–514) has presented a brief description of each item and its comparison with the 1905 Scale.

The 1908 Scale is more than a revision of the 1905 Scale. It could be more nearly represented as a refinement of the 1905 Scale with a considerable addition of new items based upon empirical evidence. Probably the major difference is the fact that the mental age is now expressed as the score which is obtained where it was only implied in the prior scale. In addition, the 1905 Scale had been designed, primarily, to show that measurement to illustrate individual differences in complex mental tasks was possible; the 1908 Scale now takes that intention one step further in trying to demonstrate the extent to which such differences exist. Binet and Simon believed that in this test they had demonstrated that the items were arranged in the actual order of increasing difficulty in a way which had not been quite so true with the 1905 Scale. The actual placement of items in this scale, too, was dependent upon empirical data and not upon any logical or philosophical premises about the intelligent behavior of children. They found, for example, and report that the abilities of most children were more limited than they thought they would be. This result was confirmed in later investigations as well. In any event they found some distinction and some difference between what they thought a child should be able to do at a given age and what he could actually do. The latter condition, what the child could actually perform, became the primary means of placement of items.

The criterion for a child to pass was based upon his performance at any given lage level. Binet and Simon, apparently arbitrarily, decided that a child passed a given age level if he passed every item but one. In looking at the scale it becomes apparent that this leads to some score differences from the very beginning, since there are some age levels which have only three or four items while other age levels may have six or seven. Some experimental verification that this is an adequate procedure for determining the mental age level of a child, then, is necessary. As a check of their assumption, Binet and Simon took a group of children and examined their test performances to determine items passed beyond determined mental age level. Some 70 children were used for this purpose and they found not a single instance where the child had in fact passed items at a higher year level than that where he passed all but one of the items. This seemed to confirm their belief that they had an adequate criterion for determining the mental level of the child.

A second experimental procedure used to determine the adequacy of the scale and the placement of the items involved the testing of some 203 children of different ages available to them primarily in the schools of Paris. Binet and Simon operated on the basis that, of any unselected group as large as some 200 children, part of them should be above average in terms of their age level, part of them should be below average, most of them should be about average. This meant that in the administration of the scale to this sample of 203 children they should find a distribution approaching normality with about equal numbers above and below average for their age groups. There should, however, be more children at age level, rather than either above or below it. The experimental results generally seemed to confirm Binet and Simon's assumption. Of the sample, they report that 103 children ranked as normal in ability, 42 were advanced by one year, 2 were advanced by two years; 44 were retarded by one year, 12 were retarded two years. There were, thus, more at age level than above or below it, but they were somewhat surprised to find more children classified as retarded by this scale than were classified as advanced. This reflects some imbalance in the distribution of intelligence in the sample. The results of this study are reported in Table 3.1. As may be seen in this table, there are not equal numbers of children at each age level, with only 10 at age three and 11 at age twelve, while there are 23 at ages five and eight. There is, in addition, the discomforting fact that the numbers do not turn out to be the same as reported by Binet and Simon. There are apparently only 93 children who tested at age level in a total sample of only 192. In addition, there seem to be 43, rather than 44, who are retarded by one year. Despite the discrepancy in numbers, however, the essential contention of Binet and Simon is confirmed that most children of a given age test at age level, while some will be above average and some below average.

TABLE 3.1*

NUMBER OF PUPILS SHOWING AVERAGE, ADVANCED, AND RETARDED INTELLECTUAL
TEST PERFORMANCE AT AGES THREE THROUGH TWELVE

Test Per-formance	Ages										
	3	4	5	6	7	8	9	10	11	12	Total
Average	3	9	13	5	7	16	11	14	13	2	93
Advanced 1 Year	3	2	6	8	7	5	9	2	0	0	42
Advanced 2 Years	0	1	0	0	0	1	0	0	0	0	2
Retarded 1 Year	4	4	4	6	3	1	2	9	5	5	43
Retarded 2 Years	0	1	0	1	1	0	0	3	2	4	12
Totals	10	17	23	20	18	23	22	28	20	11	192

* From Binet, A., and Simon, T., "Le Développement de l'Intelligence chez les Enfants," *L'Année Psychologique,* 1908, p. 73.

Other Checks

One means used by Binet and Simon to test validity of the scale was to have teachers identify those children who were superior in ability in terms of classroom achievement. In each instance in which this was done they found that the child also tended to be above his age norms in test performance. By contrast, some 14 children who were retarded by three years in academic achievement were found in terms of test performance to be retarded mentally on the average about two and a half years, with the range being from one to six years of absolute retardation on the scale. Though one might assume from this that Binet and Simon equated intellectual ability with scholastic performance, in point of fact Binet believed that certain characteristics which entered scholastic performance did not reflect intellectual ability. For example, he pointed out that in school the child who is successful must demonstrate certain kinds of traits, skills and qualities that may not benefit him on a scale of intellectual measurement.

He must be attentive, he must have a good deal of desire to succeed in school, he must have a certain kind of character, as Binet put it, some regularity of habits, and a certain amount of conformity and adaptation. Above all, he said, there must be some continuity of effort on the part of the child in school and toward school subjects. All intelligent children, Binet believed, did not demonstrate such traits and, therefore, a number of them would not do as well in school as their abilities would warrant. These should be quite good in terms of test performance, despite the fact that they might not look very good in school. The assumption is being made here by Binet, of course, that such children, though they do not perform well in school, will attempt to perform as well as they can on his test. This assumption may have less validity than Binet believed. Overall, Binet and Simon believed that the rankings of children on their scale would certainly be a more accurate reflection of intellectual ability than would their overall ranking in school. They also report that bright children tended to perform well on the test regardless of their school work and, in turn, that those children who were retarded also found the test interesting and apparently did their best.

Using the 1908 Scale

Binet and Simon drew the conclusion that they had in point of fact developed an instrument which would allow them to assess rather accurately the intellectual development of children between the ages of three and twelve years. In addition, the use of the scale appeared to them to be quite convenient, easy to give, practical in its outcome, and rapid considering the amount of time needed for administration. They state that if one wishes to know whether or not a child has the intellectual level of his age-mates one need only to administer the items at his chronological age. His performance will demonstrate whether he is at his age level or whether he might be advanced or retarded. This test should take no more than ten minutes or so. For greater precision, in those cases where apparent retardation or acceleration exists, one might administer other tests adjacent to the age level of the child in order to determine how much advanced or how much retarded he might be.

One of the primary values of this scale, Binet and Simon believed, was that the results could be used to help determine when and what kind of instruction should be given to all children. They thought that a child should be taught something only when he has reached the intellectual maturity to understand it and to deal with it; otherwise, instruction time is wasted. Knowing the mental level of the child as determined by this test should be useful in terms of determining when a child is ready to learn some particular topic, and the amount of subject matter. Thus the scale should have great applicability to the child who makes normal progress in school learning. However, Binet and Simon advocate that the greatest utility may not be with this group at all; it might rather be in terms of determining who are inferior in ability and who should have specialized kinds of instructional procedures. Thus more than only the degree of retardation could be determined. What might reasonably be used for instructional materials and procedures could be more adequately determined on the basis of the mental level of the child, as compared with children of an analagous mental level. It could also determine what and how they can learn.

Implementation of some of the suggestions made by Binet and Simon will depend to a large degree upon the quality of intelligence reflected by the measure taken. Binet maintained that there are two different kinds of intelligence which are sometimes confused. One of these he refers to as maturity and the other as rectitude of intelligence. To a large degree, at least, maturity of intelligence refers to mental growth that accompanies age. Sometimes, however, it can be found in a small child if he is precocious. There is in this maturity of intelligence some quality that goes beyond the merely experiential and objective in responding to certain kinds of problem situations. For example, Binet and Simon report that this precocity of intelligence that reflects maturity is particularly reflected in such tests as the giving of definitions, the construction of a sentence to include given words, explaining pictures, arranging weights. In his performance on such tasks, the child who is mature in intelligence will show a superiority in terms of the quality of response which is given; that is, he will not restrict himself merely to how an object is used or how it is directly related to him. Instead, he will interpret. By contrast, rectitude represents some degree of correctness in responding. The young child shows rectitude in the sense that his answers are meaningful, they are accurate, they are direct. He avoids absurdities in making responses.

Just how far this distinction in types of intelligence should be pursued is not clear from Binet's work. He states that it should be accepted on a tentative basis only until further data is available. Certainly, if the differences are meaningful ones, some items of the 1908 Scale should reflect rectitude, others should reflect maturity, while still others might allow both types to be expressed.

Degrees of Deficiency

Binet and Simon point out again the lack of agreement in the use of terms such as idiot, imbecile, and moron to describe varying degrees of mental subnormality. The vagueness of behavioral specifications leads to a good deal of disagreement in terms of diagnosis and this, of course, must affect prognosis. In point of fact, according to Binet and Simon, it was possible for a child of normal intelligence to be labeled as subnormal. This condition would occur when an intellectually normal child was brought to a clinic. The frequent attitude taken by the clinicians was that whoever appeared before them was expected to be deficient. In this atmosphere, Binet and Simon believed, the child would usually be found to be deficient. This inability to distinguish normality from subnormality they thought to be quite widespread. The reason they gave for it was that the clinician, whether he be physician or not, did not know what represented normal behavior. It was not possible for him to compare the child who appeared before him with a normal child, and thereby to determine if the child was in point of fact average or above average in intelligence. They pointed out that a child seven, eight, or nine years of age who was so severely retarded that his behavior could not be mistaken would surely be diagnosed correctly; that is, as deficient. There were many cases, however, where degrees of deficiency were not evident, and some decision must be made about borderline cases. They report having found at least a few instances of such misdiagnosis, their decision about misdiagnosis being based on test performance by some children in an institution.

Once again they use the traditional terminology of moron, imbecile and idiot as means of establishing degrees of retardation. Each of these is then described in terms of test behaviors which would limit the use of the term. The label "idiot" is reserved for that person who cannot communicate with his fellow beings by means of language. He does not speak, he does not understand speech, he cannot communicate. His behavior corresponds to that of a child of normal intelligence who is less than two years of age. To make a distinction between this individual, the idiot, and the next higher degree of subnormality, the imbecile, would require the use of the following tests, according to Binet and Simon: (1) Giving verbal orders, such as touching nose, mouth and eyes. (2) Using verbal labels to identify familiar objects that are in a picture. The idiot will fail on this test because he does not use labels to substitute for objects. In the scale these kinds of items are contained at the year-three level. Binet and Simon point out that, in all probability, they are as representative of two-year-olds as they are of three-year-olds.

The imbecile can use language in a way that the idiot cannot; yet Binet and Simon say he can be as easily distinguished from the moron as he is from the idiot. The primary distinction between the imbecile and the moron is that written language cannot be achieved by the true imbecile. He does not read nor does he understand writing, he cannot write from dictation, he cannot use language in written form and in a spontaneous manner. In test performance on the 1908 Scale, he begins to fail at year eight.

Finally, there is the problem of separating moronity from normal intelligence. Binet and Simon point out that this is a more complicated matter because there are no fixed limits which would clearly distinguish the moron from the average child, as there are for the greater degrees of intellectual deficiency.

Binet and Simon present a quite general formula as to what constitutes normal intelligence. An individual is normal, they say, when he conducts himself in his life without the need of being taken care of by someone else, when he can perform work in such a way that he is doing something worthwhile and can be paid for his services, and when his intellectual level is of such a nature that he maintains the same social rank as his parents. Verification of these degrees of intellectual deficiency was obtained by Binet and Simon in some studies done in Parisian hospitals with adults who were known to be deficient. They were able by means of the 1908 Scale to determine the degree of deficiency of each of these adults. In no instance did one of these adults exceed the level of performance of the average nine- or ten-year-old child. While it is true that some of these adults were able to answer, with some degree of exactness, the kinds of questions which could be answered through experience, there were other tests which none of these persons apparently could handle as well as a much younger child. Binet and Simon found that, where language was used by the adult imbecile, such items as naming the days of the week, naming the months, recognizing and naming correctly colors and other such items could be handled by them as well as by the average child of eight, nine or ten. Apparently, experience is helpful in dealing with these kinds of items. However, on some other kinds of tests these adults could not perform even as well as children of five years or so. Examples of these kinds of items included comprehension questions, constructing a sentence given three words, defining abstract terms, interpreting pictures, making rhymes, and arranging weights. Though some of these tests might be passed by a few of the individuals, not one of these adults was able to pass all items or even as many as three of the six. Binet and Simon state then that these six kinds of items acquire particular importance in determining whether or not an adult is normal or a moron. Though they qualify the statement, Binet and Simon state that it is not unreasonable to consider that any adult who cannot pass these six items may be considered feeble-minded, while all those who can may be considered to be normal. In the scale, these items occur between years nine and twelve.

Though somewhat definitive statements may be made about the adult, making decisions about the degree of retardation and its seriousness in the younger child is less possible. With the child, age becomes a significant factor in determining the use of the label. On the basis of evidence available to them, Binet and Simon recommend that, since intellectual retardation of one year occurs quite frequently, such an absolute amount of retardation may be considered to be insufficient for diagnostic purposes. However, retardation by two or more years is quite rare. As a matter of fact, they say, only in seven cases out of a hundred was retardation of two years in absolute mental age found. In cases then where two years or more of retardation occurs in test performance, the question may be raised as to whether or not the child is subnormal, and in which category he should be placed. One may then use the schema already provided by them; that is, in an older child idiocy is reflected by behavior like that of normal children of two years of age or less, imbecility by behavior in the range from two to seven years, moronity by eight-year-old behavior. For a child less than eight years of age any diagnosis which is made obviously must be tentative. A seven-year-old child who obtains a mental age of five years would be called imbecile under the criteria used. However, as Binet and Simon point out, with the passage of time the diagnosis may change.

Evaluations of the 1908 Scale

The 1908 Scale was more widely used than was the 1905 Scale, although the earlier Scale had been translated into English, German, and Italian. One of the earliest critiques and criticisms of the 1908 Scale came from Belgium where Decroly and Degand (Decroly and Degand, 1910) used the scale in a private school as they had in 1905. As before, they offer criticism and suggestions for improvement of this scale. One of their major criticisms was that the test tended to be too easy for young children and too difficult for older ones. This would indicate some bias in the scale which would overestimate the abilities of young children, underestimate those of older children, and lead to the conclusion that intelligence declines with age.

Because of other criticisms, including those of placement of items, Binet and Simon requested and received the data which Decroly and Degand had gathered. Under analysis it appeared to Binet and Simon that the children used in the Belgian study were not of the same social class as those upon whom the test was standardized. Since the Belgian children were from a private school they tended to be of a superior social class, and they also tended to test much higher than the children who had been used in Paris. On the average, as a matter of fact, Binet found that the Belgian sample was about one and one-half years accelerated over the norm. This difference suggested to Binet that social class might be a very important feature in the use of the scale, and he began a systematic study of differences among social classes in performance on the 1908 Scale. He further studied the superiority of performance of the Belgian children as compared with the Parisian sample and concluded that the Belgian children were most superior on those kinds of subtests where language and home training were the most important. Least differences were found in terms of formal academic training. Admittedly, the data upon which this conclusion was based were quite limited. In studies done in Paris, Binet and several of his colleagues found approximately the same acceleration for children of the superior social class that had been found for the Belgian sample.

Binet and Simon had already expressed some regrets that many persons attempting to use the scale and coming up with criticisms of it had not been trained by them. A major breakthrough against this attitude, then, occurred when Kathryn Johnston visited Binet's laboratory in 1910 and was trained in the administration of the Scale. She returned to England, and conducted experimentation with children in the schools of Sheffield (Johnston, 1910; 1911). One of the major results of these studies was a confirmation of that cited by Decroly and Degand that the tests were too easy at the lower end of the scale and too difficult at the upper end of the scale. This finding was also confirmed in the United States by Goddard (1911), and Terman and Childs (1912), and by Bobertag (1911) in Germany. Though these findings were too late to influence work on the 1911 Scale, they indicate some kind of agreement even across cultures. Peterson (1925, p. 220) has quoted Stern (1914) who saw in this kind of agreement perhaps the strongest evidence of the validity of the Binet method for measuring intellectual differences. As Stern stated it:

> That, despite the differences in race and language, despite the divergencies in school organization and in methods of instruction, there should be so decided agreement in the reactions of the children—is, in my opinion, the best vindication of the *principle* of the test that one could imagine, because this agreement demonstrates that *the tests do actually reach and discover the general developmental conditions of intelligence* (so far as these are operative in public school children of the present cultural epoch), and not mere fragments of knowledge and attainment supplied by chance. And this confirmation of the principle may also lead us confidently to expect that the discrepancies that have been revealed at the same time in some of the details of the system can be obviated in the future.

The scale generally was well received as a means of classifying degrees of defective intelligence. Though some criticisms were offered of individual items, Binet made the strong point that in combination they might yield the kind of measure which makes differentiation possible. This, of course, is the underlying defense of the measure of general intelligence. Both the success and the criticisms which followed the publication of the 1908 Scale led Binet and Simon to attempt a second revision, the 1911 Scale.

The 1911 Scale

Just as the Whipple *Manual* (1910) is an invaluable source for direct translations of the 1905 and 1908 Scales, a translation by Town (1914) of the 1911 Scale is available. This scale uses most of the items from the 1908 Scale, a few of the items from the 1905 Scale and two new items.

Changes in This Scale

One of the most immediate changes that may be noticed is that now, in every instance but one, there are five items at each of the year levels. Partial credits for the year could be assigned depending upon how many items a child passed. As a result, scoring rules were changed slightly in this revision. The procedure suggested by Binet and Simon was as follows: Take the highest year level at which all of the tests were passed. This will be equivalent to what is now called a basal age. Additionally, however, the child will be given credits for each item which he passes at any year beyond that which constitutes the basal. If a child passes all items at year seven, for example, he receives seven years' credit plus one-fifth of a year credit for any items which may be passed at year eight, nine, and so on.

In looking at the replacement of items, it is evident that Binet and Simon made some attempts at adjustment in terms of criticisms made about difficulty level. This procedure was intended to reduce the difficulty level of older age levels and increase it for younger ones.

Reliability and Validity Estimates

For the 1911 Scale, Binet for the first time became concerned about some kinds of measures of reliability. By this he seems to have meant consistency in the way that the child would perform from one testing to another testing on the scale. He had already proposed that one means of obtaining such information would be to take a group of individuals, test them at one time, then fifteen days later retest them with the same test. This should indicate whether or not children maintained approximately the same results. Binet believed, in fact, that some differences should be obtained in scores. Because of his previous research on attention and adaptation, he assumed that children would make significant score gains from one testing to another. Peterson (1925, p. 239) reports a study done in 1910 by a colleague of Binet to determine whether or not such score gains did occur. Five children were tested with a 14-day interval between tests. For these five children, gains were obtained from the first test to the second test, with an average gain equal to five months. Such a large amount of gain in a two-week period was of some concern to Binet and the items on which gains occurred were left out in the 1911 revision. Binet also pointed out that a fifteen-day interval might be too short, that if an interval of a year were allowed such gains might not occur. Undoubtedly, as Peterson says, if Binet had lived longer he would have studied more intensively this problem of reliability and applied his findings to the test.

As a means of determining the validity of the scale, Binet and Simon tested 97 children who were within two months of their birthdays. These children were unselected in terms of their mental status. However, they were placed in grades which were equivalent to their ages. To determine the accuracy of the scale, Binet and Simon computed the deviation of the grade of each child from the school-grade average for his age, as well as the difference of his mental age from his actual age. Differences were then taken between these two scores. On the average, there was only seven-tenths of one year difference between the two scores. As an added check, a table of correlation coefficients was constructed which indicated a very high correlation, though not perfect, between academic placement and mental level of each child. Binet and Simon felt that the evidence supported the validity of the scale.

The primary use of the scales was to be in public-school settings. For this reason, validity must be considered in terms of teacher utilization and teacher judgments about intellectual level, as well as the actual test performance for the child. Some persons believed that a teacher could judge the level of intelligence of a child at least as accurately as could be judged with the test of Binet. As another evidence of validity of the scale, then, Binet began a study of teacher estimates of intelligence.

To determine teacher reliability in estimating the intelligence of students, Binet conducted a survey asking teachers about the proportion of errors which they believed they made in judging the intelligence of children. He also asked the means by which they determined as exactly as possible intellectual competencies of their children. Only some forty teachers participated in this study, the answers which they supplied to Binet ranging from very short one-paragraph ones up to as many as ten pages. One of the more obvious results was that the teachers were not in very good agreement. A few of them claimed that they made no errors at all in estimating the intelligence of their students, while others said that they found it very difficult to rate intellectual competency particularly as they came to know their students better and better.

One reason for such divergence in opinions as to correct estimation of intelligence lies in the fact that teachers used different standards of assessing a child's ability. Binet pointed out that with lack of precision, accuracy must suffer. Terminology was not common from teacher to teacher, and grades of superiority certainly were not equated. Just as physicians use terminology like moron and imbecile in different ways, so teachers used terms reflecting degrees of superiority and inferiority without very much agreement. In the absence of a similar scale or procedure for rating degrees of intellectual competency, differences among teachers must be expected. As a matter of fact, Binet said, those teachers who have the least exact criteria for judging intelligence are the ones who are apt to be most pleased with their conclusions.

Generally, teachers tended to judge adequacy of intelligence on the part of their students in fairly unstandardized ways. This lack of standardization led to increased error, Binet believed. The most frequently reported means of estimating intelligence, on the part of teachers, was performance in class. The child who learned subject matter material most easily and quickly and retained it best was generally considered by the teacher to be the most intelligent student. Whatever subject the teacher taught tended to be looked upon by him as being the most important for purposes of determining intellectual competence as well. Though there certainly is some defensible basis for this, the point made by Binet that knowledge is insufficient for judging intelligence is well made. Acquisition of knowledge will include such things, Binet said, as memory, attention, comprehension, and efficient work methods. But these qualities cannot be separated from the direction of others as compared to self-direction. Under an efficient teacher, the child may appear more competent than he actually is.

To further determine teacher methods of estimating intelligence, Binet invited three teachers to come to his laboratory and demonstrate their procedures in judging intellectual levels of children. They would work with pupils selected by him and who were strangers to the teachers. Five children were used, and each teacher spent an afternoon attempting to determine the intellectual level of each of these children. The teacher was allowed to use for this purpose whatever methodology he felt to be most workable.

Again, the overall drawback that Binet found was lack of standardization, not only from teacher to teacher, but even for a single teacher from child to child. For example, a teacher might ask highly specific questions of one child relative to the part of Paris in which he lived. For another child some other set of questions would be used. Just how one might make comparisons as to the intellectual level of each of these children Binet felt to be very questionable. In addition, the measure would be biased by the fact that one child was dealing with highly specific experiences as compared to more general ones that another should have picked up in the matter of living. In some instances, the questions were leading in the sense that there would be only one of two alternatives possible for an answer; and the child might either be able to judge from the teacher's expression or looks what answer was acceptable or, at worst, would have a fifty-fifty chance among the alternatives. The teachers also tended to be inconsistent in evaluating responses. Binet cites the fact that with two children who gave essentially the same answer a given teacher scored one higher than the other because she had already concluded that the one child was brighter than the other child.

It is not surprising that from this study Binet took the position that some degree of standardization is absolutely essential if comparisons among children in intellectual level are to be made. The content of the test also becomes an important criterion in making judgments among children. Some definite set of questions needs to be used, derived on the basis of empirically established norms. The content of the questions must not be specific to some circumstances and not to others. The questions should reflect the kinds of things which an individual could learn, if he were intelligent enough, from everyday experiences common to all. In terms of mental content, the items should reflect higher mental processes.

Peterson (1925, p. 253) makes the point that, despite the fact that teacher judgments were not very good, as demonstrated by Binet, procedures used by teachers in judging intelligence were quite indispensable to the building of a scale. It was necessary to establish a pool of bright youngsters as compared to dull ones on some criteria. Teachers were in the position of being able to provide such a set of criteria. Basically, the criterion should reflect actual achievement in school. The kinds of items that would clearly differentiate between those who were successful in school and those who were not might be a device for determining more closely intellectual differences beyond the school setting. Within the school context, Binet generally found that those children who were youngest in their grade group tended to be the more intelligent, in terms not only of achievement in school but also of the test measures themselves. By contrast, those children who were overage in grade tended to be intellectually duller than their age-mates.

Binet's Theoretical Conceptions

In the introduction to the 1908 Scale (Binet and Simon, 1908) a position had been taken defending theoretical conceptions as pertinent only to empirical work. Thus, Binet says that theory is necessary since it does provide some kind of direction to the empiricism which must follow. However, unless there is empiricism, unless there is experimentation, theory is of little or no value. Binet felt so strongly that the scientific method was the best means of achieving knowledge about human behavior that it is not too surprising that he does not really state a clearly defined theory of intelligence under which he operates. Certainly some of the theoretical conceptions that directed his effort can be gleaned from his writing. But at no time did he present a systematic model which might be used and labeled as the "Binet theory of intelligence."

The essential first feature in viewing Binet's conception of intelligence is to remember that he took a strong position against the use of sensory tests as the means of reflecting individual differences and intellectual competence. This view was diametrically opposed to that of most of the psychologists of the day. The work of Galton in England had been particularly influential in terms of the development of German and American psychological laboratories. Binet believed that sensory-motor measures would not offer reliable information about intellectual competence because the behavior required was too far removed from the trait desired. For this reason, then, he recommended the use of measures of higher complex processes. These higher complex processes are not specifically defined. As a matter of fact, Binet makes it clear that it would be difficult to try to classify particular kinds of items as measuring memory or attention or judgment or comprehension or whatever other traits are assumed to be higher complex processes. The reason for this difficulty lies in the fact that probably all of these forms enter, to some degree, any higher mental operation. Until the specific traits which are significant of complex processes can be defined and measured, some general measure of intelligence would seem to be a superior one, since it would reflect to some degree all of these at work.

His first writings stressed memory and imagery as the kinds of traits which would reflect intelligent behavior at its highest level. His studies of imagery left him disappointed. Lack of consistency in results persuaded him that perhaps imagery was not a very usable concept for measuring intelligence. By *memory*, he apparently meant something more than associative memory. He included within the concept some degree of attention on the part of the child. He believed that the child with a good memory must show direction of his mental powers in order to be successful. At one point, for example, he speaks of the memory-for-sentences task as being a "virtual dynamometer of attention." Though the role of memory as a direct reflection of the general nature of intelligence becomes less as Binet continues writing and experimenting, task content reflecting memory remains heavy throughout all the scales. This state of affairs is really not so anachronistic when we consider that it is impossible to conceive of any task in which memory does not play a part.

Because of some results on memory tasks, Binet also conceived early in his career that suggestibility might be one means of differentiating the young child, or the intellectually inferior one, from the older, or intellectually superior one. Despite the fact that suggestibility tasks remain in the scales, they proved to be less usable than Binet had hoped and in efforts following his have been largely ignored.

By the turn of the century, Binet begins to use the concept of attention more directly as perhaps a direct reflection of intellectual competence. By attention he meant mental adaptation to some situation which is relatively new to the individual. Apparently, then, he meant what the learning theorist would call *transfer* or *generalization* by his use of the term *attention*. However, the tests that he devised to measure attention seemed to fail. The reason for this failure was most probably the fact that they were not very good tests of transfer. If Binet actually meant by the word attention what he would now call transfer and generalization, then a logical position favoring such a construct might be defended. Certainly there is some evidence that the child who is of higher intellectual ability does tend to utilize his experiences, that is, to transfer them, more readily than the child of lesser intellectual abilities. However, Binet ran into measurement problems and so abandoned the attention tasks he had accumulated.

Now Binet turns his attention to the possibility of a complex combination of mental functions. He still admits that there are probably certain general functions which might be described, labeled, and measured to some degree. Among these would be included such things as attention, judgment, comprehension. By 1905, with the publication of the first scale, judgment had become the essential characteristic which Binet believed would reflect this complex of mental functions. But he now says that judgment is not a simple process, nor a single one. Judgment includes a diversity of intellectual aptitudes, some of which he felt he could describe, others of which he thought perhaps could not be so easily described. And indeed by the time of the publication of the 1908 Scale, Binet admits that intelligence is much more complex than he had initially thought it could be. He now tries to avoid reference to any single term to describe the diversity of intellectual aptitudes that he felt must operate on the part of any individual.

In 1909 Binet published a study based upon cognitive processes in defective children (Binet and Simon, 1909). From the data available, Binet had come to the conclusion that what he called *thinking* is actually some kind of mental trial-and-error behavior, in which we grope our way, choose among alternatives, and gradually become proficient in our mental adaptations. This position would seem to underscore again the transfer process which he had cited earlier as the basis of intellectual behavior. He also proposed his first attempt at some kind of model of how intelligence may express itself. He speaks of three dimensions, overlapping but not continuous. The first of these, and the lowest in terms of intellectual behavior, he calls *direction*. The second level is what he calls *adaptation*. The highest level is one of *autocriticism*.

A requisite of all intelligent behavior, Binet believed, was fast, effective, thoughtful behavior. This behavior must primarily keep and maintain a definite direction in conjunction with some stated goal. Peterson (1925, pp. 260–266) describes the various levels of this Binet model and gives examples of each of them. For example, if a child is asked to perform some fairly routine task, such as picking out black buttons from white ones and putting them in separate boxes, he may easily be distracted from this goal. If he shows distractability, Binet would maintain that he cannot keep his direction of thought. A child of higher mentality or an older child certainly would be able to pursue the task until some definite closure is reached. There is the implication here that the child has to keep in mind what is to be done—that is, the goal to be achieved —and continue to work critically at the task until this goal is achieved. Binet believed that differences in ability to maintain direction in thinking was significant for differences in intelligence. Direction can be expressed in terms of simple versus complex tasks, and it may also be expressed in terms of its persistence.

The next level is described as adaptation. By this, Binet meant adapting means in order to achieve some signified ends. As he has already said, thinking is choosing between various ideas; and these ideas become clearer as means of accomplishing goals as we have more and more experience. To Binet ideas serve a vital function, they exist to help us reach some end. However, a child or an intellectually inferior adult would be too greatly influenced by immediate circumstances and by responses to immediate stimuli. The more intelligent child and adult would consider remote consequences as well as the immediate ones. The goal must be kept in mind then; that is, apparently direction has to operate in some degree in order that adaptation might operate as well. Binet was not much concerned about the goal which the individual might choose. Goals he considered to be generally based upon emotional, sentimental, or instinctive factors rather than intellectual ones. However, once the individual has chosen some set of goals for himself, adaptation in terms of alternative means to achieve the goal becomes important.

Binet has already made the case for trial and error adaptation in mental behavior. Intelligent action in the sense of adaptation must reflect this kind of trial and error choice among possible alternatives. In most instances, Binet believed, we do not choose among alternatives in some magical and automatic fashion. There is nothing mystical about the behavior that he calls adaptation. Our initial attempts will be trial and error. As we have successive experiences and successive trials we will become better, within the limits of intellectual level, in terms of choosing among the alternatives that are available to us. It is in this matter of relatively accurate and adequate choice among alternatives that the child who is deficient will begin to diverge markedly from the child who is much brighter. Even if we attempt to provide the same kinds of experiences to all children they will not be able to benefit from them equally. Since there will be differences in the effects of experience on the intellectual input of the child, we must expect differences in terms of adaptation as Binet uses the term. If children differ in the degree to which input occurs in the first place, and further differ in how they can use whatever input they have, then the concept of Binet about adaptation assumes extreme importance to our understanding of how intelligence works.

The final level referred to by Binet in this particular article he calls auto-criticism. By this he seems to have meant some kind of critical spirit, with the ability to make a satisfactory judgment about action. Some calm, objective perception of one's behavior and how to change it in order to function more creditably reflects this dimension. There has to be some appearance of control of the situation by the individual. He has to control his sentiments and emotions in such a way that they will not interfere with his intelligent behavior. In any situation, there is some objective aspect which must first be comprehended by the subject. To be intelligent, he must then evaluate critically and reflectively the objective aspects of the situation. The retardate or the less bright individual will not be able to see the inadequacy of his attempts, so that he does not adapt himself by trying better responses. To Binet, auto-criticism was the very highest level of intellectual behavior that might be achieved. Furthermore, he believed that very few persons ever achieve it.

In a book appearing in the same year (Binet, 1909), he refined somewhat the presentation presented in the earlier work. The concept of adaptation, that mental trial-and-error choosing among alternatives, is divided into two kinds of behavior. One of these he calls "comprehension," the second "invention." To function on either of these levels, and thereby to show one's mental adaptation, it is necessary first to comprehend the elements in the situation and, in some instances, perhaps utilize directly responses already available. Under other circumstances, however, it may be necessary to utilize past experiences to come up with a somewhat different response. This would represent the dimension of invention. Together these concepts of comprehension and invention reflect the need actively to organize responses in terms of whatever complexity exists in the behavioral situation.

There are now four dimensions to intelligence hypothesized by Binet. The lowest of these is direction. We should find the child developing first on this continuum. Once he has developed sufficiently in terms of direction, it is possible, but not assured, that he will begin to develop on the dimension of comprehension. As he matures mentally, he may then begin to develop in invention. Finally, if he is one of the few great intellects of his time, he may develop to some degree on the dimension of auto-criticism.

In considering the essential nature of intelligence, Binet must be classed among those individuals who look on intelligence as being a unitary function. He admits in a number of his writings that there are probably a multiplicity of faculties which exist. What these faculties are he does not himself specify and leaves as a task for others to explore. However, whatever number and type of faculties may exist, they serve only one function: some expression of a general nature that permeates all of behavior. They must operate in some combination such that the individual can adjust to the conditions of his environment, and so that he may continue in some sort of reasonable adaptation to life. This adjustment to environmental features of life will be reflected in the degree to which the individual has developed in direction, comprehension, invention and auto-criticism.

If Binet had lived longer, it would not be unreasonable to expect further changes and refinements in this schema that he has presented. Certainly all the prior work that he had done indicated his willingness to accept data as a means of influencing the opinions that he held. As a scientist and an empiricist, whenever he found that data did not agree with his conceptions, he believed the data and changed the conceptions. It is of some interest as well that Binet did not allow his theoretical conceptions to influence to any great degree his scales. The continua proposed in the 1909 publications, for example, cannot be detected particularly in the 1911 Scales. Thus, Binet's theoretical conception did not influence what went into the test. Though one might be able to select certain items which seem to reflect a degree of direction or invention or one of the other variables, these would be only sporadic. The reason is that Binet believed that each of these continua probably influences to some degree behavior on any given kind of task which truly taps higher intellectual processes. The measure derived then is one of general intelligence.

The conception of general intelligence expressed through items which discriminate between children judged to be relatively bright and relatively dull, and the methods of achieving these items, are the major contributions which Binet made to the testing movement. It would be impossible to overestimate their importance.

References

Binet, A., *Les Idées Modernes sur les Enfants.* 1909.

———, "Nouvelle Recherches sur la Mesure du Niveau Intelluel chez les Enfants d'École," *L'Année Psychologique,* 1911, 17, 145–210.

———, and Simon, Thomas, "Le Développement de l'Intelligence chez les Enfants," *L'Année Psychologique,* 1908, 14, 1–94.

———, and Simon, Th., "L'Intelligence des Imbéciles," *L'Année Psychologique.* 1909, 15, 1–147.

Bobertag, O., "A. Binet's Arbeiten über die Intellektuelle Entwicklung des Schulkindes," *Zeitschrift fur angewandte Psychologie,* 1911, 5, 105–123; 1912, 6, 495–538.

Decroly, O., and Degand, J., "Les Tests de Binet et Simon pour le Mesure de l'Intelligence: Contribution Critique," *Archives de Psychologie,* 1906, 6, 27, 130.

———, "La Mesure de l'Intelligence chez les Enfants Normaux d'apres les Tests de Binet et Simon: Nouvelle Contribution Critique." *Archives de Psychologie,* 1910, 9, 81–108.

Getzels, J. W., and Jackson, P. W., *Creativity and Intelligence: Explorations with Gifted Students.* New York: Wiley, 1962.

Goddard, H. H., "The Binet and Simon Tests of Intellectual Capacity," *The Training School,* 1908, 5, 3–9.

———, "Two Thousand Normal Children Measured by the Binet Measuring Scale of Intelligence," *Pedagogical Seminary,* 1911, 18, 232–259.

Johnston, Katherine L., "An English Version of Binet's Tests for the Measurement of Intelligence," *Report of the British Association for the Advancement of Science,* 1910, 80, 806–808.

———, "M. Binet's Method for the Measurement of Intelligence: Some Results," *Journal of Experimental Pedagogy,* 1911, 1, 24–31.

Peterson, J., *Early Conceptions and Tests of Intelligence.* Yonkers-on-Hudson, N.Y.: World Book, 1925.

Stern, W., *The Psychological Methods of Testing Intelligence.* Translated by G. M. Whipple. Educational Psychology Monographs, 1914, No. 13, p. 160.

Terman, L. M., "Genius and Stupidity: A Study of Some of the Intellectual Processes of Seven 'Bright' and Seven 'Stupid' Boys," *Pedagogical Seminary,* 1906, 13, 307–373.

———, and Childs, H. G., "Tentative Revision and Extension of the Binet-Simon Measuring Scale of Intelligence," *Journal of Educational Psychology,* 1912, 3, 61–74, 133–143, 198–208, 277–289.

Town, Clara Harrison, *A Method of Measuring the Development of the Intelligence of Young Children.* Chicago: Chicago Medical Book Co., 1914.

Whipple, G. M., *Manual of Mental and Physical Tests.* Baltimore: Warwick and York, 1910.

4

Lewis M. Terman

In the United States, Lewis M. Terman brought Binet's methods, concepts, and testing procedures to common use. Though such psychologists as Goddard (1908, 1911) translated the Binet scales and used them in institutional settings, it was Terman who first recognized the validity of the Binet approach and who made a strong case for its utilization against what represented the sensory-motor approach of Galton and Wundt. In many respects the approach of Terman was as antithetical to the prevailing sentiments in this country as had been that of Binet in Europe.

Terman and the Mental-Test Movement

Because of laboratory studies, work in this country on the measurement of individual differences persisted in using the method of the German psychologists and of Galton. Though some combination of the German method with the Binet approach had been advocated not only by Sharp (1899) but also by some others, little utilization of Binet's approach occurred. In fact there was virtually no implementation of the Binet approach as such. In 1906, however, Terman published an article entitled "Genius and Stupidity" (Terman, 1906). This article is noteworthy because it represented a firm movement in the direction of the Binet approach. Not only did it influence all of the work which Terman did after that, but it also gave the mental-test movement a new impetus.

The Study of Intellectual Extremes

Psychology, as a field, must be related in many respects to life; that is, it must show some practical utility. One of the problems in this regard is illustrating the exactness of psychology as a science. In so far as psychology can be considered a science it may make the same kinds of practical discoveries as are found in the other sciences.

Since the subject matter of the psychologist is the individual mind, there are problems of determining what specifically the psychologist studies. Terman surveyed the attitudes of a number of eminent psychologists of the day, and centered his attention on the matter of mental testing. He pointed to problems in determining whether or not the mental-test movement fell under the general heading of a scientific or an artistic endeavor. One problem in determining the scientific status of mental testing was the fact that observable traits are not so easily defined. Where such differences may be defined, however, they are probably as great as those observed, say, by the zoologist.

A need for the precision of science in psychology as a field does not preclude quite practical outcomes. Certainly, when the field of psychology invests its energies in a mental-test movement, the outcomes should be highly usable in such areas as education. Much of the writing in the psychology field, including that of such authorities as Binet, had indicated the practical outcomes of such work. The great expectations expressed by such persons as Binet and Spearman, however, had not been achieved at the time of the writing of Terman's article. Terman points out that eventually there must grow in the field of psychology a group of expert individuals who will be as important to the psychological development of the individual as the physician is to his medical nature. However, he warns that if premature results are applied to the field of education more harm may be done than good. One of the purposes in a study such as this one, then, is to try to determine to what degree the mental-test movement may have applicability to the general educational setting.

Terman says that there are two means by which mental tests may be studied. First, there is the use of a relatively large number of superficial tests used on a fairly large number of individuals. Under this general heading, it is possible either to use a fairly large number of tests—say ten to twenty—and to administer all of them within a short time period, say an hour or so. As an alternative, a relatively small number of tests may be administered to a large number of subjects under very highly controlled conditions. This approach by and large tends to yield quantitative differences that support correlations, but the individual is lost in the interpretation of results.

A second approach, Terman believed, emphasizes some qualitative analysis of the process which makes up the mental capabilities of the individual. Here, a small sample would be quite carefully studied. Mental differences among the subjects who make up this sample would be analyzed quite carefully. Frequently the tests will not be scored yes or no, plus or minus, but will allow for different kinds of answers, different kinds of errors, and different methods of correction. The study reported in Terman's 1906 article is of this latter type. He particularly states that it is based on the Binet experimental study of intelligence (Binet, 1902).

The sample used in Terman's study came from school children in Worcester, Massachusetts. Terman attempted to identify clearly different extremes in intellectual competence. For this reason he went to teachers and asked them to estimate among the boys enrolled in their classes those who were the brightest and the dullest. Some twenty-four boys were so identified, half of them believed to be exceptionally bright, the other half exceptionally dull. Since the school population comprised some 500 boys, these samples probably do represent the extremes which Terman desired. Of the twenty-four so cited by teachers, fourteen were willing to participate in the experiment and did so throughout its duration. Terman points out that each of the boys received a small fee if he completed the entire experiment. However, he believed that such payment would not have been necessary because of the apparent motivational nature of the tasks used and the general interest level of each of the boys. The work continued six hours a day, six days per week from January until May, 1905.

Terman realized that the use of terms such as *brightest* and *dullest, genius* and *stupid,* may be restricted in their meaning. In asking teachers to select those boys who would fall within either extreme, he cautioned them to base their judgments upon the child as a whole not merely upon his classwork in school. To what degree this caution was exercised cannot be known. Terman admits that teacher judgments under these circumstances would hardly be infallible, but he feels that what he got in terms of the samples achieved was what he wanted: extreme differences in general intellectual ability. He uses the terms *bright* and *dull,* then, in a most general form. At the same time, he believed that most people would tend to agree in the classification of extremely bright or extremely dull and as a result he could study the fundamental intellectual differences between these two groups. Like Binet, he pointed out that a number of such studies will allow us to define more precisely what terms mean.

One of the characteristics in which the two samples differed was that of age. The sample of bright boys averaged something less than eleven years of age, with a range of ten years two months to eleven years five months. The dull group, by contrast, averaged almost twelve years of age, with a range from ten years four months to thirteen years nine months.

As Terman points out, the discrepancy should favor the dull group since they will have had more experiences than the bright group will have had. All of the subjects seem to come from good home backgrounds; none of them was from extremely economically poor parents or gave any physical evidences of lack of health. By and large, Terman concludes that the environmental backgrounds of the subjects should be conducive to their overall intellectual development and favorable to his study.

Terman used eight kinds of tests in this study. These he classified as: (1) inventiveness and creative imagination; (2) logical processes; (3) mathematical ability; (4) language mastery; (5) insight; (6) ease of acquisition; (7) powers of memory; (8) motor ability. Each of these will be considered briefly in terms of purpose, definition, and representative tasks used for measurement.

Inventiveness and Imagination

Terman explains that he believes invention is largely dependent upon constructive imagination. As such it is necessary for the individual to use his present and past experiences to apply to new situations. The importance of this characteristic is illustrated by Terman's statement that rarely will intellectual differences among men depend upon some kind of native retentiveness or sense discrimination. Much more important than this will be the use of sense data in memory and imagination. This is what he calls invention. With invention, the individual can acquire genius. Therefore, it is a kind of ability that every great mind exhibits. If his assumptions are correct, then one of the problems of psychology is to attempt to determine the nature of invention, and the reason for differences from individual to individual. He cites at least three kinds of invention: mechanical, artistic, and scientific or philosophical. To the external viewpoint, and therefore in terms of measurement, the differences among these kinds of invention appear to be quite small. And at this stage Terman makes little attempt to differentiate among them in the practical sense. He devised some ten tasks, each of which he believed was a measure of invention in the sense in which he used the term. The purpose, then, of these tasks was to try to demonstrate differences in constructive imagination and invention and to see if there would be differences in terms of the development of logical processes among the subjects used in this study. Terman predicted that some differences would be found in methods of solution to the problems he proposed. The dull boys he believed would tend to emphasize more the method of trial and error and use perceptual thought rather than conceptual thought. For practical purposes, then, the first two abilities to be tested, namely invention and imagination and logical processes, were combined. Terman describes each of the problems used, the conditions under which they would be administered, and the results obtained.

Terman summarizes these two kinds of tasks by pointing out that the boys who were defined on the basis of teacher judgments as being brightest showed superior powers of imagination and a stronger tendency to economize in their efforts. He speaks, for example, of them using their eyes rather than their fingers, mental experimentation rather than physical manipulation, studying things out before beginning an operation, abstracting from particular problems, and using general rules. If, indeed, they began in a haphazard manner, they more quickly eliminated errors and took a more logical, reasonable approach to their problem solution. In contrast, the dull boys tended to take more trials than the brighter ones, even persisting at a task where failure seemed to be evident. Thus, brighter individuals will recognize when they cannot solve a problem and give up. The duller individual may persist even though he cannot do the problem.

Mathematical Ability

To test mathematical competence Terman uses a number of tasks beginning with quite simple problems of the fundamental processes and going up to solutions based upon developing a rule. Some eight tasks of increasing difficulty were used.

Language

Terman begins by an explicit statement about the necessity of language to intellectual development. Without language there can be no conceptual thought. In every child's development there are stages that represent peculiar language interests, language development, and language capabilities. As a single source of information, language growth probably gives more information about a child's intelligence than any other kind of data. In a reading test, Terman found that the dull boys as a group were decidedly inferior to the bright boys. Not only did they read less fluently but they tended to miscall more words and they had less expression in their oral reading. Additionally, their reading rates tended to be much slower than those of the bright boys. Terman believed this difference in rate was a significant feature of general intellectual differences. He even compares the reading of the dull boys to that of normal individuals who are reading nonsense material. Apparently, then, the dull boy simply does not become much involved in whatever written matter he is dealing with.

The word-making task, where letters randomly assigned must be used to form words, also gives some information about differences between the groups. Terman comments that vocabulary is an important aspect of success at this task, as also are ability to spell and habits of word analysis in general. But in addition to these advantages it is also necessary for the individual to have a rational plan. Randomness of behavior tended to be a function of the dull group more often than it did of the bright group. For the mutilated-text task, Terman used the Ebbinghaus procedure. The results led him to take the position that this kind of task is quite good for discrimination between intellectual levels. Particularly does such a task give information about fluency in the language behavior of the individual. The fourth kind of task, spelling, he defends against criticism which might be leveled on the basis of its lack of relationship to general mental ability. He did find differences in spelling ability favoring the bright boys, and felt these to be quite significant.

Insight

What Terman refers to as insightful behavior was tested by means of intepretation of fables. In every instance, he reports that the dull boys were inferior. Two kinds of behavior distinguish them from bright boys. First, the dull boys tend more frequently to miss the point of a story altogether. Second, the dull boys are deficient in terms of abstraction. Though they may at times correctly interpret a fable, they tend to express their interpretation in highly concrete terms related only to the given situation. They tend, therefore, not to generalize as well as the bright boys do.

Ease of Acquisition

For this purpose Terman used chess. He found differentiation between the two groups and advocated that it needed further study. The time needed for such investigation, of course, is so great that it is not surprising that sufficient follow-up did not occur.

Memory

Terman states that memory tests had proved to be largely unsatisfactory. It is not possible to get to pure retention, he said, because our memories tend to be influenced by interests of the moment and by perceptions. Even if we could get to pure memory Terman is not sure that it would be worthwhile to our study of logical and creative processes. He agrees with Binet in pointing out that memories tend to be largely specific and particular rather than general. As a result, he dismisses the memory tests as of little importance to his overall results which tended to favor the bright boys over the dull.

Motor Ability

One reason for including motor tasks in this particular study was their historical significance. As Terman points out, many authorities believe that there is some correlation between motor ability and general intellectual ability. Because of the small sample size he does not attempt to report any correlation, however.

Results

In analyzing his results, Terman reports the bright boys to be superior to the dull boys in all of the mental tasks, but inferior to them in the set of motor tasks. On all of the mental tasks except those he calls invention, the bright boys are clearly superior to the dull boys. On the invention task, though superior, the differences were much less. By and large, each of the subjects tended to hold about the same ranking throughout the various tests used. Terman interprets this to mean that intelligence does not develop along specific lines. The accuracy of this statement would depend upon demonstration that the tasks measure somewhat different intellectual traits. Since there is no real evidence of this, one may quarrel with Terman's conclusion.

Aside from the data collected, Terman also discusses observable differences in other forms of behavior. For example, the group of dull boys seemed to him to be as persistent in their attack upon problems as the bright boys were. At the same time, the bright boys seemed to accomplish more in a shorter period of time than the duller boys did in a much longer time period and with more effort. However, the bright boys also were more easily distracted. They would frequently talk about things other than the task at hand. Terman comments for example about their talking about unrelated matters after interrupting work on a task. His interpretation of this fact leads him to the conclusion that the bright boys tend to have mental associations that are spontaneous and more apt to be expressed. As he puts it, the work methods of the bright boys are ". . . mental associations that are more volatile, more spontaneous, and based on more subtle resemblances; on the part of the dull boys, associations that are close, matter of fact, and labored." Interests also seemed to differ between the groups. The bright boys preferred reading as an activity to playing games, while the dull boys inevitably chose game playing over reading. Terman points out that it would be interesting to determine whether or not there was some kind of internal aversion to physical exercise on the part of the bright boys or whether other conditions might account for the difference in interests. He speaks of finding emotional differences between the boys as well; and he believed these to be closely associated with observed intellectual differences. Over all, he concludes that there seems to him to be more evidence of the greater importance of heredity over environment, though he admits his tasks and results do not offer any evidence on the issue.

A First Scale

In 1912, Terman and Childs published "A Tentative Revision and Extension of the Binet-Simon Measuring Scale of Intelligence." Because of the limited number of items in the 1908 Revision of Binet, Terman suggested a number of supplementary tasks which he thought might be included in such a scale. Though these have significance for the 1916 Stanford Revision, they are not as important at this stage as are some theoretical and practical suggestions made by the authors. They direct their attention toward the school setting, advocating that there should be attempts to determine the qualitative nature of retardation and acceleration, both in terms of the native intellectual endowment of the child and in terms of educational outcomes. Measures of retardation and acceleration in educational outcomes should be fairly easy to accomplish, they state; yet few attempts to that time had been made to devise appropriate measures. Indeed, almost no communication existed from school system to school system as to what represented grade standards for any given level.

The determination of intellectual retardation and acceleration would be a more difficult task than that of educational status. In point of fact, educational performance has within it whatever qualities of intellectual retardation or acceleration exist. They make the point, however, that the influence of intelligence can never be truly divorced from that of training. As they state it, without ideas intelligence cannot work. For this reason the psychologist must be concerned about the quality and number of ideas which the individual has available to him, and these are dependent upon what they refer to as accidents of environment. What we obtain with a measure of intelligence is some kind of ability plus training. The problem is to make the measure as much as possible a reflection of intelligence as such. The best way to achieve this task, they state, is to make sure that tests which are used have contents which will reflect differences in training and experience as little as possible. Thus the tasks, in order to be considered a measure of intelligence, must have a content which is fairly common to all individuals taking the test. Such a state can never truly be achieved, but for practical purposes they believe that it can be reasonably approximated.

A first step must include norming procedures. For whatever kinds of performances about which we wish knowledge, age norms must be determined for each kind of performance. It is from this standpoint that the Binet Scale of 1908 becomes important. Though there are limitations within this scale, Terman and Childs point out that the test does attempt to determine different levels of intellectual competency. These are expressed through the mental age that is yielded by the scale. Through extension and through further study the items included in the Binet and Simon Scales can be extended and refined so as to meet the purposes of determining different levels of intellectual competence. The tentative revision offered by Terman and Childs, then, is an attempt to accomplish this purpose. Specifically, they mention as purposes: (1) determination of the adaptability of the Binet test to American conditions; (2) discovering what changes are needed in arrangement of items to make them more reliable; (3) to try out other kinds of tasks which could supplement the Binet tasks; and (4) to draw conclusions about the psychological and educational value of the items individually and collectively.

For these purposes, the 1908 Binet Scale was administered to 396 children in and around Stanford University in 1911. The children were not selected, and came from homes where the wage earner ranged from college professor to laborer. The children varied in age from four years through teen years. The numbers at each age level differed greatly, however, with the largest number being 83 at age five and the smallest number being 2 at age fifteen.

One of the problems with the use of the Binet Scales is the procedure followed in the determination of the mental age, the score achieved with the scale. Terman and Childs report two variations from the procedures generally followed with the Binet and Simon scale. First, the child's test age was computed by giving him the year equivalent of the lowest year in which he passed all the tests or all but one and then crediting him with an additional half year for every three tests that he satisfactorily passed beyond this point. Because of different numbers of items in the 1908 Scale, of course, it was not possible to rigidly enforce such a system throughout the entire scale. A second difference, not with the Binet method but with other procedures of scoring, was in the fact that a year level was assumed to encompass a chronological year. Thus by an eight-year-old is meant all children between the ages of eight and nine years. The median age then is actually eight and one-half, not eight. Terman and Childs state there is no problem with this procedure so long as what has been done is recognized. Then the appropriate interpretation of the mental age can be made.

In the use of the Scale with these California children, Terman and Childs found what Johnston in England, and Decroly and Degand in Belgium had also found. Younger children scored better than they should have if proper item placement had occurred, while older children scored more poorly than they should. Terman and Childs remark, rather kindly, that the items are poorly placed for an American sample. As they further state, certain items would have to be moved as much as three years to be correctly placed for their sample. As a result of such errors of placement, and because of a limitation in the number of tasks at certain ages, Terman and Childs made specific suggestions about some items which may be added and a procedure for equating the number of items at each age level. Still, in this revision there are not equal numbers of items at each level. In most instances there are six subtests; however, in certain instances there are five and in two instances there are eight.

Characteristics of the Scale

Because of dependence upon formal training, certain items were deleted from the Binet-Simon Scale and replaced with new items. Whether the items were from the original scale or were new ones, the decision on item placement was based upon percentage passing. Thus, Terman and Childs concluded, without any given reasons, that about two-thirds of the children of any age ought to pass a task to make that test characteristic for that age. Though it might seem reasonable that each item should show a fifty-percent-passing criterion for a given age group, this procedure actually is not workable. If all the tasks at a given year level are passed by exactly fifty percent of a norming group of that age, the task would be too difficult when used with the general population. The choice of a sixty- to seventy-percent-passing criterion is a better one for this reason. Since, however, it is not possible to find sufficient items which exactly meet a criterion such as sixty percent, such a figure is usually used as an average. Thus, one item at a year level may be passed by approximately fifty-five percent, another item by say seventy percent, another by sixty percent, and so on.

The content, according to Terman and Childs, sampled from a number of areas which would be characteristic of mental ability. They thought that each child, regardless of his age, should be tested with a variety of items which cover such things as memory, comprehension, reasoning, tests of observation, linguistic invention and association. In their view, the responses to such items should give a picture of the general level of intellectual functioning of the child at the time of testing.

Terman and Childs state that a test of this content is of significance, not because it displays the child's intelligence in its totality, but for determining and identifying the type of individual who is most apt to profit from his social environment. Thus, for any one kind of item, a child may show consistent failure. If, however, he fails a number of the variety of items, the failure has considerable significance. Particularly will such behavior be of importance for classroom purposes. The authors point out that there are no standardized norms of acquisition ability except for the quite crude ones contained in the curriculum. Where the child cannot successfully do school work, the assumption is made that he is mentally subnormal. Terman and Childs say that in most cases this is not an unjust assumption. But there will be a fairly high degree of error in the identification of such cases. It is at this point, then, that a scale such as this one becomes of considerable significance. Its utility, they believe, is undoubted.

The Terman-Childs (1912) article closes with some suggestions about means of assigning credit in an age scale such as this one. As they point out, Binet gave differential amounts of credit to the different age groups simply through the uneven number of items. Though equalizing the number of items at each year level as suggested by Binet in the 1911 Scale would be a step in the right direction, they believe it is not sufficient. Terman and Childs advocate that each item should be assigned appropriate value so that partial credits may be allowed for any given child. A child begins at some point in the scale where he can be successful. Once the level at which he can pass all items has been determined, testing continues until he can no longer pass items. He would receive partial credits for each item he passes above the so-called basal age.

Despite the limitations that they have pointed out in the Binet-Simon Scale, Terman and Childs conclude that it is still a most worthwhile approach to determining intellectual competence. The results on such a scale give a more reliable estimate of a child's ability in relation to normal children of his age than can be achieved by most teachers who have contact with a child over a period of a school year. Teacher standards tend to be in terms of whatever constitutes the qualities of the class she presently teaches. Since each class is not a fair representation of the range in extent of intelligence in the population, her observations may be quite biased. If she has a group which is over all low in ability, she will tend to overestimate the intellectual abilities of the relatively better students in the class. On the contrary, with a group of quite high ability, the teacher may tend to underestimate the competencies of some of the children. Since some teachers use only a rather vague and transcendent "average," the problem is even further complicated. Using such a scale as this (1912 Scale), Terman and Childs believe, will avoid problems in judgment for the teacher.

In closing, Terman and Childs suggest other developments which should be employed. For one thing, they believe that the revision they offer should be subjected to trial with a much larger sample. Specifically, they talk about thousands of children, representative of appropriate variables. Further, additional kinds of items should be tried out, they say, to determine their adequacy and applicability to such a scale. It would be well, too, if norms could be established for children who are above the ages of thirteen and fourteen. In view of the lack of knowledge at this stage, they suggest that sex differences might be investigated to see to what degree they should be controlled in a norming procedure.

Implementation in School Settings

The matter of utilization of test results for academic purposes was further stressed in a book published by Terman in 1919, and following the publication of the first Stanford Revision. This book, written for school people and for those who were to be teachers, reviews principles of testing, analyses some of the components of individual differences, and reports data on children of differing grade levels in terms of differences in intellectual abilities. There are chapters dealing with mental-age standards in terms of grade placement of children, using the I.Q. for predictive purposes, and some data relevant to intellectually superior children.

The Galton suggestion of the sinking of shafts to determine a man's intellectual qualities is cited by Terman and discussed from the standpoint of its implementation in the Binet-Simon Scales. He points out that the measure obtained with the now available Stanford Revision of 1916 gives a measure of a person's general intelligence, not of special abilities of a particular type. What is obtained with such a test, then, for teachers is a composite picture of general, mental ability. The score yielded is a mental age, usable since the items were standardized on samples of youngsters of different ages. Terman defines mental age as the score achieved by the child. Items are arranged in year levels in such a way that the average child of a given year will earn by his performance a mental age equivalent to his chronological age.

There are two misconceptions which Terman believes must be avoided in the use of the mental-age concept. The first is that a given mental age is clearly differentiable from the mental ages above and below it. But a mental age of eight cannot be clearly separated either from a mental age of nine or a mental age of seven; there is a consecutive and gradual nature to mental development. As a result, clear separation and differentiation is not possible. This position is reinforced by the fact that usually a child will have credits across several year levels rather than only one. The second misconception deals with the fact that many individuals advocated that all children of a given age who are normal show a corresponding mental age; only those children, then, who are of some special type or degree, such as defective or genius, will differ from the mental age for an age group. But Terman says that the distribution in any one age group, as a matter of fact, will be quite large and that one of the purposes of his book is to demonstrate how great differentiation occurs in mental age for a group of children of a given chronological age. Additionally, he offers some evidence on the overlap of children of adjacent ages.

Mental age is specifically defined by Terman in this way:

> The real meaning of the term is perfectly straightforward and unambiguous. By a given mental age we mean *that degree of general mental ability which is possessed by the average child of corresponding chronological age.*

Terman believed that mental age could be used as a means of grading children so that classrooms would reflect homogeneous ability levels. To him, if all children were given a Stanford-Binet, it would be possible to place them in a grade such that their mastery of the curriculum content would be assured. Under a system where chronological age was used as the base for placement, he believed that a high level of failure must occur. One of the drawbacks of mental age is that it does not have much meaning unless the chronological age of the child is known. Given both the chronological age and the mental age of a child it is possible to express the ratio of these, a ratio termed the intelligence quotient. The use of the I.Q. as a rate measure was accepted by Terman.

Certain assumptions underlie the Stanford Revision. Among these is the assumption that any child with whom the test is used will have normal physical development and will have a reasonable opportunity to learn the language in which the tasks are given. Though criticisms had been offered about differences in social background, Terman assumed that all children who are enrolled in school will have had some reasonable exposure to the kinds of opportunity that would make success on the test possible. If there are language problems, he advocates that the highly verbal tasks such as vocabulary be omitted. He admits to problems concerned with the cultural level of the home from which the child comes and its influence on test score. However, he says that this effect has not been accurately determined. He cites a limited number of cases where most of the children in a family score relatively low but one child scores very high. Such an incident reduces the strength of the argument about cultural differences, Terman believed.

Since the Stanford-Binet Scale is time consuming in its administration, he advocates that group tests be administered first as a means of gathering general information about children. Scores on such group tests should not replace individual-test data. As a kind of testing program, every child in the fourth grade and beyond should be given a group test each year. Those who score very high or very low on the group test should then be given an individual test, the Stanford-Binet. In the first three grades, Terman states that group tests are not very usable. For this reason whatever data are gathered about intellectual status should be based upon the individual test.

He next discusses individual differences, pointing out that in any trait which can be measured a wide variation will be found within a group of individuals. This is true in school subjects as well as outside school, he says; it is also true in measures of intelligence. In any given age group in school, then, we should find some students who intellectually are well above the norms for their age group, others who are well below. These intellectual differences should influence what they are competent to do in school and what they actually accomplish. He believed this was clearly demonstrated in the schools by the fact that there was a fairly high educational-retardation incidence in each grade. Terman assumes that investigation would disclose that most of the children who are retarded educationally are also retarded intellectually. At the same time, he felt that certain other children should be accelerated not only intellectually but educationally as well. The latter group has been largely neglected in the schools, he says, and therefore has not had the opportunity to be so well disclosed. Either group would be adequately identified by the Stanford Revision.

One procedure that Terman advocates for overcoming problems of retardation, particularly, is the use of the ungraded room. In his estimation, the ungraded room would be based upon intellectual level rather than chronological age. In recent years the concept of ungraded rooms has been proposed again as a means of allowing each child to proceed at whatever learning rate is reasonable for him. To Terman, and to many others as well, such a procedure is a means of implementing mental-age placement in academic work rather than chronological-age placement.

Terman's 1919 work included data using the Stanford-Binet and demonstrating the extent of individual differences in intellectual ability for kindergarten, first grade, and fifth-grade pupils and for high-school freshmen. Terman reiterates his case for placement of a child in a grade by using mental-age standards rather than chronological age. An interesting sidelight contained in his discussion of children who are slow in learning ability deals with some problems of an explanatory nature. Terman cites certain authorities of the day who pointed to the fact that there is educational retardation for a number of reasons, none of which are intellectual. For example, Ayres stated that physical defects, irregular attendance, late entrance, high standards, and lack of flexibility in methods of promotion were primary reasons for school retardation. Terman rejected such a simple explanation and cited a study done with 108 children in Salt Lake City, each of whom was educationally retarded, and the ascribed cause of retardation was one of those cited by Ayres. For these children, Terman found mental retardation, on an average, of three years. To him, therefore, the problem was one of general intellectual functioning, not of the specific nonintellectual ones more commonly accepted. Though he discusses the problem further and cites data, it is interesting to note that the Terman concept was neglected in the years that followed. Instead, other explanations for educational retardation were accepted and still hold strong influence.

Terman reports some data on children who test superior on the Stanford-Binet. He concludes from his study of these children that they tend to be above the norms in almost all the traits which he measured. For example they were not below average in general health, their ability seemed to be general rather than highly specific, they had high moral and personal traits, they showed excellent social adaptability, their school work was excellent. Additionally, he reports that in terms of intellectual competence these children tended to be placed two or three grades below that reflected by their mental age. Their superiority showed itself very early in life, was not influenced by formal instruction, and seemed to be permanent. By and large, the sample came from superior homes. This kind of data led to the genetic studies of "genius" begun in 1921 and still in process.

In 1923 Terman published a chapter in a committee report on school reorganization. The committee was part of a Commission on Revision of Elementary Education as sponsored by the National Educational Association. The chapter written by Terman again presses for the utilization of individual tests in schools in order to identify degrees of intellectual brightness in each grade, and for the establishing of differential kinds of classes for those who are intellectually retarded and those who are intellectually accelerated.

The Genetic Studies of Genius

Though the revisions of the Binet-Simon Scales would probably be ranked as Terman's most significant contribution as a psychologist, much emphasis must also be given to the longitudinal study begun by him in 1921 and still going on today. It uses intelligence-test performance as the criterion for inclusion in the sample. The subjects of the genetic studies of genius are now middle-aged. They will continue to be studied throughout the remainder of their lifetimes. Oden has pointed out that this particular research project has yielded documentary evidence about intellectual giftedness that has either not been realized before or conflicted with general beliefs (Terman and Oden, 1959, p. xii.). She points to the influence of the findings for education and the fact that certain provisions for gifted children have now been undertaken that might not have occurred otherwise.

Important as such an outcome is, *Genetic Studies of Genius* has even greater import. The data offer evidence of a longitudinal nature which have never been collected before and demonstrate relationships of variables (of several types) to intelligence as measured primarily with the Stanford-Binet. The study is presently in five volumes (Terman, 1925; Cox, 1926; Burks, Jensen, and Terman, 1930). Four of these bear directly on the sample first identified in 1921. For purposes of summary and description, Volume V (Terman and Oden, 1959) will be used here.

The First Study

In 1921, Terman received a grant from the Commonwealth Fund of New York City for purposes of investigating the physical, mental and personality traits of gifted children. The sample was to consist of at least a thousand children having the highest I.Q.s in the schools of California. Terman believed that investigation of these children could offer information on what qualities are found in intellectually superior children, what happens to them through their lifetimes, and what kinds of factors seem to influence later accomplishments.

The sole criterion for inclusion in the sample was an I.Q. that would place the child in the highest one percent of the school population. To identify an adequate pool from which students might be chosen, three procedures were followed, depending upon the grade level studied. For grades three through eight each classroom teacher was asked to identify the brightest child in the room, the second brightest, the third brightest, and the youngest. These children were tested with a group intelligence test, and those who showed promisingly high scores were given the Stanford-Binet (1916 Revision). For kindergarden and the primary grades, the Stanford-Binet test only was used after teacher nomination since no adequate group test was available for such young children. At the high-school level, teachers nominated students who were then tested with the Terman group test as the criterion. Evidence gathered seemed to indicate that at least 90 percent of the children who should appear in such a sample had been properly identified. Terman intended that all children who were tested with the Binet should have an I.Q. of 140 or above. For various reasons, a few children with I.Q.'s between 135 and 139 were also included. Admittedly, this criterion is quite arbitrary, but it was chosen to assure that the children in the study actually were in the top one percent in general ability. Despite the title of the studies, Terman did not make any judgments that such children would turn out to be geniuses as such. To only a minor degree, additionally, are any data gathered which would bear upon genetic factors influencing their performance as well.

The sample finally selected in 1921 and with some additions through 1928 consisted of 1528 children, 857 of whom were males. For those tested with the Binet, the mean was 151 I.Q. For the high-school group, the mean on the Terman test was 142.6 I.Q. No child achieved an I.Q. of less than 135 on either test. It would appear that Terman is safe in his conclusion that he has identified a sample of highly gifted children, at least as measured by traditional intelligence tests.

Given such a sample, additional information of various kinds was gathered. Terman and Oden summarized the characteristics of this group of gifted children (Terman and Oden, 1959) as follows. Though there are a number of exceptions, the typical gifted child seemed to come from a superior background. Not only was the cultural and educational level of the homes from which they came higher than average, but apparently there was also a superior hereditary basis. Because of this superiority in background and heredity, the children were superior physically to the normal child of the same age in the general population. On the average these children tended to be accelerated educationally in terms of grade placement. However, as measured on achievement tests used by Terman, these children appeared to be further advanced than their grade placement in school would indicate. This confirms again the belief of Terman that the only educationally retarded children in school are those who are gifted.

Interests found in these gifted children are spontaneous and of a varied nature. They read easily and extensively. At the same time they were engaged in a number of activities so that they were not merely sedentary. They had great knowledge of games and plays, considerably more than that found in their age-mates. They seemed to prefer the kinds of activities that their chronological age peers preferred. However, their interests tended to be more mature than those of their age group on the average of two or three years beyond the age norm. In character, for the traits selected and tested, the group was above average. In point of fact, Terman and Oden comment that the typical gifted child at age nine tests as high in character as the average child of age twelve. A summary of rankings by teachers of these gifted children is given in Table 4.1 It will be noted that teachers and parents tended to confirm the findings with their estimates.

To summarize the findings on characteristics of the initial sample, Terman and Oden say:

> Three facts stand out clearly in this composite portrait: (1) The deviation of gifted children from the generality is in the upper direction

TABLE 4.1*
PERCENTAGES OF GIFTED SUBJECTS RATED BY TEACHERS
ABOVE THE MEAN OF THE CONTROL GROUP

	Percent	
1. Intellectual traits		
General intelligence	97	
Desire to know	90	
Originality	85	
Common sense	84	
Average of intellectual traits		89
2. Volitional traits		
Will power and perseverance	84	
Desire to excel	84	
Self-confidence	81	
Prudence and forethought	81	
Average of volitional traits		82.5
3. Emotional traits		
Sense of humor	74	
Cheerfulness and optimism	64	
Permanence of moods	63	
Average of emotional traits		67
4. Aesthetic traits		
Musical appreciation	66	
Appreciation of beauty	64	
Average aesthetic traits		65
5. Moral traits		
Conscientiousness	72	
Truthfulness	71	
Sympathy and tenderness	58	
Generosity and unselfishness	55	
Average of moral traits		64
6. Physical traits		
Health	60	
Physical energy	62	
Average of physical traits		61
7. Social traits		
Leadership	70	
Sensitivity to approval	57	
Popularity	56	
Freedom from vanity	52	
Fondness for large groups	52	
Average for social traits		57.4
8. Mechanical ingenuity	47	

* From L. M. Terman and Melita Oden, *Genetic Studies of Genius. Vol. V: The Gifted Group at Mid-Life.* Stanford, California: Stanford University Press, 1959, p. 14.

for nearly all traits; there is no law of compensation whereby the intellectual superiority of the gifted is offset by inferiorities along nonintellectual lines. (2) The amount of upward deviation of the gifted is not the same for all traits. (3) This unevenness of abilities is no greater for gifted than for average children, but it is different in direction; whereas the gifted are at their best in the "thought" subjects, average children are at their best in subjects that make the least demands upon the formation and manipulation of concepts.

Finally the reader should bear in mind that there is a wide range of variability within our gifted group on every trait we have investigated. Descriptions of the gifted in terms of what is typical are useful as a basis for generalization, but emphasis on central tendencies should not blind us to the fact that gifted children, far from falling into a single pattern, represent an almost infinite variety of pattern. (Terman and Oden, 1959, p. 16)

The First Follow-Up

Between 1922 and 1928 some data were gathered through information blanks sent to parents and teachers of these children. However, the first true follow-up occurred in 1927–28 when a number of field workers visited the homes and schools of the children. This first follow-up in 1928 indicated that the findings of 1921 were still accurate. By now the average age of the children was 16 to 17 years. Most of them were in high school. They were tested for intelligence, school achievement, personality, and interests. Additional information on home factors was gathered through an information blank plus the use of an interest blank filled out by those children who were under 20. For children still in elementary and high school, teachers also gave some information on school matters. Once again parents and teachers were asked to rate certain selected traits; of the 25 used in 1921, 12 were selected for use in this 1928 follow-up. No information on medical status or physical measurements was obtained at this time.

The findings indicated that the composite picture of the sample had changed very little over the period from 1921. The group still tended to be superior intellectually—most of them still within the top one to two percent of the general population. Some changes had occurred in I.Q., most of them being decrements. However, the tests used may account for this since there was not sufficient "top" for these children to show how well they might perform. In school achievement, the performance of the sample was still most superior. Less grade skipping occurred after the age of 12, but quality of work continued to be exceedingly high. The predominant grade made by this group in school was *A*. These findings assume added importance in view of the fact that as these children get into high school and college, the characteristics of the group against which they are competing become less diverse.

Despite the fact that for the various traits measured the group is above average on means, Terman and Oden point out that in individual cases there are great amounts of deviation from the group average. In 1928, in all the traits used the range of variability tended to be greater than it was when investigated in 1921. Such a finding follows the development of traits in the general population. The fact that the group on the average tends to remain above the mean of the general population on all the traits may be of greater significance than Terman and Oden were willing to state.

A Second Follow-Up

In 1936 a mail follow-up was attempted and gathered some information usable to the study. Of most importance was the fact that subjects who were located were by now adults, and many of them had left home. As a result of this procedure, some 90 percent of the original subjects were located and information was gathered. In 1939 a second field follow-up was undertaken. Now the average age of the subjects was 29.5 years. It was important to determine to what degree traits first measured some 19 years earlier would show stability in the adults, and which traits would show instability and in what direction. Once more, intelligence tests were given not only to the members of the sample but to their spouses and children as well. An interest inventory also was used with the men of the sample. Ninety-eight percent of the living subjects were contacted and some data gathered. Complete data were available for 96 percent of the original sample. Conclusions drawn from this sample of young adults included: The group showed average or below average incidence of serious personality maladjustment, insanity, delinquency, alcoholism, and homosexuality. For those who had tested I.Q. 170 and above as children, evidence was gathered that they were more often accelerated in school, received better grades, and went further in school than those who had made I.Q.s lower than this in the original sample. Equally, the children of those with 170 I.Q. as adults were not as prone to serious maladjustment and showed greater vocational success than the lower-scoring members of the sample.

For those children who were accelerated in school, contrary to the opinion of some school people, adjustments both in terms of personality and general health were better than the average, they tended to do better school work than their age-mates, and they continued to go further educationally. As might be expected, vocationally they were more highly successful than those who had not been accelerated. The intellectual level of the adult sample was still at the ninety-eighth percentile and above.

For the whole group, vocational success was above the norm of the general population. Choices made and success in those choices, however, depended upon motivational factors and personality adjustment at least as much as upon ability. For the group, the number of individuals in the higher professions was about nine times what would be expected from an unselected sample. Not only did the group tend to exemplify societal values in marriage, but they also were better adjusted in their marital status than the general population. The divorce rate was no higher than that in the general population and in some instances was less. Sexual adjustment in marriage was normal, according to data gathered. As was predicted by Galton, the children of these adults tended to show regression toward the mean in the traits measured. However, the group was not producing children at a rate high enough to assure continuation of the stock.

A Third Follow-Up

In 1950 the most recent field follow-up began and it was concluded in 1952. The average age of the sample was now forty-one years. However, in this middle-age sample, with only a few exceptions, the individual had maintained his superiority over the general population in nearly every measured trait. Of course, as had been true throughout their lifetime the superiority was not equally great in all traits measured. Greatest superiority was found in intellectual ability, in school achievement, and in occupational achievement. Since the death rate was less than that of the general population and health ratings were generally good, physically the gifted group continued to be above average. In terms of personal adjustment and emotional stability, despite measurement problems, the group apparently did not differ from the general population in terms of personality and adjustment as measured by the number of mental breakdowns, suicides, and marital failures. In terms of social problems such as alcoholism and homosexuality the gifted group had lower incidence than the general population. Delinquency was such a rare occurrence in these gifted individuals as to be almost nonexistent. Terman and Oden conclude that desirable traits tend to go together. In point of fact, no negative correlations are reported between intelligence and such factors as size, strength, physical wellbeing, or emotional stability. Where correlations occur, these tend to be positive in direction.

Superiority in intellectual ability was as extreme as it was in 1921. The group still showed most of its members in the ninety-ninth percentile in measured mental ability. Even where the individual had not been notably successful vocationally, his intellectual level tended to be extremely high. As Terman and Oden point out, the real test of great mental ability is the use made of the competence. On the basis of evidence available, it appeared the capacity to achieve beyond the average can be detected quite early in life through tests of general ability. What direction this ability will take cannot be predicted accurately, and such features as personality breakdown or accidents may somewhat reduce the accuracy of prediction. Still, the chances are excellent that the child who has very high measured ability will succeed at whatever it is that he undertakes.

Educationally, the group was outstanding. Of the eighty-five percent who entered college, almost seventy percent graduated. As might be expected, honors such as Phi Beta Kappa occurred much more commonly than in the usual college population. Roughly a third of the sample achieved some academic distinction upon graduation. For those who graduated, about sixty percent of the women and sixty-seven percent of the men went into graduate study. A doctoral degree was achieved by fourteen percent of the men and four percent of the women. In the general college graduate population less than three percent achieved such a degree.

Because of factors which influenced occupational status of the women, distinctions in the area of vocations are discussed separately for men and women. Though fewer women entered professions and the business world, where they did so they tended to be highly successful. Most of the women of the sample had become housewives. Among the men in the sample, over eighty-five percent were either in the professions or semi-professions and in higher business. Not a single one of the group was found in the lowest levels of occupational listings. There had been many scientific contributions made by members of the gifted sample, and a number of them had achieved important administrative positions. Terman and Oden reported that about sixty books and monographs and nearly two thousand scientific and technical articles had been published by members of the sample; they had also been granted over two hundred and thirty patents. Other members of the sample had written novels, short stories, and plays; and over two hundred and fifty miscellaneous articles had been published by members of the group. Of course, Terman and Oden were most concerned about vocational achievement in terms of what might be predicted from the high level of intellectual ability. Though by and large the record is significant, there were a few individuals from the original sample who must be considered failures. There were another eighty or so men whose vocational accomplishments were much less than the general standards for the group. Since all of these individuals were equally competent intellectually, there were apparently other factors that contributed to notable achievement besides intelligence as such. From follow-up data available, the primary contributors in this regard seemed to be nonintellectual factors of a personality nature. Generally, correlation coefficients between vocational success and mental health, emotional stability, and social adjustment were positive rather than negative. Since the average age of the sample in 1952 was about forty-one years, Terman and Oden point out that careers are pretty well set throughout the rest of their lives. Future follow-ups should indicate some increases in administrative responsibilities, promotions, and so on, but relatively few changes in vocational work undertaken.

Terman and Oden were also interested in the perspective that the members of their sample had on life and what constitutes success in life. For this reason they included a question: "From your point of view, what constitutes success in life?" Though there was no consistent agreement as to what constituted success in life there were certain responses which tended to occur with a high degree of frequency. The most frequently mentioned definitions of life's success by members of this intellectually competent sample are as follows:

A. Realization of goals, vocational satisfaction, a sense of achievement.
B. A happy marriage and home life, bringing up a family satisfactorily.
C. Adequate income for comfortable living (but this was mentioned by only twenty percent of women).
D. Contributing to knowledge or welfare of mankind; helping others, leaving the world a better place.
E. Peace of mind, well adjusted personality, adaptability, emotional maturity. (Terman and Oden, 1959, p. 152)

It would seem that in such a group as this many of the recognized social responsibilities and goals are accepted as important in one's life. Merely being successful vocationally is not enough. One must accomplish other things with his life as well.

A tribute to the life and work of Terman has been well expressed by Sears (Terman and Oden, 1959, p. viii).

And so we reach the end of one stage in this extraordinary research enterprise. When Professor Terman came to Stanford in 1910, as an Assistant Professor of Education, the scientific study of the intellect had scarcely begun. In Paris, Alfred Binet had constructed an ingenious test for measuring academic ability in school children; at Columbia University's Teachers College, E. L. Thorndike had begun work on the measurement of school achievement. But it remained for Lewis Terman to conceive the development of a rigorous intelligence test that could select the ablest children, and thus allow society to focus its full educative power in developing their potential. In 1916, Terman published the Stanford Revision of the Binet-Simon test. In the last years of World War I, he was a prime mover in the construction of the Army Alpha and Beta tests. After the war, with both individual and group tests available, he turned to the problem that enthralled him ever since his days at Clark University. Although he made two useful excursions into other fields— the measure of masculinity-femininity and of marital happiness—his main concern for the rest of his life was the research on gifted children. What he started, now remains to be finished. . . . We can be grateful for the courage and vision of the man who finally broke the barrier of the limited lifetime allotted to any one researcher, and got underway a study of man that will encompass the span of the *subjects'* lives, not just those of the researchers. . . .

Though Lewis M. Terman died in 1956, his work will continue for years to come. The influence of his ideas and their implementation will be felt until at least the middle of the twenty-first century. Few men in history will have had such an impact.

A Comment on Terman's Theory

Like Binet, Terman took no specific position on a theoretical model to direct his test efforts or research. Perhaps one of his closest statements to a strong theoretical position occurred in the 1921 Symposium in the *Journal of Educational Psychology.* Here Terman takes the same position as Binet but with a more explicit statement. He defines intelligence as the ability to carry on abstract thinking (Terman, 1921, p. 128) and attempts throughout the rest of his discussion to demonstrate what is meant by abstract thinking, the kinds of tasks which will reflect it, and the outcomes of its nature. An examination of the Binet-Simon test as revised by Terman, as well as of those for which he was directly responsible, demonstrates his continuing dedication to abstract thought and its intellectual expression. Primarily, he looked for the kinds of things which the bright child does and the dull child does not do. In this regard, verbal taks of an abstract quality he felt to be superior.

References

Binet, A., *L'Étude Experimentale de l'Intelligence.* Paris: Schleicher Frères et Cie., 1902.

——, and Henri, V., "La Psychologie Individuelle," *L'Année Psychologique,* 1896, 2, 411–465.

Burks, Barbara Stoddard, Jensen, Dortha Williams, and Terman, L. M., *Genetic Studies of Genius. Vol. II: The Promise of Youth.* Stanford, California: Stanford University Press, 1930.

Cox, Catherine Morris, *Genetic Studies of Genius. Vol. II: The Early Mental Traits of Three Hundred Geniuses.* Stanford, California: Stanford University Press, 1926.

Decroly, O., and Degand, J., "La Mesure de l'Intelligence chez les Enfants Normaux d'après les Tests de Binet et Simon: Nouvelle Contribution Critique," *Archives de Psychologie,* 1910, 9, 81–108.

Goddard, H. H., "The Binet and Simon Tests of Intellectual Capacity," *The Training School,* 1908, 5, 3–9.

————, "Ten Thousand Children Measured by the Binet Measuring Scale of Intelligence," *Pedagogical Seminary*, 1911, 18, 232–259.

Hollingworth, Leta S., Terman, L. M., and Oden, Melita, "The Significance of Deviates," Chapter 3, Part 1, 43–66. In *Intelligence: Its Nature and Nurture*, 39th Yearbook, Part I, National Society for the Study of Education. Bloomington, Ill.: Public School Publishing Co., 1940.

Johnston, Katherine L., "M. Binet's Method for the Measurement of Intelligence: Some Results," *Journal of Experimental Pedagogy*, 1911, 1, 24–31.

Sharp, Stella Emily, "Individual Psychology: A Study in Psychological Method," *American Journal of Psychology*, 1899, 10, 329–391.

Sumption, M. R., Norris, Dorothy, and Terman, L. M., "Special Education for the Gifted Child," Chatper 14 in *The Education of Exceptional Children*, 49th Yearbook, Part II, National Society for the Study of Education. Chicago: University of Chicago Press, 1950.

Terman, L. M., "Genius and Stupidity: A Study of Some of the Intellectual Processes of Seven 'Bright' and Seven 'Stupid' Boys," *Pedagogical Seminary*, 1906, 13, 307–373.

————, *The Measurement of Intelligence*, Boston: Houghton Mifflin, 1916.

————, *Intelligence of School Children*, Boston: Houghton Mifflin, 1919.

————, "Intelligence and Its Measurement: A Symposium," *Journal of Educational Psychology*, 1921, 12, 127–133.

————, *Intelligence Tests and School Reorganization*. Yonkers-on-Hudson, N.Y.: World Book, 1923.

————, *Genetic Studies of Genius. Vol. I: Mental and Physical Traits of a Thousand Gifted Children*. Stanford, California: Stanford University Press, 1925.

————, "The Discovery and Encouragement of Exceptional Talent," *American Psychologist*, 1954, 9, 221–230.

————, and Childs, H. G., "A Tentative Revision and Extension of the Binet-Simon Measuring Scale of Intelligence," *Journal of Educational Psychology*, 1912, 3, 61–74; 133–143; 198–208; 277–289.

————, and Oden, Melita, "Status of the California Gifted Group at the End of Sixteen Years," Chapter 3, Part, 2, 67–74. In *Intelligence: Its Nature and Nurture*, 39th Yearbook, Part I, National Society for the Study of Education. Bloomington, Ill.: Public School Publishing Co., 1940.

————, and Oden, Melita, "Correlates of Adult Achievement in the California Gifted Group," Chapter 3, Part 3, 74–89. In *Intelligence: Its Nature and Nurture*, 39th Yearbook, Part I, National Society for the Study of Education. Bloomington, Ill.: Public School Publishing Co. 1940.

————, and Oden, Melita, *Genetic Studies of Genius, Vol. IV: The Gifted Child Grows Up*. Stanford, California: Stanford University Press, 1947.

————, and Oden, Melita, *Genetic Studies of Genius. Vol. V: The Gifted Group at Mid-Life*. Stanford, California: Stanford University Press, 1959.

Wissler, C., "The Correlation of Mental and Physical Tests," *Psychological Review Monograph Supplement*, 1901, 3, No. 6.

5

Edward L. Thorndike

Thorndike's work in intelligence represents only one facet of his contribution to all factors of human learning. He was one of those rare individuals who presents a theoretical system that is inclusive of such a variety of behaviors that any one is essentially inseparable. Thus, when Thorndike deals with learning theory, the components of the operations of intelligence are as clearly a part of the explanation as would be any other human behavior. Thorndike is responsible for the viewpoint of learning called by him "connectionism," which is the forerunner of all current and widely accepted theories of reinforcement. In this viewpoint, learning is conceived as the formation of associations. As the organism is exposed to stimulation throughout his lifetime, responses are made. As a response is made to a specific stimulus or set of stimuli, an association or connection is formed. Thorndike believed this connection to be neurophysiological in its basis, with each connection representing one bit of experience from the life of the organism. There are, then, as many connections as there are experiences.

Intelligence plays its role within this theory by the fact that all organisms do not have equal ability to form connections. There must be some difference of a hereditary nature among organisms and individuals within phyla to explain differences in number of connections. To Thorndike, the human being who has the greater potential for neural connections will behave more intelligently than an individual of lesser potential for the forming of connections. Essentially, he will take better advantage of the multitude of experiences offered to him: the variety of stimulation to which he is exposed, and to which responses may be connected.

The basis for this position was first presented in Thorndike's doctoral dissertation which was published as a monograph supplement to the *Psychological Review* of 1898. This dissertation, entitled *Animal Intelligence,* was a significant contribution to experimental psychology. The subjects involved in the study were dogs, cats and chickens, each of which was confined in an enclosure from which it might escape by some fairly simple act. For instance, the animal might escape by pulling a loop of cord, or pressing a lever, or stepping on a platform. To induce a desire to escape from the enclosure, Thorndike deprived the animal of food to the stage where it would be considered hungry. This, plus some assumed desire to escape, led the animal to behavior it might not ordinarily show. There is a very obvious relation of this procedure to the work of B. F. Skinner, a debt acknowledged by Professor Skinner (see Jončich, 1968, p. 506). Though something of an oversimplification, Thorndike found the animals to be not very intelligent; that is, they could not learn associations with the ease which he had assumed they could. Though Thorndike continued to study animals over the next several years, he turned his attention readily to the animal most intelligent and most worthy of study: man. A considerable portion of the work in the remainder of his life dealt with the learning of man, particularly in the formal educational setting.

Associationism in Human Behavior

Thorndike was concerned about the application of psychology as a science to human behavior. One of his early works was an explication of at least Thorndikian theory as it might apply to many everyday situations and was published in the form of a novel. This book, called *The Human Nature Club,* was by his own admission nontechnical and somewhat superficial. However, the essential theory advocated by him is clear within the context of the book. The events are centered about a household determined to obtain a better grasp of the reasons for some of their behaviors. Why certain stimuli will be responded to and others ignored, why many actions appear to be so automatic as not to be thought about, why certain things appear to be so difficult to learn and others so easy, are the kinds of questions to which the group addressed itself. The theory of connectionism is evident early in the book and throughout the remainder of the presentation.

Specific material dealing with intelligence centers around the experiential content of the mind. To Thorndike, mind was synonymous with brain. Any separation of mind from some physiological base is greeted with derision, as the following quote illustrates:

> . . . I remember once hearing a man at a teacher's institute compare the mind to a big machine. "Sensations are thrown into the hopper at one end," he said, "attention makes them clear and intense, perception, imagination and memory in turn work them over. They are changed into general notions by the action of conception, and are then subjected to the influence of the reason, which turns out the finished product." Of course, that sort of view is all bosch. (Thorndike, 1900)

Though one might consider such a statement today as obvious, it certainly was not obvious in its day. For example, in his review of this book, Charles H. Judd (1901), one of the leading psychologists of the day, criticized Thorndike for presenting such a viewpoint to the public. Though he agreed there might be some basis for it he felt that the linking of mind and brain would lead to unwarranted assumptions on the part of the general lay public.

Regardless of its acceptability at the time, Thorndike proposed that special training has little or no effect upon general ability as such. The specific kinds of subject matter studied in school, then, will have little or no effect upon a person's general-ability level. Indeed, each separate experience must be stored as an association to be used in situations to which it is directly applicable. Though it will contribute to a general store of knowledge, it cannot increase the person's general mental competence. Some empirical evidence for this position was available from a study done by Thorndike and Woodworth and published in 1900. Thorndike makes the distinction clear in a note to the chapter dealing with mental training. He points to the general belief that observation, attention and reasoning have a facilitative effect from a specific instance to all examples of observation, attention, and reasoning. This viewpoint he rejects on the basis that the mind is actually a number of particular abilities, particular acts, and particular memories. The purpose of the brain is to connect those ideas which exist discretely and particular muscular adjustments with situations to which they apply. Though, under appropriate circumstances, special ability might contribute to general ability, these conditions are indeed rare.

In a chapter on Heredity and Environment, Thorndike takes a position favoring a heredity basis for intelligence. He quotes Francis Galton, and seemingly agrees with much that Galton proposed about inheritance. Without taking a quite strong position, Thorndike advocates that general mental ability as well as any specific mental traits which we might possess must be due to some hereditary basis. Though he does not say so specifically, it would seem reasonable that whatever these constitute are based upon some inherited tendency for association-forming. In any event, he rejects the role of environment or education as being the chief contributor to outstanding mental ability. Though intelligent parents would tend to train their children in a more intelligent manner than less intelligent parents, this will not account for the vast array of differences found within children both of highly and less intelligent parents.

Improving Mental Function

More detailed data dealing with the improvement of mental function through training appeared in articles published in 1901 by Thorndike and Woodworth. The approach taken by them was to measure some function, give training in some other function until improvement was demonstrated, then to test the first function again. The experimental issue, then, is whether or not changes occur in the function which did not receive direct training. The findings seemed to indicate either little or no improvement, or improvement of an irregular type, in the experimental task. With the crude analysis attempted, the conclusion may be drawn that improvement did not occur in related activities where specific practice was provided.

Thorndike speaks of the vast differences in mental connections found among individuals in his *Elements of Psychology* (1905a). He proposes that the differences noted among individuals and the amount of knowledge possessed are due to differences in mental connections. Further, where a person shows errors in his thinking, these represent incorrect connections. Ignorance is no more than the absence of the connections. He speaks of the differences that exist in amount of time necessary for one idea to bring about another idea. Even in so-called normal children, the differences in time for such connections are clearly identifiable. The degree of such differences is of importance to psychology, of course, but must be demonstrated in some fashion more precise than observation. In an unselected group of children, even of the same general-ability level, the differences are obviously great. What kinds of differences will be obtained, however, if twins are compared as well as siblings? This issue Thorndike deals with in a study published in 1905 (Thorndike, 1905b). For the purpose, fifty pairs of twins were used and compared with a sample of siblings. Thorndike believed that the data collected should offer some information about the comparative importance of the original nature of these individuals and the effects of training.

Thorndike comments that twins showed resemblance in mental traits roughly twice that of siblings. However, there were little or no differences between older twins and younger twins. The results indicate to Thorndike that heredity is a stronger influence in mental behavior than is environment. In Thorndike's view, correlational relations in physical traits for twins also point to the importance of inheritance. He admits that there is no evidence from his study as to the possible effects of environment prior to the age of the youngsters tested. Thus, quite early childhood influences may be of significance in the results obtained in the years covered by this study. On purely logical grounds, Thorndike rejects any such influence.

Though written as a means of challenging assumptions made by Spearman about the presence of *g* (general factors) in large numbers of behaviors, an article by Thorndike, Lay, and Dean (1909) bears upon this issue of improvement through special training. A sample of 37 women students in a teacher-training institution and 25 high-school boys was used to study the correspondence of specific traits to general ability. Members of the sample drew lines of different lengths as accurately as possible, and filled boxes with shot to approximate weight as accurately as possible. Additionally each judged his fellow subjects' general ability and in turn each was judged by his teachers. Thorndike *et al.* found only a low positive correlation among these factors, rather than the perfect one advocated by Spearman. Indeed, Spearman draws the conclusion that all kinds of intellectual activity share some fundamental function with a remainder that is dependent upon a specific trait. Thorndike *et al.* propose an "equally extravagant one," that there is nothing common to mental functions or to any part of them. Relationships certainly will exist, but these will represent only shared elements between the traits tested.

Yet another comment on the independence of traits is found in Thorndike's presidential address to the American Psychological Association (Thorndike, 1913b). The address is an attack upon the commonly-held beliefs that an idea produces an act, or at least produces that act which it resembles. To Thorndike this was anathema, since he felt that a mental state can have no dynamic potency. The mental state that exists has a physiological correlary which may act to produce whatever response is connected with it. Unless the physiological connection is inborn or has come about through experience, an idea cannot produce an act. This again emphasizes the one-to-one correspondence between stimulus and response and the connection which this correspondence represents. In such a viewpoint, intellect will be some summation of all the connections which can exist and do exist from the person's experience.

Theoretical and Empirical Developments

In 1913, Thorndike published a classic in the field of educational psychology, a three-volume work entitled *Educational Psychology*. In Volume Two, subtitled *The Psychology of Learning*, and Volume Three, subtitled *Mental Work*, direct reference to intelligence and intellectual factors is made. The constant feature of each of the volumes included in this major work is the connectionist theory, based upon stimulus-response relations from the organisms' experience.

Intelligence and Behavior

In a discussion of mental functions, Thorndike points out that all learning represents connections and man is superior because he forms so many more of these than other forms of life. Through his experience, man becomes an elaborate and intricate organism comprising millions of connections. One form of these in man is called intellect; others might be called character, skill, and temperament. In terms of the intellect, such descriptions as information, habits, interests, and ideals help to define certain groups of connections. A more discrete kind of listing would include such things as ability to add, ability to read, interest in music, and business honesty. Whatever the category, and however basic it may be, it is defined in terms of the number and kinds of connections which occur. By intellect, then, is meant some series or groups of connections which may be signified by some more general title. These connections are as important to the learning of a list of nonsense syllables as to some qualitative assessment on the part of the individual. Because of the fact we can define the former, however, measurement and description will be much more precise than in the case of the latter. To Thorndike, at least, there is no difference in what constitutes the basic entity of either.

To determine man's intellect, it might be possible to determine man's original nature and to trace every formation of each individual bond from the very beginning of life for the individual until the point is reached at which the study is undertaken. Obviously such a procedure, as Thorndike says, is impossible. An alternative viewpoint, then, is to consider each function in terms of the stimulus-response connections which constitute its complexity. One may then study each of these in terms of each element as it is added to the behavior repertoire of the individual. Unfortunately, reducing all acts to such basic components is more difficult than might seem possible. Most of the descriptive terminology which is used is of a very vague and composite nature. As a result, studies of learning have not described the basic connections comprising the traits studied. The basic components are the functions which psychology and education have emphasized and, even though they are vague stimulus-response relationships, they are the basis upon which some information is available.

Within this context, the psychologist must restrict himself to overt behavior. Admittedly, there are covert behaviors which influence man's behavior. However, our knowledge must be restricted to what may be reported and measured. There are consequently problems to the under-standing of mental functions. First, it is impossible for us to get to the neuronal components, the connections, which underlie each behavior. Second, even should we question individuals, we receive different kinds of reports depending upon what is selected out by the individual to report. Indeed, each individual must be somewhat selective in what he reports, since there are specially hidden conditions which influence him in a particular way and of which he may not be aware. There is even the problem of what kinds of scales and units to use. The imperfection of the scales available to us for determining presence and degree of mental functions complicate their study immeasurably.

Any mental function contains either a single set or a series of sets of connections. As a result there can be differing degrees of complexity of the mental function to be studied. Thorndike reports that some functions such as sensitivity to pain may use a relatively few number of connections. By contrast, some such mental function as executive ability may be very complex in the number of connections used.

As a result, Thorndike defines a mental function as consisting primarily in an attitude or an ability. The law of effect, that is the satisfac-tion or annoyance that accompany acts, influences many mental func-tions. Only events which are observable and measurable in behavior can be considered a mental function in the Thorndike sense. This means that whatever mental functions are discussed psychologically in point of fact cannot be related directly to the physiological conditions which are re-sponsible for the functions. The connections which constitute any given act cannot be so precisely defined. As Thorndike points out, we know that ability to spell a word such as 'cat' must be reflected in some connections among neurons, but what connections and what neurons must remain unknown. Mental functions may be compared on the basis of the scalable and measurable amounts of qualities or things or facts which exist among them. To improve a mental function, then, would mean nothing more than adding to or subtracting from the amounts of qualities which are measurable.

Overall, mental functions are described in a quite unsatisfactory fash-ion. Though considerable opinion may be expressed about given mental functions and how they operate, the data to support such opinions is highly limited. Essentially, we are reduced to some score expression or combinations of scores to make statements about a function's efficiency. This may be vague or defined, precise or rough, but it is all that we have. The law of effect will operate to a high degree in determining improve-ment of any mental function. In point of fact, Thorndike says that im-provement in any mental function is reducible to additions and subtractions of connections and of the present readiness.

In Volume Three of *Educational Psychology*, Thorndike discusses units and scales for measurement. He is particularly concerned in this volume about the measurement of individual differences. Differences in human nature which are commonly discussed reduce primarily to a difference in amount of one trait or some aggregate of differences among traits. This is more usually quantitative than qualitative, though qualitative differences in such areas as knowledge certainly do exist. Even qualitative differences reduce to some quantitative explanations. Thorndike considers it scientifically useful, then, to think of human beings as measured upon some series of scales, each expressing amount, and each being comparable. In measuring aspects of human nature, and thus individual differences, the scale used must identify in some way a quantitative amount. It must be objective, so that competent individuals making the same measurement would get essentially the same results. Additionally, there should be some type of scaling such that defined points are clear and the distances between these points are of some definable degree. The individual may then be placed at his point on the scale and compared with any other individual in terms of his placement.

In measuring various kinds of mental traits, one commonly obtained result is great variability in the mental measurement. This variation, Thorndike believes, is usable and illustrates the trust which we may place in the measures which we use. Variation expresses itself along a number of dimensions. One of these, for example, is sex differences in ability. Such differences do exist as demonstrated in the variation. The necessity or importance of such differences is not demonstrated by the mere fact of variability, however.

In discussing sex differences in ability, Thorndike points out that there are several things which must be kept in mind quite aside from the results obtained. For one thing, sex differences in abilities do not necessarily imply that there should be differences in school and home training for boys and girls. As a matter of fact, one reason for sex differences may be because of different training which has already been received and not clearly discriminated. Certainly, physical differences should not be confused with mental differences, if any such exist. By and large selective factors in occupations available to women have tended to discriminate against them in a way that is unrelated to sex. From this discussion, it can be seen that differences in variability of the sexes will be found which may or may not be proved to be due to sex as such. Thorndike reviews a number of studies on sex differences and reports most such differences to be slight, though systematic. The greatest differences seem to occur in variation. Men show a wider variability in such a trait as intelligence or energy than do women. Whether or not such differences are in point of fact true sex differences is left unexplained. Thorndike makes the point that, overall, sex is the cause of only a small fraction of differences among individuals. The differences of men from men and of women from women are almost as great as any differences which may be disclosed between men and women.

Another area within which individual differences may be found is that of ancestry or race. Thorndike begins with some discussions of problems involved in denoting intellectual differences among races. There are at least two unknown quantities that must be considered. For one thing, racial purity is an extremely difficult thing to determine and define. There may be differences between groups which are distinct to some degree and yet go undiscovered, or unmeasured. When this is complicated by the fact that there are unknown differences in terms of training, then racial distinctions and racial comparisons are on difficult grounds indeed.

When differences between races are considered in terms of achievement, apparently large differences are noted. Thorndike points out that when actual measurements are used, however, what appear to be quite large differences become relatively small ones. He found no evidence that any two races have ever been measured which do not overlap mentally whatever the trait may be that is measured. Any position of true racial differences in such a thing as intelligence, therefore, is of doubtful validity. Frequently, observation by the layman is not concerned with mental traits as such but with indirect consequences which the layman is apt to misinterpret. For example, Thorndike says, the layman looks at customs not moral capacity, he looks at habits not energy, he looks at knowledge not intellect. The layman then draws a conclusion about differences in intellect which have no basis in fact. Thorndike concludes that differences between even "pure" races would be relatively small. Though such differences might be stable and demonstrable, educational practices would remain unchanged. Since all races will show a wide variability in intellect, and since there would be considerable overlap between the races, education must concern itself with providing experiences for connection-forming from which the individual may benefit. He states that the differences in original nature within a race are many times greater than between races.

If racial differences present a problem in determining influence on intellect, immediate ancestry or family presents even greater problems. Over all, Thorndike concludes from the available evidence, limited though it is, that heredity determines whatever similarities and differences exist in the original natures of men, with the effects of environment in terms of present behavior being relatively small. This does not mean that environment does not have a significant role to play. Indeed, providing the best possible environment will lead to the greater possibility of connection-forming for all kinds of individuals. They will not all achieve equally under these conditions. Those who have the greater hereditary possibility for connection-forming will benefit from the better environment more than those who have less hereditary possibility for connection-forming. All of them however can benefit, and this becomes the educational key.

Thorndike also points out the importance of maturity as the individual grows. There are observable differences in mental traits as the individual matures, irrespective of training. Even if in some fashion we could find a large group of children who were completely alike in terms of sex, ancestry and training, differences in terms of mental development from year to year would still be expected and found. Thorndike believes that the kinds of studies which had been conducted, at least to 1913, were not very good for demonstrating development of mental traits with age. What was needed was measurement and repeated measurement upon the same individuals over a long period of years. Some direct specification of the kind of training which the individual has received would be an important component in such studies. Nevertheless, with the data available, Thorndike concludes that children all across the spectrum of intellectual competence show differences in terms of maturity. This belies the well-accepted notion, at that time, that only the extremely bright or extremely dull showed differences in maturity. It was rather widely accepted that children of average or nearaverage intelligence were so much alike as to be indiscriminable. Thorndike rejects any such conception.

Issues in Measuring Intelligence

An article by Thorndike which appeared in 1924 clearly states the theoretical basis that becomes the source for *The Measurement of Intelligence,* published in 1927. This 1924 article, then, was of a theoretical nature at the time of its presentation. The ideas underlying the Thorndike theory which was implemented with its tests, the CAVD, are clearly delineated in this article. Thorndike points out that the various tests then currently available to assess intelligence had come from three sources. First, there was the interview, most directly exemplified in the Stanford-Binet. Second, there was the school examination; and, third, various tests of sensory acuity, memory, and so on. These latter two were exemplified in the Army Alpha examination. Despite the fact that dramatic gains in precision of measurement and utility had resulted over the first quarter of the twentieth century, there were still three fundamental defects which Thorndike recognized and discussed in this 1924 article.

The first of these defects Thorndike titles "ambiguity in content." He points to the variety of different kinds of items and subtests found in the most widely used tests of the day. The kinds of problems presented in

many instances were very familiar to the subjects; in certain other instances the material was very novel. Speed was a factor in some tests and
items of tests, and it was absent in others. As a result of these and other
factors, the score that was obtained on any given test represented a
composite which was not clearly discriminable nor related to other tests
of the same general type. Though one may rationally present the argument that any one of these tests represented some careful sampling of
tasks with a scoring plan that weighted the responses to each item differentially, Thorndike maintains that the argument is spurious. The reality
was that the tests tended to approximate representativeness of item content and suitability of weighting.

The second defect noted by Thorndike in the then-currently available tests is one he entitles "arbitrariness of unit." Two scoring procedures were commonly used in tests. The first of these, and the more
commonly found, was to grade intellect on the basis of number of positive
credits achieved. In this method, one simply added up the number of
correct answers to the problems presented. A second procedure concerned itself with gradation of difficulty of tasks in determining the point
on a grade of difficulty to which the subjects could correctly respond.
Whichever procedure might be used, the arithmetical values achieved
could not be taken at face value. Differences between score units were not
at all clear, with the result that direct comparisons from one test to
another, or even from one form to another of the same test, were not
possible. The true zero point was not known, thus limiting many kinds
of comparative statements between score values. One problem facing the
testing movement then was to try to determine meaning for various credit
summations and difficulty levels and apply these to some absolute scale
if possible.

Thorndike admits that the argument that such a score unit as the
mental age does not require equality of units, that in point of fact it may
even be an unnecessary refinement, is a fairly valid one. This is true
because one may say that a score of mental age twelve achieved by a child
corresponds to performance on the test like the average twelve-year-old
child, regardless of chronological age. This is convenient, it is practical,
it is understood easily, and it is realistic. However, all of this utility ceases
around the age of fourteen, since this represents the top of the mental
age scale (at least in the case of the Stanford-Binet), and beyond this point
mental age has little or no meaning. Thorndike raises the question of
what the average fifteen- or sixteen- or nineteen-year-old can do intellectually for purposes of assuming a mental age. He sees as a better procedure than the use of age units, the implementation of some kind of
standard score. If this procedure is followed, units of mental ability at
various age levels should be at least approximately equal.

The third defect cited by Thorndike is called "ambiguity in significance." Since the test score that is obtained is some composite of credits not equally weighted, the meaning of the score in terms of the individual's intellect depends upon the intuition of the examiner, or upon some correlation between the score and observable effects of intellect, or upon a combination of these two. Obviously, it is impossible to get to intellect as such. It is not possible then to determine the correlation of test score with this trait which is supposedly measured. Though we accept the fact that the systematized interview such as the Stanford-Binet, or a battery of tests such as the Alpha, do measure somewhat the same trait, this assumption is based upon correlations between the two tests. Since there is a generally accepted agreement among authorities that each of these tests in fact reflects something about a trait which may be called intelligence, the further assumption is made that we are measuring some effects of the trait.

The assumption is made in all the tests that are available that the individual being tested will perform at the best level possible for him. The validity of this assumption is highly questionable. We are further limited by the fact that the measures which are used are measures of intellectual products, not of intellect itself. One child is assumed to be brighter than another child simply because he performs better on a test, that is, gives more correct answers or more precisely defined answers, than the other child. There is always in this matter of intelligence testing, then, some kind of value placed on the work of the individual.

This matter of value has three criteria which must be met in order for the test scores to be usable. The first of these Thorndike says is truth. He defines truth as some insight into the real world, evidence that knowledge may be used accurately for prediction. In this sense, measures of intelligence really reflect the accuracy of man's predictions. However, Thorndike points out that a number of kinds of tests of intelligence actually do not get to truth in terms of ability to make accurate prediction. If such instruments as the Army Beta, or the Ebbinghaus completion task, or a standardized interview reflect something about the ability of the individual to get at the truth, it is merely due to accident rather than design. Though one might argue that this predictive value might be what we need to obtain with intelligence tests, Thorndike points out that very few of those who devise tests or who use tests think that it would be a sufficient factor.

A second criterion of value is concerned with development by age. The essential feature of the Binet scale, it will be recalled, was to determine what it is that five-year-olds could do that four-year-olds could not, or within an age group what the bright children of five years could do that the dull children of five years could not. With increasing age, the criterion

of what represents ability is increased. There is the further matter that
Binet did not take into account all the psychological features of any one
age group. Revisions of the Binet Scale in this country by Terman and
others have carried this idea of value and its significance in intellectual
performance to a greater degree. Thorndike believes that this is the
procedure that should have been followed. The content of tests should
be restricted only to those items which may be determined to be intellectual in their content.

The third criterion of value is concerned with the ability to learn. One
of the most commonly espoused definitions of intelligence is its alliance
with the ability of the individual to learn as a result of the amount of
intelligence present. This may mean learning either more difficult things
or learning the same thing much more quickly than some other individual. Such a viewpoint seems to be circular. For example, if we use ability
to learn more difficult items, the discrimination is made in terms of
percentages of those who can perform one item as compared with another item, and this becomes the proof as well as the discriminator.
Because of the lack of evidence, Thorndike suggests that we should not
desert the rather mixed approaches to measurement in most tests by
substituting ability to learn more things or to learn the same thing more
quickly.

There are two other less important means of reflecting value. One of
these is in terms of response to novelty, which Thorndike believes to be
ill-suited to problems of measuring intelligence. The other is what he
calls "relational thinking." Though he accepts this as an important part
of intelligence, he rejects it as a sole basis because of its limited features.

Though man's intellect should enter all forms of behavior, the content of these has tended to be quite limited in selection. One reason for
this is convenience. The content generally used is chosen also because
it deals with more general forms of behavior and these are felt to be more
valuable for assessing a person's general level of intellect than particulars
in behavior. Sometimes the test has tended to emphasize external behaviors in performance on the task, at other times tests have tended to
emphasize some kind of internal processes which the person uses in
solving the task presented to him. Regardless of which of these may be
emphasized in any given test, there is a great variety in terms of the form
by which the content, whatever it is, may be presented. The individual
approaches the test content in terms of its external appearances: questions to be answered, sentences to be completed, errors to be corrected,
definitions to be given, and so on. To perform satisfactorily on such
presented material, there are certain things which must occur internally:
the individual must attend to some stimuli and ignore others, certain
things must be retained in his memory, certain inhibitions must be exer-

cised, and so on. Presumably, then, the individual does use attention, retention, relational thinking, abstraction, deductive reasoning, and the like.

Within whatever form is used, and considering whatever values may be applied, Thorndike proposes that measurement may be expressed on one of three dimensions. The first of these he calls altitude or level or height, and is equivalent to difficulty in tasks to be performed. The second of these he calls range or extent or breadth, and includes the number of items which may be performed at any given altitude. Certainly he considers these two to be related to each other, but for the time being at least he feels that they should be kept separate for certain kinds of measurement. The third factor which he advocates for inclusion in measurement is that of speed. With equality in altitude and range, for example, the individual who could perform tasks more rapidly than another would be considered somewhat more intelligent. As he states:

> For the practical purposes of estimating intellect, a battery of tests in which *level, extent* and *speed* combine in unknown amounts to produce the score may be very useful. For rigorous measurements, however, it seems desirable to treat these three factors separately, and to know the exact amount of weight given to each when we combine them. (Thorndike, 1924, p. 241)

Thorndike advocates that each of these three factors is essential. Each of them influences the performance of an individual, and in somewhat different ways. For this reason he would be most pleased with a test which gives a measure of each of them independently, as well as in combination. The test he devised for this purpose is called the CAVD and it was used extensively in Thorndike's major work on the measurement of intelligence.

The Measurement of Intelligence

Based upon conceptions of learning presented thus far and from the number of research studies done by him, Thorndike's major contribution to the understanding and measurement of intelligence appeared in 1927 with the publication of *The Measurement of Intelligence* (Thorndike, Bregman, Cobb, and Woodyard, 1927). This book not only presents a systematic theoretical approach to the nature of intelligence, but it also provides methods by which such theory might be implemented, and includes descriptive item material which comprises a test measuring the components of the theory.

The first chapter of this book is a recapitulation of Thorndike's article which appeared in 1924 and was discussed above. As mentioned in that discussion, the theoretical components of altitude, range, area, and speed are described, and in this text they are defined more explicitly and demonstrated in measurement. Thorndike, *et al.* point out that the individual does not display the same level of intellect in every behavior nor in every behavioral situation. There is some kind of average status of intellect around which his behaviors will vary from time to time. If in some way there can be determined the distribution of the variations and level of intellect for the individual, then it would be possible to compare differences on performance of tasks so as to determine the actual difficulty of the task. The authors report such a procedure whereby they studied variation within individuals on repeated tests of intelligence to determine if possible the distribution of performance from time to time. This study was undertaken in order to specify equality of units in testing and thereby to avoid some of the arbitrariness currently true of intellectual measures. The results indicated to them symmetry in terms of variation of performance from one time to another, with most conditions neither depressing nor accelerating scores to an extreme degree. Indeed, the result suggests that if scales of ability having equal units were available, the variation of the individual in performance from one day to the next would be the same regardless of whether his ability level is quite low, superior, or somewhere in between. One evidence of this fact is found in plotting the distributions of different age groups on several scales where equal units have been used. With this procedure, Thorndike, *et al.* found the distributions to be unimodel, symmetrical, and approximating very closely the normal probability curve.

If all that were needed were such distributions in order to determine the intellectual difficulties of tasks, the problem would be solved. As Thorndike and his coauthors point out, however, much more is required. What is reflected in the performance curve of the groups used is not the kind of pure intellectual difficulty desired. Intellect is of course involved but other factors than intellect are involved as well. The result is some measure of difficulty of an item, but not intellectual difficulty of the item. There is the measure of intellect plus error. What the nature of this error is and how much of it is present in any given short intellectual task has to be a part of the evaluation procedure to estimate intellectual difficulty. The authors then attempt to deal more exactly and rigorously with intellectual difficulty of tasks.

Several assumptions are made by them in approaching the assessment of intellectual difficulty. These assumptions are: (1) that man has some quality that may be called "altitude" or "level of intellect;" (2) that the amount or degree of this level is reflected in the number of tasks that a person can do on a series of intellectual tasks ranked for difficulty; (3)

that any individual may differ in the amount or degree of level of intellect which he has available to him from one time to another time; (4) different individuals will differ in the amount or degree of intellectual level available in terms of generalized averages. Intellect then becomes the ability to perform intellectual tasks. It is necessary for the authors now to define what is meant by an intellectual task. There are two possible approaches to this problem. One may assume, first, that certain abilities, such as understanding directions, and seeing relationships, are on the whole intellectual. Such tasks may then be described, some credit or weight attached to each as precisely as possible, and they may be placed in a series so that the individual may attempt to deal with each item. The second possibility is to rank individuals from a very low degree of ability to an extremely high degree of ability on the basis of a consensus of opinion.

In most available tests there is some combination of the two approaches. For example, test constructors have normally taken tasks which they assume to be of an intellectual nature and then put them into some order. At the same time they have used for validity purposes rankings of teachers and school achievement of children as a means of demonstrating correlations of the performance on their tasks with the criterion. The procedure, then, has been largely arbitrary on the part of most test constructors. Using either procedure, a series of tasks is devised, administered to all the individuals of a specified group and ranked according to percentage passing. Thorndike and his colleagues followed such a procedure, deliberately restricting themselves to a fairly narrow choice of tasks. They avoided tasks which might reflect, for example, what they call social intelligence and mechanical intelligence, and concentrated on the kinds of tasks more commonly associated with abstract intelligence. The result is a test which they refer to as intellect CAVD: C standing for completion items, supplying words so as to make a statement true and sensible; A standing for arithmetic, the solution of arithmetical problems; V standing for vocabulary performance; and D standing for directions, understanding connected discourse as in oral directions or in reading a paragraph. Examples of the items used are cited in the text (Thorndike, *et al.*, 1927), and the CAVD test is available in published form.

Intellect is defined, then, as whatever it is that produces intellectual products, whatever it is that allows success with intellectual tasks. As such, a strong component of educability is included within the test itself. Thorndike did not agree with the criticisms which may be leveled at such a procedure. Though he admits that it would be well to measure inherent capacity which a person might have for accomplishment of intellectual tasks, he believes that enterprise would not be so important as the measurement of intellect as it functionally operates. Indeed, the inclusion of items in which education is not a part might lead to a collection of items irrelevant to the use of intelligence by the individual. Thorndike reports data illustrating the relation of intellect CAVD to commonly used group-intelligence tests and the Stanford-Binet mental age. The correlations obtained indicate a systematic agreement in what is measured.

The authors conclude as well that some collection of tasks must be used rather than single tasks or small numbers of tasks. Though difficulty of a single task is an important component within a test, intellectual difficulty can be measured really only in terms of composites which contain a sufficient variety of tasks to represent a reasonable sampling of intellect.

To obtain the best estimate of an individual's altitude, several levels should be administered. By administering more than one level, the best estimate of an individual's overall average level can be obtained. Generally speaking, the estimate that is desired is the level at which he would obtain exactly fifty percent of the items correct. Since in very few cases will exactly that number of items be passed by an individual, this matter of estimating an average over several levels is superior. Each of the levels in the CAVD contains forty items, ten of each of the subtests. The most practical approach, at least the one followed in the actual administration of the CAVD, is to administer five levels to the individual. Thus there is a possible score of 200. If the levels are adjacent and well chosen, as they should be, the individual will probably have a high number of successes at the lowest level and very few successes at the very highest level. Thorndike, *et al.* advocate that scores near zero or 40 should receive very little weight because they will be affected by factors other than those desired in the estimation of intellect CAVD. For scoring purposes, then, they advocate using the three successive levels whose sum of correct responses is nearest to 60, and thus an average of 20 at any one level, and to give equal weight to each of these three levels. This is the procedure used by them, for which tables are prepared.

Given performance over several levels to best estimate altitude, some estimate of range or width may also be achieved. There are two measures of range which may be obtained with the CAVD. One of these involves the number of levels at which the individual scores correctly on at least half the items. The other expression of range involves the average number of items across the various kinds of tasks, C, A, and so on. For all practical purposes, the estimate of altitude is essentially an estimate of range. Area of intellect is defined as the number of successes in either the sample used or in an entire inventory of tasks which have been or can be assembled. Just as with range, area of intellect is best reflected in altitude. In summary, then, altitude becomes an adequate single measure from which some inferences may be made about range and area if needed. The authors plotted performance on altitude and range with increasing intellectual level and found a result approximating a funnel shape figure.

One of the concluding chapters of this book is entitled "The Nature of Intellect." In this chapter, Thorndike and his associates present a working definition and a set of systematic hypotheses related to and derived from their work with the CAVD. They begin by pointing out that intellect had been considered to be the ability to succeed with intellectual tasks. This represents a practical state of affairs since its measurement is noted but through an inventory of tasks arranged in levels of intellectual difficulty and scored in terms of the number of tasks at each level with which the individual can succeed. The procedures followed assure that altitude, range, and area will be closely interdependent. As they state, any defined intellect could be treated in exactly the same way as they have treated CAVD.

Despite the practical consequences of this approach, there was some dissatisfaction over its explanatory value. They present a working definition of intellect based upon the general position that the nature of intellect which is sought is reflected in the ability to deal with things or persons or ideas.

A commonly held view of the time was that intellect could be divided into two parts. The lower part of intellect was reflected in connection-forming or association of ideas. Through this part the individual acquired information and specialized habits. The higher half of intellect was thought of as involving abstraction, generalization, seeing relationships, and the like. This level of intellectual behavior was not conceived of as being based upon connections which are formed physiologically. Indeed, there had been little differentiation as to what the corresponding physiological process might be. Thorndike, *et al.* propose that in point of fact both kinds of intellectual behavior have as their base connection-forming. The only difference between the lower forms of intellect and the higher forms is in the number of connections which are required for the behavior to be displayed. By extension, then, the individual who is of higher intellect differs from a person with lower intellect not because of some different kind of physiological process but because he has a larger number of connections available to him. The expression of intelligence is on a continuum consisting of a quantitative display of connections which have been formed.

The principal assumption made by those most interested in intellectual competence, namely teachers and test makers, has been that intellect reflects some power to respond correctly. Quality of response becomes a primary basis upon which to judge the degree of intelligence possessed by the individual. To such persons, correct judgment and valid inferences would require a great deal more intelligence than the making of wrong judgment or the drawing of false inferences. Thorndike accepts this view but separates the original intellectual capacity which a man may possess from the actual intellectual products and their quality which he produces. The quantity of ideas that a man has, the adequacy of the judgments that he makes, even the validity of the inferences that he draws, are due largely, Thorndike says, to the kind of training which he receives. The position taken here limits itself to original capacity, not training. If one man possesses, due to original nature, a greater tendency for good judgment, or discrimination between good and evil, or better inference drawing, this is due to some anatomical basis. Essentially, the hypothesis advocated by Thorndike, *et al.* is concerned with some quantitative reflection of anatomical cause for qualitative differences among individuals, at least as far as such qualitative differences are due to original nature. If individuals of equal environmental training possess a different amount of connections, this difference must be due to the physiological cause. Since differences do obtain between individuals of equal training, there seems to be some support for the hypothesis that by original nature individuals differ in the number of connections which they may form and which in point of fact they do form during experience. Differences in intelligence, then, basically express the adequacy of the individual to benefit from the experiences which he has, the stimulus-response relationships which may be encountered. In terms of measurement, if a test may be devised which will offer an adequate inventory of tasks to measure the anatomical basis, intellectual capacity will have been measured. This of course could be done at an early age and yield highly stable predictive results.

Despite the importance of the anatomical basis for connection forming, Thorndike admits that there are other causes of intellect in original nature. Two persons may have identical physiological potential and have identical training throughout their lives, yet differ in intellectual achievement. Among the factors which may lead to differences between them, even under these similarities, are such things as curiosity, reinforcement value of dealing with ideas, competition from nonintellectual activities and interests. Certainly, differences in energy level or in health will be important to the introduction of differences behaviorally as well. At the same time, Thorndike maintains that even with these qualifications, the hypothesis is a valid one to hold.

Further Work of Thorndike

Though Thorndike continued to interest himself to some degree in the measurement and meaning of intelligence (see for example 1928) he returned to other aspects of human behavior and particularly to human learning. A book on adult learning appeared in 1928 (Thorndike, Bregman, Tilton, and Woodyard, 1928). This was followed by *Human Learning* in 1931 and the *Fundamentals of Learning* in 1932. Certainly, within the context of Thorndike's theory, one may find references to intelligence and intellectual behavior in these works. Even so, what has been said to this point is reflected in work following 1927.

In the 1940's, Thorndike turned his attention to language behavior and published a series of papers (1943 and 1946, for example) on the origin of language and the psychology of semantics. This represented something of a new field to Thorndike and undoubtedly would have brought a considerable amount of his interest and competence to bear on basic issues in language. Unfortunately, Thorndike, now old and very tired (see Jonçich, 1968), was unable to invest much of his vitality and energy in the task. In 1949, Thorndike died. As was true with other individuals discussed in ths text, the contributions of his life stand as his major epitaph.

References

Jonçich, Geraldine, *The Sane Positivist: A Biography of Edward L. Thorndike.* Middletown, Conn.: Wesleyan University Press, 1968.

Judd, C. H., "A Review of Thorndike's *The Human Nature Club,*" *Psychological Review,* 1901, 8, 626–628.

Thorndike, E. L., "Animal Intelligence: An Experimental Study of the Associative Processes in Animals," *Psychological Review,* 1898, No. 8, p. 109.

———, *The Human Nature Club: An Introduction to The Study of Mental Life.* New York: Longmans, Green, 1900.

———, *Elements of Psychology.* New York: A. G. Seiler, 1905a, pp. 249–250.

———, "Measurement of Twins," *Journal of Philosophy, Psychology and Scientific Method,* 1905b, 2, 547–553.

———, *Educational Psychology. Vol. I: The Original Nature of Man; Vol. II: The Psychology of Learning; Vol. III: Mental Work and Fatigue and Individual Differences and Their Causes.* New York: Teachers College, Columbia University, 1913a.

———, "Ideo-Motor Action," *Psychological Review,* 1913b, 20, 91–106.

———, "Measurement of Intelligence," *Psychological Review,* 1924, 31, 219–252.

———, "The Resemblance of Siblings in Intelligence," Chapter 3 in *Nature and Nurture: Their Influence Upon Intelligence,* 27th Yearbook, Part I, National Society for the Study of Education. Bloomington, Ill.: Public School Publishing Co., 1928.

———, *Human Learning.* New York: Century, 1931.

———, *The Fundamentals of Learning.* New York: Teachers College, Columbia University, 1932.

————, "The Origin of Language," *Science*, 1943, 48, 1–6.

————, "The Psychology of Semantics," *American Journal of Psychology*, 1946, 59, 613–632.

————, and Woodworth, R. S., "The Influence of Special Training on General Ability," *Psychological Review*, 1900, 7, 140.

————, and Woodworth, R. S., "The Influence of Improvement in One Mental Function Upon the Efficiency of Other Functions," *Psychological Review*, 1901, 8, 247–261. 384–395; 556–564.

————, Lay, W., and Dean, P. R., "The Relation of Accuracy in Sensory Discrimination to General Intelligence," *American Journal of Psychology*, 1909, 20, 364–369.

————, Bregman, Elsie O., Cobb, M. V., and Woodyard, Ella, *The Measurement of Intelligence*. New York: Teachers College, Columbia University, 1927.

————, Bregman, Elsie O., Tilton, J. W., and Woodyard, Ella, *Adult Learning*. New York: Macmillan, 1928.

6

Charles Spearman

Where the work of Binet and Terman centered upon the practical outcomes of intelligence with little attention to theory, and where Thorndike combined to some degree theoretical and practical matters but still with a greater emphasis upon the practical, the work of Charles Spearman is almost entirely in the area of theory, at least as far as intelligence is concerned. His work is no less ingenious because it tends to be theoretical, particularly since his theory might apply to all kinds of tests already available. His two-factor theory, maligned though it was throughout his lifetime, was the basis upon which certain other developments occurred, particularly tests which use measurement of specific abilities. Spearman's importance in psychology would be assured even if restricted only to an assessment of his statistical contributions (for example, 1906, 1907, 1910, 1913, 1931c, 1934a; with Holzinger, 1930). When these are combined with notions of the presence of general (g) as well as specific factors (s) in intellectual behavior, Spearman's significance is increased.

Unfortunately, there was considerable criticism of Spearman's work, both statistically and theoretically, and to most of these criticisms he reacted in a defensive manner. He spent about as much energy in defense of his procedures and ideas as he did in their verification. Though the citations of argument are long (1905, 1916, 1922a, 1922b, 1927a, 1928a, 1929a, 1929b, 1930a, 1930b, 1931a, 1931b, 1932, 1933a, 1934b, 1937a, 1940, and 1941), his positive contributions to conceptions of intelligence should not be underestimated. One might take the position that, of all theories of intelligence proposed, Spearman's must rank as one of the most brilliant and potentially the most usable ever given. Its theoretical importance can be demonstrated for both informal and formal situations, and if the quantifications of g and of s's as proposed by Spearman are valid, their practical implementations in such areas as curriculum building and assignment would also be easily demonstrated (see Edwards and Scannell, 1968, pp. 23–26).

The Proposal of Two Factors

In 1904 Spearman published two articles, one dealing with the essential procedures in correlation techniques, and the other applying this procedure to measures that he called "general intelligence." In the first of these articles (Spearman, 1904a), Spearman pointed out the presence of partial relationships that exist in many scientific areas. Particularly in psychology, he felt, it is difficult to find relationships which are perfect. Yet psychologists have tended to conduct studies based upon some premise of significance which the results do not deserve. His purpose in this paper, then, is to demonstrate the procedure of correlation and to apply it, in the second paper, to the concept of "general intelligence."

In his discussion of correlation as contrasted to accidental deviation, he points to the need for accuracy. Unless there is some stability in the results that are obtained, the findings may not be trusted. One means of determining the stability of the correlation achieved is through the probable error. Any method which yields the least probable error will be the one which is most acceptable to the correlational technique. Spearman presents the conventional formula which may be used with variables that yield quantitative measurement. He then points out, however, that in most psychological traits some degree of exact quantification is not possible. Some other procedure will be needed and for this purpose he recommends and discusses comparisons by ranks. Not only are formulae presented for the various correlational techniques which he discusses, but there are also data given to use as the basis of computation.

In dealing with psychological traits, as well as with physical ones, some form of universal correlation is not possible even though it may be quite desirable. As a result, Spearman says, we must deal with certain kinds of restrictions such as the constitution of the sample or problems in quantifying the trait. Such restrictions reflect those hypotheses, in terms of causation, which underlie the purpose of the study in the first place. From this standpoint, they are not so restrictive as they might otherwise be considered. However, they do allow the occurrence of certain kinds of errors about which Spearman believes we shuld be much concerned. First, unless the restrictions are explicitly recognized, they may lead to quite trivial and unscientific results. He uses as an example of this a study which had been recently published in which children's grade placement in school was shown to be correlated with height, weight and strength. As Spearman points out, since age had not been taken into account in this study, the reasonable conclusion that might be drawn is that as children grow older they get larger in size and move up in the grades in school. The second source of error deals with careful delineation of the problem. Spearman says that, even though the underlying basis may be good, unless the experimenter has carefully stated his problem so that he may control for restrictions the results will be ambiguous and in certain instances useless. The final source of error lies within the statistical technique itself. Only if one can determine the factors which are involved and control for these will the relevant ones be included in the correlational technique. In so far as irrelevant factors are included, the correlation will tend to be impure. Spearman discusses in more detail the kinds of error introduced by such impurities.

Spearman maintains that, at least to the time of the publication of his first 1904 article, psychologists had remained blissfully ignorant of the kind of work which Galton began and which was continued by Pearson. Most psychologists doing experimentation had little knowledge of the necessity for precise quantitative expression in the use of correlational techniques. As a result, findings which had been published were to be examined with great care. Finally, Spearman discusses the need for a sample size sufficient to afford stability. At the time, Spearman felt that samples of two to three dozen subjects should be sufficient, particularly since the use of this technique was still in the experimental stage. He also points out, however, that size alone was not sufficient. Indeed, if the relationship between variables was strong enough then a small sample might be sufficient to demonstrate its systematic relationship.

In the second article appearing in 1904 (Spearman, 1904b), Spearman discusses the fact that the laboratory method had yielded little useful data, despite its increasing acceptance in many parts of the world. Though most persons had tended to criticise the laboratory method for the fact that it did not deal with important or complex problems, Spearman felt this criticism to be somewhat unfair. In every field initial efforts must deal with basic matters before the more complex matters may be considered. To him, the true limitation lay in the fact that there was a lack of relation between the matters studied and quantified and the traits desired. There was, primarily, the study of such traits as intelligence in an indirect manner. This matter becomes particularly important when the lack of correlation between the measure and the trait cannot be specified.

Psychology, in common with the other sciences, has two identities. The first of these Spearman calls "uniformity of function," the fact of having like relation under like conditions. The second identity, however, differs from other sciences in the fact that psychology depends upon introspection. Spearman speaks of this as a conceptual uniformity. As such, its scientific precision cannot really be specified. He points out that experimental psychology to that day had dealt only with the first of these identities and had ignored the second completely. Since the second may be as significant as the first, in his second article Spearman attempts to present a means of estimating conceptual uniformity. For this purpose he intends to investigate those "psychical tendencies" which may be reflected in mental tests in terms of their relationship with psychical activities of greater interest in general. Specifically, general intelligence was to be investigated: the relationship of this general intelligence to sensory discrimination (behaviors most commonly investigated in the laboratories of the day) and, hopefully, the definition in some objective manner of what is meant by general intelligence, thereby providing some precise means of measuring it.

In reviewing the experimentation done to that time, Spearman comes to a pessimistic conclusion. Whatever approaches were used, either of high similarity or great diversity, inconsistency of the findings had been most frequent. In fact, Spearman makes the point that frequently diametrically opposite conclusions are drawn by equally competent experimenters. This must mean either that there is no such thing as general intelligence, and therefore there are only a number of mental activities which are completely independent of each other, or the kinds of tests which are being used in the laboratories are of such a nature as to be inapplicable to the quality which is noted as general intelligence. Since functional uniformities have not been demonstrated, what Spearman has called "conceptual uniformities" must be the basis of investigation. In such a procedure, the experimental work in the laboratories is suspect.

According to Spearman, there are several deficiencies in the approaches taken in the laboratory. For one thing, there is a frequent assumption that what is "labeled" is congruent with content. Terms like "voluntary attention" are commonly used and yet the means of measuring voluntary attention (that is, the content of the test or items) may be a poor sample to demonstrate what is labeled. In point of fact, this dilemma still faces us in many of our tests today. It is not unusual to find among widely used tests subtests bearing certain labels. The content of the items included in that subtest are not always clearly discriminable from the content of the items used in some other subtest with a different label. In the absence of demonstrated predictive efficiency, then, it is doubtful that such labels have any meaning beyond some experimenter's belief.

The second problem encountered in laboratories of that day was the attitude toward numbers of subjects to be used for experimental purposes. Most experimenters seemed to feel that large numbers of subjects would be detrimental rather than helpful. Despite the deficiency in the number used, quite sweeping generalizations were frequently drawn from the data, Spearman says. These he feels are unjustified considering the lack of representativeness of the sample.

There are even more precise deficiencies which might be described in the then-current approaches to the study of intelligence. First among these is the fact that there is seldom a precise quantitative expression used for the data studied. Though masses of data may appear in tables, rarely are they reduced to any single exact result. Hence, frequently, the data are interpreted to fit the theory of the experimentalist and his inferences thus lack the impartiality necessary for interpretation and extrapolation.

Because of the lack of precision in quantitative expression, a second major deficiency occurs along this line: the lack of a calculation of the probable error when a correlation coefficient is reported. The correlation may then express nothing more than accidental coincidence since it cannot be judged in terms of its excess over error.

The third deficiency lies in the fact that in many cases there is no explicit statement of the problem investigated. In consequence, not only must a large number of qualifications be attached to any single experiment, but in addition comparison of results among experiments becomes quite difficult. Some method which will allow the effects of all factors to be discriminated and expressed would be superior.

As a final deficiency, Spearman speaks of the many errors of observation which occur. Most frequently there are differences between the measures that are actually obtained and the reality which the experimenter wishes to achieve. Again this circumstance only leads to greater error.

To Spearman, the investigations to that time had been inadequate. Rather than leave them at this stage, however, he offers an alternative which he believes will be superior. He discusses means by which the deficiencies just presented may be avoided or eliminated. As one should expect, the correlational technique is the thing that is advocated.

This procedure will depend upon the demonstration of reliability and validity. Spearman maintains that in his experimentation and use of the statistic he has controlled adequately to assure reliability. Validity, though desirable certainly, is not so well assured either in this study or others.

In the material reported by Spearman in his second article of 1904, the approaches to estimating intelligence advocated by Ebbinghaus and Binet are rejected for an approach using sensory measures. Sensory data are used primarily because of their simplicity and exactness, not necessarily because of their superiority for reflecting intelliegence. Specifically, measures of hearing, sight, and touch represent the sensory measures used. Some five experiments were conducted, using children of different ages as well as adults, though not with the same tasks in every instance nor even with measurement on all the tasks represented. Intelligence was estimated in terms of a child's placement in school, his rank, and his rank by age. Additionally, teachers categorized each pupil as bright, average, or dull. Finally, older students rated the rest of the sample in terms of their common sense as demonstrated on out-of-school tasks. To this kind of data the correlational technique was applied.

Spearman points out that the meaning of the results which he obtains is in opposition to the kind normally reported. For one thing, his direction of inquiry is reversed over the usual laboratory experimentation. He has restricted himself to computing the correlational relations between the several tasks used by him. Admittedly, he could not comment about what faculties may be reflected in the behaviors, but he feels no need to do so anyway. Beyond the commonality present in two measures, the possibility exists for extension to more exact relationships in future work. Over all, Spearman reports a consistent and fairly high relationship between the sensory tasks used by him and what he calls "life intelligence" as based upon the school rankings and judgments of teachers. When the various tasks are combined to produce a measure of general discrimination and general intelligence, Spearman concludes not only that there are such factors but that the functional correspondence between them is very nearly absolute. From these facts, Spearman draws an important conclusion:

> . . . *Whenever branches of intellectual activity are at all dissimilar, then their correlation with one another appear wholly due to their being all variously saturated with some common fundamental function (or group of functions)* . . . *(p. 273).*

This, of course, is a statement of g as he will use it in the future and even at this stage Spearman speaks of the momentous importance both theoretically and practically of this concept.

Spearman also reports correlation coefficients obtained between school subjects as well as between performance in a given subject and the measures of sensory discrimination. Some information on musical performance was also obtained from the school. The results are reported in Table 6.1.

A further step was taken by computing the correlation of each kind of activity with general intelligence, and then determining the ratio of the common factor to the specific factor. This procedure included not only the concept of g (general intelligence) but also the first steps in the direction of specifying s's (specific intelligences) and ratios of each s to g. Spearman makes the point that one important outcome of such procedures may be decisions made for individual children about a curriculum in their school work.

TABLE 6.1*
RELATIONSHIPS BETWEEN FACTORS STUDIED AS A PART OF
"GENERAL INTELLIGENCE"

Tasks	(1)	(2)	(3)	(4)	(5)	(6)
(1) Classics	.87	.83	.78	.70	.66	.63
(2) French	.83	.84	.67	.67	.65	.57
(3) English	.78	.67	.89	.64	.54	.51
(4) Mathematics	.70	.67	.64	.88	.45	.51
(5) Discrimination	.66	.65	.54	.45	—	.40
(6) Music	.63	.57	.51	.51	.40	—

* From Spearman, 1904b, p. 275.

Though greater explicitness is evident as future work develops the theory, these articles published in 1904 are the clear delineation of the two-factor theory, how it may be expressed, and its implications.

The Abilities of Man

With the publication of *The Abilities of Man,* Spearman's theory had reached its most precise point. A phenomenological viewpoint is quite clear, for he states in his first chapter that the indvidual is aware of himself in his environment. The person perceives his world and himself in this world and thinks about himself and his world. As a label to denote such perception in thinking, psychology uses the term cognition. But Spearman maintains there is more to intellectual life than cognition since various appetites, aversions, impulses and so on are a part of perception and thinking. To denote these, Spearman speaks of the conative and affective or, as he puts it, striving and feeling components of man's behavior. Though admittedly the person exists in some totality, the major content of this book by Spearman deals with cognition. Spearman defends this approach by speaking of the fact that cognitive ability may be regarded as a part or organ at the disposal of any of the conative activities of the person. The purpose of the book, then, is to carefully examine this ability which he calls "cognition" with special reference to how it varies in terms of efficiency from one individual to another.

Spearman discusses at some length widely held views of the nature of intelligence. Most of these definitions he finds ambiguous, inadequate, and very frequently overlapping, but without giving much information about the nature of the trait itself. He quotes some advice from Hart: "We shall have to give over the front of our giving words and begin to face facts. Our intellectual joust is over; it is time to plant some beans" (Spearman, 1927, p. 15). It is probably not unfair to say that Spearman managed to ignore his own advice, since there are tremendous numbers of words argued over within the context of the first part of the book, covering some nine chapters. Because of the numerous attacks from all direction on his theory, Spearman has become quite defensive in his writing. He quarrels when quarreling would seem to gain him little either in terms of acceptance or furtherance of his own ideas. One example is his treatment of a statement by Terman in *The Measurement of Intelligence* (1916). He quotes Terman's contention that it is not necessary to present a complete definition of intelligence before the measurement of it. Terman further discusses the point using electricity as an illustration. Despite the fact that the nature of electricity was unknown, the utilization of its effects for mankind's welfare was continuous. Terman speculates that in the same way intelligence may be unknown in its true nature and yet its effects may be investigated, measured, and used. Spearman maintains there was a fallacy in Terman's argument, based upon the confounding of two quite different things. Though the true nature of electricity need not be known, its manifestations must be, according to Spearman. He then states: ". . . Analogously, we may perhaps dispense with knowing the 'pure science' of intelligence; but assuredly we cannot test it without having decided which mental operations belong to its domain. Popularly and roughly expressed, we must needs know if not *what* at any rate *which* it is" (Spearman, 1927, p. 16). He continues here pointing out that this procedure has not been followed in the investigation of intelligence, so that no decision has been reached as to whether intelligence should include memory, imagination, attention, sensation, comprehension, or anything else. As a result, Spearman maintains we are as ignorant about intelligence as the physicist who is unaware of which galvanometer to take into account. Though one may accept some legitimacy in the arguments offered by Spearman, the question is to what extent does he improve upon the situation in *The Abilities of Man.*

Spearman speaks of three approaches to definitions of intelligence that were currently popular. The first of these he calls *monarchic* as a doctrine because it emphasizes intelligence as a unitary function—some kind of sovereign power that is measurable and reflected in a single value. Such an approach he believes to be very popular with the layman as well as with many psychologists, such as Binet and Terman. Increasing criticisms of that viewpoint had led to some awareness of its invalidity, Spearman states. Essentially he believes it to be a label used indiscriminately with all sorts of things and for which there is an assumed reality which does not exist.

A second, though less popular, explanation of intelligence he labels *oligarchic.* The emphasis here is on discrete faculties or powers, including as typical labels such presumed factors as judgment, memory, invention, and attention. Since each of these is presumed to be a separate function or behavior unit of its own, measurement must be conducted for each separately. This oligarchic viewpoint stands in diametric opposition to the monarchic viewpoint but Spearman makes the point that it is implied almost as universally as is the monarchic viewpoint. Thus, when an individual's ability is to be determined, the various single traits such as judgment and memory are assessed. One result is the construction of rather elaborate mental profiles with each trait receiving its own measurement but plotted on a single dimension. Spearman believes that the doctrine is dangerous because of its application to large numbers of individuals in industry, determining their fate without an adequate foundation.

Yet another doctrine about intelligence Spearman calls *anarchic.* The oligarchic viewpoint that there are several different faculties or types of intelligence fell victim to its own assumptions, according to Spearman, since it became apparent that each of the so called faculties could be broken down into subfaculties. There were many more mental operations required, then, than were expressed by the faculties proposed. The approach may even be carried to the extreme that Thorndike proposed whereby intelligence operates for every response and thus any and every connection between stimulus and response represents intelligence.

Even so, certain behaviors tend to cluster with other behaviors such that intercorrelations may be found among responses. The correlational procedure which would demonstrate such relationships had not been followed as well as it might, according to Spearman. Instead, the belief in some general level or average or sample of a person's abilities had become widely accepted, a doctrine referred to by Spearman as anarchic. The most common procedure of determining this general average— pooling a number of tests indiscriminately—Spearman maintains is not justified by the theory and does not yield the kind of general level or average which it is assumed to yield. The approach used by Binet and others to achieve this averaging Spearman titles as a promiscuous pooling, despite the brilliance with which Binet executed his tasks. Since there was little to defend the procedure theoretically, however, more trouble was created than solved.

The solution to all of these problems of course lies in Spearman's approach, one that he calls eclectic in nature, and including the doctrine of two factors. The eclectic doctrine is based on the correlations between abilities. Spearman had noted in a number of studies a peculiar arrangement in terms of the correlations obtained between measures of different abilities. Included in these abilities were test scores, school-subject grades, estimates of general ability, estimates of specific competencies, and so on. This arrangement which resulted from such correlations presented itself in a form that allowed a distinct mathematical formulation. This formula, called the tetrad equation, is expressed as

$$r_{ap} \times r_{bq} - r_{aq} \times r_{bp} = 0$$

The r stands for any correlation coefficient while the subscripts a, b,, p, and q stand for abilities that are intercorrelated. If the tetrad equation is true, then any four intercorrelations among ability scores may be substituted in the formula and always yield the appropriate value of zero.

Spearman tells us that when the tetrad equation holds throughout a table of correlations but *only* when it does so, then every individual measurement of every ability including any variable that enters the correlational table can be divided into two parts. One part he calls a general factor and denotes it by the letter g. This is some quality which varies greatly from individual to individual although it is a constant for any one individual in terms of the correlated abilities. The other part is what he calls a specific factor and denotes by the letter s. Not only is there variation from individual to individual but even within the individual from one ability to another. By 1927, Spearman believed that the formal proof of this theorem was complete. The precise expression of the division into two parts is given with the following equation:

$$m_{ax} = r_{ag} \times g_x + r_{as} \times s_{ax}$$

In this formula, m_{ax} is the measurement obtained for any individual x on a variable a; g_x is the amount of g possessed by the individual, the common factor in all the variables; s_{ax} is the amount the individual has of the specific factor s_a. In every ability for which the tetrad equation holds, both g and s will be present. However, they will not bear the same relationship for each ability. The g tends to be of much greater importance for some kinds of behaviors than for others. To illustrate this, Spearman computed ratios of g to s in given traits. In terms of success in study of the classics, for example, he found a ratio of 15 to 1, indicating that g is of much greater importance to this behavior than is some specific talent. On the other hand accomplishment in musical performance showed a ratio of one to four, indicating that some kind of specific talent is of greater influence here than is general intelligence as such. The relative magnitudes of g and s in a given trait should not be taken as some indicator of the importance of the trait.

Spearman is clear that g is not some concrete thing, but only a value or magnitude. There is a further point that the magnitude does not define the quality or energy which represents g. It represents an objective measure which may or may not be intelligence. When the tetrad equation holds, *g* may be computed. However the tetrad equation will not hold in all situations. Correlation coefficients between abilities must differ, that is, they must not be overlapping, in order for the tetrad equation to be valid. Under certain circumstances specific factors do overlap. These overlapping specific factors Spearman calls group factors. As an example, he mentions the cancellation test where measurement first occurs for cancellation of *a*, then separately for cancellation of *e*. These two performances would be very much alike and would share not only a *g* factor in common but also have a large overlap in respect to the *s* factor necessary to success. The tetrad equation would not hold in such a case due to the presence of the group factor. In Figure 6-1, this outcome is demonstrated. The upper left circle indicates the specific factor operating in *a*-cancellation, the upper right circle represents the *s* factor in *e*-cancellation. Since the two share a common specific ability there is an overlap between the two. The bottom circle indicates the *g* present in both *a*-cancellation and *e*-cancellation tests. As mentioned, the tetrad equation is not valid in such a case as this. A problem exists for the theoretical position, then, if there are very many such group factors operating. In certain theoretical and statistical writing following Spearman's work, just such a position is taken. Factor analysis is an example of the technique used to demonstrate group factors.

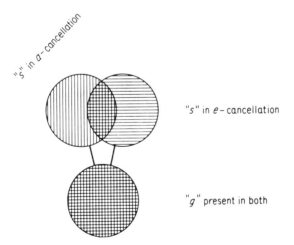

Fig. 6-1. Example of overlap in specific factors. (From Spearman, 1927b, p. 80.)

Having offered what he believes to be a satisfactory demonstration that *g* and *s* are divisible and measurable, Spearman then attempts to explain what *g* may be. He reviews the many attempts at defining general intelligence. Some psychologists considered *g* to be equivalent to intelligence. Whenever tasks which were designed to measure something called "general intelligence" were analyzed, apparently there were large loadings of this general universal factor running throughout the performance. Beyond this demonstration of the presence of some universal factor, however, there is no demonstration as to what intelligence means.

Spearman proposes the possibility of g as a mental energy. There is in ordinary, waking life, according to Spearman, the phenomenon of universal mental competition working. By this he means that the beginning of any given mental activity causes other activity to cease. The converse of this, cessation of any activity causing another activity to commence, is believed equally probable. Essentially, then, mental activity is like physical activity, showing consistency of total output in an evervarying manifestation. Just as such physical activity is denoted as energy, so should the mental activity be noted. By mental energy he meant the consistency and constancy of mental activity on the part of the individual. Since energy does not operate in a vacuum, Spearman advocates the possibility of some kind of "engine." The so called engines represent neural systems which allow mental output for the expression of the general energy called g. In the theory of intelligence proposed, the energy is used to explain g, while the concept of engines is used to explain s's.

In order to test and define the limits of g, Spearman includes the entire field of ability. He applies the tetrad equation to correlation coefficients in every psychological areas where measures were available and data could be gathered. He reports overwhelming evidence for the presence of g whenever such tests are used. Admittedly, the universal nature of g applies to man's cognitive nature and not to the more dominant influence of the affective and conative natures of man.

An important practical corollary is denoted by Spearman as the theorem of indifference of the indicator. For purposes of indicating the amount of g possessed by the individual, Spearman states that any test does just as well as any other provided the correlations with g are equally high. This may mean that even quite ridiculous tasks and stunts may be used if the amount of g necessary to their performance is as high as is found in highly abstract, imaginative, or logical operations. This is the reason, Spearman maintains, that then-current tests which were called measures of general intelligence seemed to show high correlations not only with one another but also with g. The explanation lies not in the theories that underlie the tests, since these theories had been quite confused, nor even in the uniformity of construction, since these had been very heterogenous, but only because of the fact that there was an indifference of the indicator. This theorem would allow even for very grotesque-appearing tests, tests on a logical basis not related at all to the measure of general intelligence, yet showing a comparable measure of g and, indeed, correlating quite well with other tests considered to be much more adequate.

In summary, evidence is offered by Spearman that *g* is a factor which enters the measurement of abilities of all kinds. Furthermore, the amount of *g* present to the individual remains constant regardless of the kind of task to which it is applied. Because of its mental-energy nature, *g* is not affected by education and its quantity cannot be increased by any specialized educational procedures. This, of course, is not true of *s* since any given *s* can be greatly influenced by the educational procedures used. Heredity apparently is a great factor in the amount of *g* present to the individual and to a lesser degree in specific intelligences as well. As far as Spearman is concerned, neither race nor sex are of any particular importance in terms of determining amount of *g* present to the individual.

Further Refinements of Spearman's Theory

An essential condition for the acceptance of *g* and *s* lies in the hierarchical structure of correlations between abilities. There had been a number of attacks upon this observed hierarchy as reported by Spearman, most of the explanations centering around chance factors or what was sometimes called sampling factors. Spearman attempted to disprove this viewpoint with an article appearing in 1928 (Spearman, 1928b). The criticisms centered around the chance distribution which occurs through tossing coins or throwing dice and the like. The assumptions underlying such procedures are not acceptable to Spearman since there is no attention to fundamental qualities or mental elements discoverable by introspection. Spearman maintains that every performance or ability depends on a randomly selected group of quite numerous independent elements. The correlation between two performances has to be due to the elements common to both groups. He attempts to demonstrate mathematically both for a case of numerous elements and for moderately numerous elements the untenability of a chance explanation. He concluded that there is no general theory of chance, but only special theories that involve it. His theory of two factors cannot be explained, then, on a chance basis since it is a quite general theorem allowing analysis of variables which yield functions designated *g* and *s*. Both logical and statistical arguments are presented to support his case.

This problem was considered further in an article published in 1930 (Spearman, 1930c). Some critics had maintained that tetrad differences would have to be obtained for more than four tests; in fact, in some instances there was the call for at least 10,000 such differences being computed. Only with a large number of cases would a random sample of elements be adequately controlled. Under conditions with a large number of cases, the critics maintained, a small probable error would be found and any observed tetrad differences would be more likely to disclose themselves. If tetrad differences other than zero were consistently found, then the theory of a general common factor must be rejected and random distribution of ability from one element to another adopted instead. Only if tetrad differences were found to be zero through such a consistent number of cases would the general factor hold. Spearman rejects such an argument on logical grounds and even proposes an alternative.

Perhaps, he says, the two theories are not antithetical at all. Where numerous cases are used, and tetrad differences become significant in comparison with probable error, further proof of the general factor might be derived. Though under ideal conditions the tetrad conditions should be zero, under practical conditions the probable errors do indicate departures from zero. But Spearman maintains there are other disturbances than just probable error, or errors in sampling, which account for increases in departure from zero. In order to test the theory of a general factor, then, it is necessary to compare the observed tetrad differences not only with their probable errors but also with the aggregates of all the disturbances which according to the theory should occur. If out of the aggregate of expected disturbances there is not a match with those actually observed, then the general-factor theory must be amended. To that date, such a procedure had not been followed, and it was the purpose of Spearman's paper to offer preparatory work.

Spearman lists as the kinds of disturbances which would lead to departure from zero in tetrad differences such things as the probable errors, group factors, accidental linkage between abilities, and heterogeneity of subjects, especially in terms of age, sex, education, and the like. Such sources of departure Spearman says he had indicated since he first proposed the theory. Further refinement had indicated the importance of these factors as disturbing influences. In this list would now be included accuracy or speed of performance taken separately, testing of subjects in separate sections, and assumptions that abilities are linear functions of g and s. Undoubtedly, Spearman says, other sources of tetrad differences will be disclosed with further work. He concludes the article with an analysis of scaling as it would affect tetrad differences. Under conditions where scaling of variables reflects a normal frequency distribution, very little departure from zero tetrad differences would be found. In an article published in 1931 (Spearman, 1931c), further statistical and logical arguments are presented to substantiate the two-factor theory.

The various arguments, formal proofs, and logical derivation of evidence to support the two-factor theory are presented in a series of articles published by Spearman in the *Journal of Educational Psychology* (Spearman, 1933b, 1933c, 1934c, 1934d, 1934e).

Final Contributions

Further work of Spearman continued to clarify and define the essential theoretical conceptions first presented in 1904. Among his writings were the two-volume work entitled *Psychology Down the Ages,* dealing not alone with intelligence as the term is more commonly used but with other aspects of the phenomenological self. The sections dealing with intelligence in both volumes attempt to state more precisely the hypotheses that had been stated in the past. Continued data collection was utilized to demonstrate the presence and extent of *g,* and as an argument against the opponents of the concept. Over all, Spearman attempts to simplify the hypotheses he has presented in the past, and to communicate in a fashion that had not been true in several of his immediately preceding works. In Volume One, he repeats an idea which he had presented before, clarifying what he believes to be his posiition in the history of the measurement of intelligence. In a review of the use of the term intelligence in contemporary times, Spearman credits Galton with having brought the word intelligence back to the Latin meaning of the word. In this sense, according to Spearman, intelligence is the power of distinction and selection. Galton's procedure of attempting to describe the intellectually ablest individual on the basis of tests of discrimination Spearman believes reflected very directly this original meaning. With Ebbinghaus, the process of elaborate analysis was begun with the conclusion drawn by Ebbinghaus that intelligence represents some power of combination. Spearman points to the variety of tests advocated by Binet and used by him in research in developing the scales. However, Binet made little if any use of the notion of intelligence as such. The item content reflected what Binet referred to as certain faculties of memory, imagination, attention, suggestibility, and so on, without clearly designating which of these faculties represented intelligence and to what degree any given item measured each faculty. It is at this point that Spearman proclaims his entrance upon the stage.

> In 1904, however, the present writer proposed a new theory, wherein all such separate faculties were replaced by a single one called —with much reservation—"general intelligence." (Spearman, 1937b, p. 127)

Spearman went on then to state that Binet follows very shortly by maintaining on the one hand some doctrine of multiple, separate faculties and on the other hand tacitly adopting the procedure that Spearman had adovcated—that of general intelligence. No longer were there measures of separate single faculties (if indeed there ever were), but all measures were now thrown into a single test score. Spearman expresses his attitude toward such a procedure as: "He [Binet] wants, it would seem, to run with the hare yet hunt with the hounds."

Spearman goes on then to review and criticize the positions of Terman, Haggerty, and Freeman. Spearman points out inconsistencies between the theoretical statements of many test constructors and the content of their tests. Such efforts Spearman found inconsistent, theoretically impossible to defend since they were not based upon any consistent theory, and most often were limited to some criterion which was too restricted for life in general, such as school achievement. On these bases alone, then, he would believe his own theory to be much superior since it attempts to describe intellect more directly and to express it in a fashion that could be used for varied criteria.

In the second volume of this work, *Psychology Down the Ages,* Spearman also presents a new equation with regard to *g.* This formula is expressed as follows:

$$a = g + s$$

In this formula, *a* represents the score made by any individual on any particular test. Thus, *a* may be replaced by performance on test *b* or test *c,* or any other test which is defensible in the tetrad equation. The symbol *g* stands for the presence of one "general intelligence" which permeates all of the behavior of the individual; *s* is the specific factor entering into performance on the particular test chosen. Test performance, then, is some combination of general intelligence plus specific ability for the task at hand. The important point, here, is that *g* will remain proportional for the individual as compared with the test performance by all other persons, regardless of whether the test is *a, b, c,* or whatever. By contrast, the *s* will change depending upon the presence and degree of this specific ability within each test individually. Spearman makes the added point that performance on a given test may be divided into other ways than *g* and *s.* He believed the division presented by him to be preferable, however, since it is parsimonious as an explanatory principle.

There are some additional theoretical positions taken about the dependence and independence of *g* and *s* in this book. Spearman maintains that if a person is to possess capacity for high achievement in any of life's work, he must have both *g* and the *s*'s relevant to the particular kind of performance in very high degrees. Where there is only a moderate amount of *g* and the relevant *s*'s, then only moderate success may be achieved. At the same time, there cannot be compensation either. Thus, high amounts of *g* with relatively low amounts of *s* for any particular accomplishment or conversely low amounts of *g* with very high amount of *s* for any particular kind of work will lead at best to only moderate success. When both *g* and *s* are low, the individual cannot have any possibility of success. In this context, then, if we can indeed measure and express quantities of *g* and *s*'s it should be possible to identify fairly early in the life of the individual the areas in which he may expect success as compared with those in which he will be little successful. Such a concept should have considerable import for school guidance programs, for example, as well as for curricula chosen for individual students. This matter has been discussed by the author in another source (Edwards and Scannell, 1968, p. 23–26).

Spearman speaks directly in the matter of vocational choice. He cites research indicating that different kinds and types of occupations require *g* in differing amounts. Any person employed in a job with insufficient *g* will be inefficient in his work. At the same time, the individual employed in a job where smaller amounts of *g* are needed than he has available to him will not only be wasting much of his efforts but is apt to be discontented in his work as well. Spearman maintained that it would be possible to use the measures of *g* and *s*'s for the individuals as a final choice of a vocation except for the fact that this decision must also be based upon other factors, such as preferences, feelings and the like.

Where *g* seems to be discriminable and quantifiable and explicit, *s* factors create some problems for Spearman's theory. Since the *s* varies for the individual from one kind of task to another kind of task, its quantity can vary sharply, depending upon measurement. In addition to such differences as these, there is also the matter of breadth of *s*. That is, the *s* may be narrow or broad, it may extend over a small range of performance or over a large range of performance within any given task. If an *s* has great breadth then it may cover more than one kind of task. This means that several tasks may show some degree of overlap between two or more *s*'s. Where this occurs the heirarchy of correlation coefficients necessary to satisfy the tetrad equation will not exist. Spearman speaks of this overlap between *s*'s as group factors. The most important of these group factors, according to Spearman, is the verbal factor. He maintains that, though important, this verbal factor shows only a small percentage of loading in most usable tests. Other examples of group factors include a mechanical factor, a practical factor, and a persistence factor. This list appears incomplete and debatable, when considering the work of factor analysts which follows.

Spearman maintained that the importance of *g* was being more and more realized. In illustration of this point, he states that the determinations of mental age and general intelligence that had been in common usage up until 1937 were then being supplanted. Thus *g* as a measure would perform all the services that either mental age or some other expression of general intelligence would accomplish with the added advantage that what is expressed as *g* will be a stable, well-defined value. Changes for the individual from testing to testing would not occur as can happen with either mental age or some other expression. Indeed, even utilizing several different tests, if these tests meet the essential requirements of the tetrad equation, there should be a stable estimate of the amount of *g* available to the individual.

Nature of the General Factor

In 1946, Spearman published an article not only defending the concept of *g* on both philosophical and empirical grounds but discussing the general factor in other contexts as well (Spearman, 1946). In this regard, he speaks of the fact that some authors who had disclosed kinds of general factors maintained that these were not *g* at all. Part of this variability was accounted for by statistical manipulations, he says, and therefore were not defensible arguments. Even in instances where some kind of general group factor was disclosed, Spearman maintains that the factors were reasonably good approximations of *g*. A different case altogether was found in the so-called bi-polar factors. Here values much unlike those of *g* were found. Spearman attempts to explain these bipolar factors as more properly belonging in the area of feeling and volition, what he calls *orexis*, than in the field of intellect.

Finally, there were those cases where no general factor was found at all. Spearman says the most striking feature of these is the fact that they were extremely rare. Even in the very few cases which had been reported in the literature, he maintains that if there was not a general factor there was at least a very good imitation of it. He does not dismiss the possibility, however, that such cases may be found which are defensible. Under such circumstances, he says the *g* factor would be not so much absent as latent. The remainder of the article returns to theoretical and empirical defenses for *g* that he has offered a number of times before. The factor-analytic school had been marshalling and presenting evidence which seems to discount the two-factor theory proposed by Spearman. Spearman believes that he has now offered a bridge which would combine the statistics of factor analysis with the psychology of his theory.

Human Ability

The final work of Spearman appeared in 1951, after his death, and was co-authored with Jones (Spearman and Jones, 1951). Very little change in the concept of *g* is presented in this book although it was intended to be an extension of *The Abilities of Man* (Spearman, 1927). Perhaps the principal change is one of terminology and symbolization. Though maintaining the *g* factor to represent some kind of mental energy, Spearman and Jones propose two other factors which influence intellect. One of these they denote as *p* (perseveration), referring to inertia. The other factor *O* (oscillation) represents the facility of recuperation of the intellect after some expenditure of effort by the individual. These factors, of *p* and *O*, thus, seem to bear some functional relation to much more current research on chemical balance and the firing of neurons. The acetylcholine-cholenesterase balance and function seem to be some physiological basis for what Spearman could only imagine (see Edwards and Cawley, 1964).

Summary

The principal contributions of Spearman are theoretical and statistical. His work became the basis for the factor-analytic techniques which expanded and refuted his theory. Still, without his contributions the more sophisticated models prevalent today might have been greatly delayed.

Spearman's theory of *g* and *s*'s remains a brilliant view of intellectual expression. The inability to apply these concepts in practical situations are less a reflection on the theory than on our inability to devise sufficient tasks.

References

Edwards, A. J., and Cawley, J. F. (eds.), *The Kansas Symposium on Physiological Determinates of Behavior.* Lawrence: University of Kansas Studies in Education, 1964.

Edwards, A. J., and Scannell, D. P., *Educational Psychology: The Teaching-Learning Process.* Scranton, Pa.; International Textbook, 1968.

Spearman, C., "The Proof and Measurement of Association Between Two Things," *American Journal of Psychology,* 1904a, 15, 72–101.

———, " 'General Intelligence,' Objectively Determined and Measured," *American Journal of Psychology,* 1904b, 15, 201–292.

———, "Proof and Disproof of Correlation," *American Journal of Psychology,* 1905, 16, 228–231.

———, " 'Footrule' for Measuring Correlation," *British Journal of Psychology,* 1906, 2, 89–108.

———, "Demonstration of Formulae for True Measurement of Correlation," *American Journal of Psychology,* 1907, 18, 161–169.

————, "Correlation Calculated from Faulty Data," *British Journal of Psychology,* 1910, 3, 271–275.

————, "Correlation of Sums or Differences," *British Journal of Psychology,* 1913, 5, 417–426.

————, "Some Comments on Mr. Thomson's Paper," *British Journal of Psychology,* 1916, 8, 282–284.

————, "Manifold Sub-Theories of 'The Two Factors', " *Pychological Review,* 1920, 27, 159–172.

————, "Recent Contributions to the Theory of Two Factors," *British Journal of Psychology,* 1922a, 13, 26–30.

————, "A Friendly Challenge to Professor Thorndike," *Psychological Review,* 1922b, 29, 406–407.

————, "Material versus Abstract Factors in Correlation," *British Journal of Psychology,* 1927a, 17, 322–326.

————, *The Abilities of Man: Their Nature and Measurement.* New York: MacMillan, 1927b.

————, "Pearson's Contribution to the Theory of Two Factors," *British Journal of Psychology,* 1928a, 19, 95–101.

————, "The Sub-Structure of the Mind," *British Journal of Psychology,* 1928b, 18, 249–261.

————, "The Uniqueness of 'g'," *Journal of Educational Psychology,* 1929a, 20, 212–216.

————, "Response to T. Kelley," *Journal of Educational Psychology,* 1929b, 20, 561–569.

————, "Heterogeneity and the Theory of Factors," *American Journal of Psychology,* 1930a, 42, 645–646.

————, "A Truce to 'Barking In'," *Journal of Educational Psychology,* 1930b, 21, 110–111.

————, "Disturbers of Tetrad Differences Scales," *Journal of Educational Psychology,* 1930c, 21, 559–573.

————, "What the Theory of Factors is *Not*," *Journal of Educational Pscyhology,* 1931a, 22, 112–117.

————, "Our Need of Some Science in Place of the Word 'Intelligence,' " *Journal of Educational Psychology,* 1931b, 22, 401–410.

————, "The Theory of 'Two Factors' and that of 'Sampling'," *British Journal of Educational Psychology,* 1931c, 1, 140–161.

————, "Pitfalls in the Use of 'Probable Error'," *Journal of Educational Psychology,* 1932, 23, 481–488.

————, "The Uniqueness and Exactness of g," *British Journal of Psychology,* 1933a, 24, 106–108.

————, "The Factor Theory and Its Troubles: II. Garbling The Evidence," *Journal of Educational Psychology,* 1933b, 24, 521–524.

————, "The Factor Theory and Its Troubles: III. Misrepresentation of the Theory," *Journal of Educational Psychology*, 1933c, 24, 591–601.

————, "Analysis of Abilities into Factors by the Method of Least Squares," *British Journal of Educational Psychology*, 1934a, 4, 183–185.

————, "Professor Tryon on Factors," *Psychological Review*, 1934b, 41, 306–307.

————, "The Factor Theory and Its Troubles: IV. Uniqueness of G," *Journal of Educational Psychology*, 1934c, 25, 142–153.

————, "The Factor Theory and Its Troubles: V. Adequacy of Proof," *Journal of Educational Psychology*, 1934d, 25, 310–319.

————, "The Factor Theory and Its Troubles: Conclusion. Scientific Value," *Journal of Educational Psychology*, 1934e, 25, 383–391.

————, "Abilities as Sums of Factors, or as Their Products," *Journal of Educational Psychology*, 1937a, 28, 629–631.

————, *Psychology Down the Ages, Volumes I and II.* London: MacMillan, 1937b.

————, "Is Ability Random or Organized," *Journal of Educational Psychology*, 1940, 31, 305–310.

————, "How 'g' Can Disappear," *Psychometrika*, 1941, 6, 353–354.

————, "Theory of General Factor," *British Journal of Psychology*, 1946, 36, 117–131.

————, and Holzinger, K., "The Average Value for the Probable Error of Tetrad Differences," *British Journal of Psychology*, 1930, 20, 368–370.

————, and Jones, L. W., *Human Ability.* London: Macmillan, 1951.

Terman, L. M., *The Measurement of Intelligence.* Boston: Houghton Mifflin, 1916.

7

L. L. Thurstone
and
Thelma Gwinn Thurstone

L. L. Thurstone was responsible for a number of statistical contributions, including the innovative practice of factor analysis (1925, 1927a, 1938b, 1945a, 1947, 1948, 1954a). In the field of attitude measurement, his contributions were many and significant (1927b, 1945b, 1951, 1954b, 1959, with Chave, 1929, Patterson and Thurstone, 1933). Along with these, his contributions in the field of intelligence testing and theory, in which he was joined by his wife Thelma Gwinn Thurstone, represent a major accomplishment.

Thurstone's initial work was in vocational testing and dealt with statistical and measurement problems in this practical field. In 1919, he published two studies dealing with mental testing for specified occupational groups. In the first of these (Thurstone, 1919a), he attempted to determine whether it is possible to predict ability in telegraphy through the use of mental tests. The subjects constituted 165 men, drafted by the United States Army and in training in radio telegraphy. Data dealing with the mental-test scores and the progress in telegraphy were reported. For the sample used, Thurstone found that occupation, schooling, and age were unrelated to success in learning telegraphy. Eight tasks designated by Thurstone as mental tests were used, most of them representative of the kinds of tasks commonly used. The first of these, a rhythm test, required students to reproduce a pattern with the telegraphic key. Thurstone found that scores on this test correlated positively and moderately with his criterion scores of achievement in telegraphy. The second task, an opposites test, also yielded a moderate correlation coefficient with success. Tests of analogies, following directions, word completion, and spelling yielded low positive correlations. Performance on an arithmetic test and a sentence completion test yielded negligible correlations. A multiple correlation coefficient of .53 was found between the five most successful tests and success in telegraphy. However, the rhythm task accounted for virtually all of this coefficient. Thurstone concludes that general intelligence tests are not valuable for determining ability to learn telegraphy. Considering the content of the rhythm task, it would appear that the best means of predicting motor accomplishment is through a task the content of which involves motor performance.

The second of these studies (Thurstone, 1919b) followed much the same procedure, but in terms of predicting success in clerical work for office workers. An examination, comprising some eight parts and taking approximately ninety minutes for administration, was described and re-sults reported for 100 employees of an insurance company. Five different classes of employees were compared and the quality of office work cor-related with accuracy in test performance, speed, level of schooling, and age. Accuracy in the test correlated most highly with grade of office work ($r = .50$) with age correlating least well ($r = .35$). In combination, accuracy and speed yielded a correlation coefficient of .61 while the combination of all four variables correlated .67 with the criterion of grade of office work. These two studies have importance not so much for their direct contribution to Thurstone's work in mental testing, as in the fact that they demonstrated an early interest in discrete measures and combi-nations of subtests as means of best estimating intellectual competence.

This testing methodology was demonstrated in the presentation of an intelligence test for college students published by Thurstone in 1921. He points to problems of measuring intellectual competence of adults with the commonly-used standard of mental age applicable to children. Since mental age units are not suitable for adults, he advocates expres-sion of scores in terms of ranks, percentile ranks or *z*-scores. This study is based upon the use of about fifty different mental tests with college freshmen over a five-year period. The tests were administered as early as possible in the freshman year, and the scores were compared with schol-arship records and teacher estimates of ability when these were available. The predictive validity of the test scores for these two criteria was then computed. Thurstone points out that the estimates of professors about the abilities of their students are highly unreliable. As a result he finds their estimates unsuitable as a means of judging predictive efficiency of mental tests.

Though one may argue that there are better criteria of mental abili-ties than school achievement, Thurstone points to the practical problems involved in forecasting educational achievement, particularly at the col-lege level. Though he admits to some limitations by this procedure, at the same time he expresses the hope that scientific principles about intelligence may come from correlation coefficients of performance and ability measures. He points out that the student's retention in school is directly dependent upon his achievement, at least much more so than any other single factor. In the practical sense, then, intelligence tests, if they are to be useful to colleges, must demonstrate stable and significant relationships with the important criterion of grades. Thurstone would not even argue that perhaps the kinds of tests that he advocates using are not really tests of intelligence at all. Whether or not the tests measure some abstraction which may be called intelligence, the mental tests advocated by him may be very serviceable in a practical setting and therefore should be retained.

There are at least two criteria proposed by Thurstone which may be used to determine the adequacy of mental tests. In the first of these, one may compute the correlation coefficient between the scores obtained on the mental test and the actual achievement by the student. In the second case, the correlation coefficient may be computed between the test scores of those students who are successful and remain in school and the test scores of those students who are unsuccessful and leave school. Though the same result may be obtained in both procedures, correspondence is not always assured.

In terms of the data used in this study over the five-year period, Thurstone found that the correlation between grades and test scores varied from zero to .60 depending on the test used, the criterion and its exact expression, and the student tested. In no instance did he find a correlation coefficient higher than .60. As a matter of fact the range was mostly between .3 and .5. These correlation coefficients were somewhat lower, Thurstone reports, than were found for prediction with younger children. There are several possible reasons for this. One of these is the fact that with the college student success in school depends on many factors other than ability. An even more tenable reason, according to Thurstone, is that college students are a more select group and therefore do not show as much variability on the test-score range as children in an elementary school would show. So long as there is restriction in one of the variables used for computing the correlation coefficient, there will be a spurious depression of the coefficient itself. Thurstone reports some six subtests selected from among all those he has tried for inclusion in a battery devised for freshmen in engineering. These included:

1. *General information.* Thurstone explains that this is an excellent test of intelligence, though an indirect one. He bases this statement on the assumption that the individual who is brighter will gain a greater amount of information over his lifetime than will a person who is mentally less competent. This is based on the idea that differences in ability innately express themselves in the adequacy of benefiting from life's experiences.

As he points out, empirical evidence on this point is difficult to gather. He does report that the general-information test differentiates to some degree the students who are able to succeed in college work from those who are unable to survive the freshman year.

2. *Analogies.* No rationale is given by Thurstone for including this test except that it is a difficult task in the form in which he has presented it. Considering the select nature of the sample, perhaps this increased level of difficulty would warrant inclusion of a test for which no other rationale is given.

3. *Sentence completion.* This task employed the Ebbinghaus technique, and Thurstone reports that it has good diagnostic value for college retention. Though the correlation is only .35 for the college group, Thurstone believes that it should be retained. The principal difficulty, as he reports, is in scoring. Several different scoring procedures were tried, each of which was unsatisfactory in one or more ways. By and large, Thurstone seems to make an excellent case for retaining a logically good but empirically poor kind of test in the series.

4. *Syllogisms.* No rationale is given for the inclusion of syllogisms, except for the negative one that it does not test reasoning ability as one might suppose.

5. *Quotations.* Again no rationale is given. Essentially, the task requires the individual to read a short paragraph and answer questions concerning the paragraph, or interpret proverbs giving two meanings for each proverb. This kind of task occurs in Thorndike's CAVD test as well.

6. *Number completion.* Thurstone says that the justification for including an arithmetic task is the fact that it affords an opportunity to test an individual's ability to form generalizations. He offers no evidence that the test indeed does so.

Though correlation coefficients are not reported for each of the tasks separately, Thurstone reports that the six tests give coefficients with scholarship grades in the vicinity of .30. At this point he also discusses the presentation of items. In order to be certain that every subject has the opportunity to perform at least some of the items of each type, he gave one item from each of the six tests in cycle form. Thus item (1) would be a general-information item, (2) an analogies item, (3) a sentence completion, (4) a syllogism item, (5) a quotation or proverb, and (6) a number-completion item. He points out that this kind of test should not be used when one is interested in the diagnostic information from each kind of subtest. Total score is of importance in this procedure, then, and administratively Thurstone found it superior to the separate administration of six tests.

From such a background of dealing with quite practical and important problems educationally, Thurstone begins to develop a systematic theory of what he believes intelligence to be. However, interest in the practical problems remains, and leads eventually to the development of the primary mental-abilities test. As with most test constructors, the theory and the test content are not always equivalent.

The Nature of Intelligence

By 1924, Thurstone was able to present a clear statement of his beliefs about the nature of general intelligence. In his first such statement (Thurstone 1924a) he develops ideas proposed originally in the 1921 symposium in the *Journal of Educational Psychology* (1921, 12, 201–207). In this 1924 paper presented at the Seventh International Congress of Psychology, Thurstone points to the fact that he has now spent several years working with intelligence tests as well as with other varieties of mental tests and as a result has felt it necessary to formulate for himself some definition of intelligence. Though his definitions tend to be modified from time to time, and he expects them to be modified in the future, this statement was typical.

Any definition of intelligence, according to Thurstone, must begin with its products. There is no way that intelligence may be perceived, and there is no such tangible entity as intellect, he says, so that what we are able to accomplish by means of intelligence becomes the basis upon which its nature may be hypothesized. Several possibilities may present themselves: such things as the ability to get along in society, the ability to succeed in competition, the ability to adjust to societal demands, the ability to learn by trial and error, the ability to profit by experience, the ability to reason, and so on and on. Each one of these represents some product of our intellectual natures. They refer to things that we can do, but Thurstone indicates that they do not tell us what intelligence actually is.

Such intelligent action can be described, but the intrinsic nature of intelligence can only be speculated upon. Thurstone speculates and proposes what he believes may be the intrinsic nature of intelligence. At its most unintelligent level, behavior is of an overt trial-and-error type. Through trial and error, occasional successes behaviorally may be experienced. Such overt trial and error allows the expression of all impulses in overt conduct. The failures of the behavioral effort are recorded both on the environment and on the individual.

At a somewhat higher level, the most simple order of intelligence is what Thurstone refers to as perceptual intelligence. Because of reception, the organism may be able to perceive in the distance some percept that will allow him to achieve mentally some equivalent contact experience. Thurstone describes this level of intelligence thus:

> . . . If we perceive a puddle in front of us on the sidewalk, the visual percept is the expectation of a contact experience in the puddle, but that contact experience is only partly specified or anticipated in the visual percept. If we were moving by overt trial and error we should complete the impulse and step right into the puddle. By perceptual intelligence we have transferred the trial and error process out of the puddle to the point where we now are. We also move the trial and error process back in time. . . . (Thurstone, 1924a, p. 244)

What happens psychologically in such a level of intellectual action is a transfer of trial-and-error selection from the stage of overt completion to a stage at which the impulse is only partially formulated. This level of intelligence is of great biological value to the organism, Thurstone believes, because it gives him some control over future time and space.

The next stage moves into even greater incompleteness and lack of specification. Any percept is, in the greatest part, imaginal, according to Thurstone. The sensory nature of the percept is really only an insignificant cue. When the sensory cue is dropped from the percept what is left is a corresponding idea which is a more tentative form of action than the percept itself. Ideation then becomes the next highest level of intellectual action. The main difference between an idea and a percept is the matter of degree of incompleteness. With ideation, we can anticipate experience without having to directly encounter it. Thurstone illustrates this difference between the idea and the percept by describing a situation where a certain street is avoided before it is overtly experienced. Whatever impulse existed to walk along the original street is very roughly specified when recall occurs that the street is torn up. With perceptual intelligence only, we would go all the way to the construction work and not proceed along a different route until the street-closed sign was encountered. Ideational trial and error then is more intelligent than perceptual trial and error; indeed, the more incomplete the alternatives, the greater the intelligence.

The highest form of intelligence is what Thurstone refers to as conceptual intelligence. Here, trial and error will be carried on among quite crude, poorly-organized, highly incomplete actions that may be called concepts. By concept Thurstone means some expected conduct which is loosely organized, tentative and incomplete.

The hierarchy of levels of intelligence, then, from low to high, proceeds from overt trial and error, to perceptual trial and error, to ideational trial and error, to conceptual trial and error. At the very highest level, conceptual intelligence, we have selection among alternatives that are not physically nor spatially defined nor even particularized by the environment.

Within this conception, measurement of intelligence would depend upon determining the degree of abstraction of which the individual is capable. Thurstone mentions that the Binet-type questions have yielded some of our best measures, precisely because they do depend upon abstraction in behavior. By contrast, most nonlanguage tests are very little successful primarily because abstraction is not necessary to their solution. Thurstone questions whether nonlanguage tests can really be called tests of intelligence.

He differentiates between two types of tests of intelligence. One of these requires measuring intelligence that is at work during the test, the other kind of test measures the role of experience in intelligence. A general-information task reflects the second of these kinds of measures since the assumption is made that the amount of information available to the individual at the time of testing is some product of past experience. By contrast, an ingenuity or problem-solving task would be a more direct measure of intelligence requiring intellectual work and some degree of abstraction during the actual test taking. Thurstone does not signify that either of these is more important than the other. He does point out that educational procedures which stress particulars will not be very success-ful at training of intelligence. A liberal education, however, will allow the reduction of problems to their basic and universal status and when solved by the student will indeed educate his native intelligence.

Thurstone published in the same year a book, entitled *The Nature of Intelligence,* which explained in much greater detail the theoretical posi-tion taken in this article. He points out that psychology had assumed that action begins in the environment (the traditional *S-R* theory) but that a change was then being widely accepted. Under academic psychology the relationship among elements had been: stimulus-person-behavior. In the new psychology this hierarchy is changed to: person-stimulus-behavior. Thus all action begins in the individual and the stimulus operates to determine the detailed manner in which some purpose of the individual expresses itself on a particular occasion. Thurstone takes the phenomenological viewpoint that the individual is in constant readiness to maintain, defend, and promote the self in all its aspects. In fact this is the very essence of being alive. A psychological act is comprised of the course of events from the purpose or motive within the individual, through its imaginal form, to overt expression, leading to the conse-quences and satisfactions of the actor.

Wherever it operates through the psychological act, intelligence has as its purpose a means of satisfying the desires of the organism with the least possible physical risks. Once there is the need, there is a deliberation about the dissatisfaction. Through deliberation, when a constructive suggestion occurs the motive has become focalized. Now the motive can be more closely defined and can lead to some adjustment by which it may be satisfied. The matter of the constructive suggestion is the psychological act. From this point on there is the possibility of conscious control since imaginal behavior can carry the suggestion to its completion without necessary overt action. If the concrete experience that is imaginally anticipated gives promise of neutralizing the dissatisfaction accompanying the motive then this experience will be acted out in overt form. If it does not seem to satisfy the motive then the imaginally anticipated experience will be dropped. If the psychological act becomes focal at a very early stage, there is a possibility of a wide range of final adjustments among which to choose the particular act which will satisfy the desire. Thurstone believes that the earlier in the psychological act the motive becomes focal, the greater the possibility of intelligent behavior.

Thurstone also points out that intelligent action is usually opposed to a factor of urgency. Whenever an impulse is quite strong, whenever the demands of a situation are quite urgent, then the impulse will achieve overt expression without much anticipation or rationality. Thus, in the setting of a burning building, we are more apt to act impulsively than intelligently. By contrast, if the impulse is relatively weak, a situation arising when only a remote benefit is concerned, intelligence operates to a high degree.

In this context of the psychological act, Thurstone then discusses overt trial and error, perceptual trial and error, ideational trial and error, and conceptual trial and error. He gives examples of these levels of intelligence at work and of behaviors representing psychological action. For example, in discussing autistic thinking, he draws a contrast with realistic thinking. To Thurstone, a person thinking realistically anticipates satisfaction while the person thinking autistically lives imaginally the satisfaction. In realistic thinking, the individual strives to attain while in autistic thinking the individual lives the attainment imaginally as though it had already been reached. The content of thinking for the two forms of behavior, autism and realism, cannot then be differentiated. In both instances there is imaginally represented experience, dealing with ideational and conceptional representations of expected experience. Nor should one assume that all examples of autistic thinking are necessarily bad and to be avoided. The circumstances will determine whether autistic or realistic thinking is to be preferred.

Thurstone points out that the more intelligent the conduct, the more remote will be the expected benefit. He defines intelligence in this manner:

> The intelligence of any particular psychological act is a function of the incomplete stage of the act at which it is a subject of trial-and-error choice. Intelligence, considered as a mental trait, is the capacity to make

impulses focal at their early, unfinished stage of formation. Intelligence is therefore the capacity for abstraction, which is an inhibitory process. (Thurstone, 1924b, p. 159)

Thurstone closes by describing levels of intelligent behavior. In its lowest form, he says, every impulse of the organism will be expressed in purely random form without consciousness. Thus, reflex behavior represents the very lowest form of intelligence. A first sign of intelligence may be found among animals, since they may use perceptual intelligence. With the human, the next highest levels are possible. As the child grows, for example, ideation occurs. With adults, conceptual intelligence to some degree may be expressed.

Measurement of Conceptual Intelligence

Thurstone returned to some of the practical problems involved in the measurement of intelligent behavior in the years immediately following the publication of *The Nature of Intelligence.* Tasks of an abstract nature, no matter how good as measures of conceptual intelligence, are no better than their score expressions. This matter next attracted Thurstone's attention. One of the most common and most widely-accepted means of score expression was the mental age. Though by no means the first psychologist to question the validity of the mental age concept, Thurstone did attempt to illustrate its limitations both with logical argument and empirical data. To him the mental age concept failed in that it leads to ambiguities and inconsistencies. He felt there were at least two definitions of mental age, both of them commonly used and yet leading to the same kinds of ambiguities (Thurstone, 1926).

In the first definition, the mental age corresponding to a given test performance is the chronological age for which the test performance is the average. This is the usual sense in which mental age is used. A mental age of eight is conceived to be the level at which a group of children chronologically eight years of age performed as an average. In the second definition, the mental age corresponding to a given test performance is the average chronological age of people who make that test performance. This definition includes the possibility of comparative procedures among individuals of different chronological age, all of whom achieve the same mental age. Though this latter definition is less widely accepted or even expressed, implicitly it is the most meaningful for the interpretation of mental age. Thurstone says that these two definitions do not achieve the same numerical values. This means they are inconsistent and because of this inconsistency he maintains that there must be specific reference to indicate which of them is being used. To Thurstone, the two are not interchangeable.

Thurstone demonstrates that a plot of correlation coefficients for test performance and chronological age would yield two regression lines. These regression lines would not follow the same plot so that a different interpretation is possible depending upon which regression line is used. Obviously, inconsistencies will result, particularly if it is not clear which comparison is being made. Thurstone maintains that either of these definitions might be adopted and used so long as it is clear which is preferred. If the other expression is also desirable, some other title than mental age might be applied to it and it might be used as well.

Regardless of the applicability of either of these to children, Thurstone makes the valid point that the concept of mental age is unsuitable for adults. Beyond a certain specified chronological age level, either because of limitations in the test or the fact that intelligence actually does not develop beyond that age, all individuals will be credited with the same mean test performance. If, for example, we use the Stanford-Binet Revisions as illustrative, no adult could achieve a score higher than the mean test performance at which mental growth is assumed to stop. The individual of age fifteen, age twenty-five, or age forty finds a ceiling imposed on his test performance. A mental age of forty is the same as a mental age of sixteen or of any other age beyond this sixteen-year level. Such a position leads to fallacious assumptions and predictions if accepted. Thurstone points out that there must be some revision in terms of what is meant by mental age for all individuals who are older than the ceiling imposed by the test limitations. He questions whether an age scale is needed at all for mental development either with children or adults. He points out that the relationship between intelligence and age is imperfect and nonlinear, and that it would be better to specify test performance, on some convenient scale, directly to test performance itself. This procedure would obviate some of the problems and ambiguities attached to the first definition of the mental-age concept.

For the second definition, Thurstone sees no hope and suggests that there is no way that it may be redefined so as to avoid ambiguity. As such, then, it would represent a pointless definition. He suggests, in place of mental age, an alternative procedure that he believes would be superior. For purposes of comparison, he suggests the use of a percentile rank. This would be an unambiguous score which may be interpreted directly in terms of the child's performance in his own age group. Along with mental age, he would discard the intelligence quotient at the same time. By using percentile rank within a given age group, the determination could be made as to whether or not the child maintains his relative standing from year to year.

For at least statistical purposes, Thurstone believed that it might be preferable to use the sigma standing of the child (a z-score) rather than the percentile rank. As with the percentile rank, the *z*-score would allow the test performance of any particular child to be compared with children of the same age. Additionally, the *z*-score system would avoid all of the problems present with adults. If such a system were used for all age groups, Thurstone maintains that there would be continuity and sense that is not possible with mental ages and intelligence quotients. He maintains as well that in the use of some ranking system, such as percentile ranks or *z*-scores, a child of a particular age could still be compared with the average child of another age group. This would allow for the kind of comparison frequently desired with the mental age, particularly.

The criticism cited by Thurstone regarding the use of mental age with adults has been proven to be a quite valid one. Mental age is a meaningless concept when applied to adult ages and as a result other systems have had to be devised where adult tests were used. Additionally, criticisms concerning the mental-age concept of children have also been frequent over the years. In some tests, the mental age is avoided altogether. A score expression such as a deviation I.Q. or a percentile rank or both will frequently be used in such tests. The assumption is made that the mental-age concept is invalid, frequently on the grounds cited by Thurstone. With children, however, the mental age may have greater validity than is commonly cited for it. So very few studies have been conducted on the comparative validity of the mental age across chronological age groups that no strong position can be taken on either side. Most rejection or acceptance of the mental-age concept, unfortunately, has been on the basis of logical arguments rather than empiricism. In any event, Thurstone's arguments were accepted by many and he pursued the issue by trying to suggest better means of test scoring.

In 1929, Thurstone and Ackerson published a study in which the mental-growth curves for the Binet tests were demonstrated for several age groups (Thurstone and Ackerson, 1929). They point to the problem of studying the mental-growth curve because the units of measurement cannot be assumed to have constant increments from year to year. Thus, the increment of score from raw score ten to raw score eleven probably is not the same as the increment from raw score 100 to raw score 101. Such gross scores can be used, then, only for purposes of rank, ordering individuals within a group. Though the criticisms cited are not restricted to mental age, the same problems do exist in using mental age as some measure of mental level. The assumption will not hold, for example, that the increment in mental age from year three to year four is the same increment as from year eleven to year twelve. As with other score forms, mental age may be used for ranking individuals within a group; but they are not true measurements because they do not reflect equal incremental values. This paper of 1929 is intended, then, to determine something about the nature of mental growth by using a method of absolute scaling.

Most psychologists recognize the fact that increments in mental growth seem to be larger in young children than in older children. In observing behavioral difference, it is assumed that the child growing from year two to year three shows much more dramatic gains mentally than the child growing from year twelve to year thirteen. Thurstone points out that this belief is usually represented graphically by some hypothetical mental curve, concave in nature with negative acceleration. Whether or not this presumed curve is accurate can be tested under the procedures followed here.

A sample of 4,208 white children enrolled at the Institute for Juvenile Research was available to the authors. However, since very young children at the institution could not be measured with the Stanford-Binet, the absolute scaling was applied only to those individuals between ages three and seventeen. Though other year levels could have been selected, Thurstone and Ackerson used the standard deviation of the seventeen-year-old group as the unit of measurement for variability, and the mean test performance of four-year-old children as the arbitrary mean test performance. From these data, a formula could be derived such that mean performances for each age level from three to seventeen could be equated and their variabilities made equal. With the corrections applied to the absolute data of each year level, it was possible to plot variability against mean test performance for each age and establish an absolute zero. The specific values found and substituted in the data here collected would not be applicable to all groups since the sample used is of a select nature. The procedure would be applicable to any group with the result that the plot of mental growth increments can be generalized to other subgroups of the same age levels.

Contrary to most expectations, Thurstone and Ackerson found that the mental-growth curve is positively accelerated in the younger ages. As they point out, the finding of positive rather than negative acceleration is more reasonable since it provides a better picture of continuity for mental growth when regarded as a biological function. At the upper ages of the mental-growth curve there is an apparent asymptotic function. This would seem reasonable since one cannot expect test intelligence to rise with age indefinitely. Beginning with puberty, however, it is probable that whatever mental-growth curve exists will show some rather marked deviations, since irregularities of a sometimes pronounced degree are also found with anthropometric measures. This function is not surprising. Such irregularity does make it difficult to determine the exact course of mental growth above the age at which puberty begins. In the data presented, then, the absolute zero is more precise than the point of test maturity. There is an inflection in the curve about year eleven.

Thurstone and Ackerson point out that the curve as plotted cannot be taken as representative of the general population. They believe, however, that the form of the mental-growth curve as they have found it would apply to any group whether normal, mentally accelerated, or mentally retarded. The absolute zero probably is the same for all children but the upper asymptote is probably higher for bright children than for dull ones. They express the belief that mental-growth curves for all children would show in initial positive acceleration, some inflection point, and a later negative acceleration. The findings of this study have more than just theoretical interest. They may be of significant practical value as well.

The Primary Mental Abilities

In the area of expression of intelligence Thurstone made a major contribution in describing a set of primary group factors operating in conceptual levels of behavior. Through the mathematical technique of factor analysis, to which he made major initial contributions, the primary mental abilities were disclosed. A group test measuring each of these abilities was devised by Thurstone. One major difference between the procedure he followed and what had been typical in the past, however, is that Thurstone began with adults and worked down to children. Derivations for younger age groups are based upon the structure of the expression of intelligence first demonstrated with adults. Just as there are problems of proceeding from empirical demonstrations about intelligent behavior in children to the meaning of such behaviors in adulthood, so are there problems demonstrated in the application of a factor series derived from adults and applied to children. In point of fact, however, the tests devised by the Thurstones were more widely used with children over a period of several years than were the tests devised for adults.

In the field of individual testing, the work of Wechsler follows the same general procedure as that of the Thurstones. Again, this brings problems of testing children, which must be considered in the evaluation of the Wechsler Scales just as the problems of testing adults are considered in evaluations of the Binet Scales.

Thurstone discusses problems of conventional approaches in intelligence testing to that time, and the place of factor analytic techniques and their derivations in the scheme of things (Thurstone, 1936a). He points to the common, daily judgment about intelligence of other individuals by the layman. There is common recognition on even such unstable grounds that intellectual endowment appears to be unevenly distributed in the general population. This kind of rating leaves much to be desired, since it is imprecise and nonrigorous. For this reason Thurstone attempts to define what such ratings of intelligence imply about individuals. He concludes that the most generally accepted indicator of intelligence is some ability to perform on mental tasks rapidly and correctly, tasks that most individuals find rather troublesome and on which they tend to be slow in performance. Informal means of judging intelligence are too subjective to yield a very stable and accurate measure. The formal procedure, intelligence tests, has as its chief purpose the elimination of subjectivity in individual judgment and the substitution of objective and experimentally-demonstrated procedures.

Yet in this formal procedure of objectively measuring a trait, there are some underlying principles which remain unresolved and troublesome. Chief among these is the conception of the nature of intelligence held by the test maker. There are many ways in which intelligence may express itself, and by which it may be measured. Questions of the unitary nature of intelligence expressed as a general ability, or a large number of discrete abilities, or a number of group factors with no general factor at all influence both measurement and conception. However, in the practical situation, theoretical conceptions of intelligence and the differences among them are of small moment since it is well accepted that mental abilities are positively associated. There is the widely held conception that if a child is superior in one kind of mental task the chances are excellent that he will be superior in other kinds of mental tasks as well. Thurstone points out, however, that there are exceptions to this rule and that these exceptions are of interest since they indicate that perhaps some composite of elements represents intellectual endowment. Unless a case can be made for the fact that all such differences within the individual are due to cultural influences, the possibility of some elementary abilities crucial in differing kinds of intellectual performance must be accepted.

Thurstone next reviews the problems of scoring and score expression, a matter considered at some length above. Some complex which we call intelligence is quite useful to differentiate those who are generally accelerated intellectually from those who are generally retarded intellectually. At that same time, it was of considerable importance both practically and scientifically to try to isolate any elements which operate in intelligence. Through observation, different types of ability are noted for the individual from one kind of task to another. Such differences are not very well expressed when a single index is used. What is needed, then, is some objective experimental method which allows the expression of such differences in performance on the part of the individual. This purpose will be met, Thurstone says, by the use of factor-analytic techniques.

There is the assumption in factor analysis that, where given primary mental abilities are necessary for performance on several different tasks, abilities will not be differentiated by such tasks. If a number of tasks require different kinds of primary abilities, it is possible to demonstrate differences in these abilities by performances on the several tasks. There is the further assumption in factor analysis that the performance by an individual on a task is the sum of the contributions of the several abilities available to him. However, these abilities will not always be weighted to the same degree in performance, depending on the nature of the task. Through the use of the factor-analytic technique, Thurstone reports that seven primary mental abilities had been disclosed in work since 1932. He does not claim that these are all the possible primary abilities, but he does say that his experience leads him to believe that there are probably not as many primary abilities as some people had proposed. The basis for the derivation of these seven factors was performance on fifty-six tests of a psychological nature taken by 240 college students over some fifteen hours. The tasks used and some brief description of their content is given by Thurstone (1936b). A further discussion of the factorial procedure as applied to these tests is also included in that article.

The seven factors disclosed by the factor-analytic technique used with this sample of college students in 1936 were as follows:

1. *Number facility.* Thurstone believed that this is one of the most conspicuous of the primary abilities found in that experimentation. As would be suggested by the name, the factor is restricted almost entirely to numerical thinking and is present in the highest amount in computational-speed tests. Where reasoning or formulation of a problem in quantitative terms is involved, the content of the number-facility factor drops considerably.

2. *Word Fluency.* This factor also is quite prominent from the results of the experimentation. Here, the subject is required to supply words in a given context. The kind of performance which leads to greatest success on this particular factor of word fluency seems to be limited to recall of words. Verbal reasoning, then is not a large component in the factor.

3. *Visualizing.* The evidence for the visualizing factor was somewhat less demonstrable than for either of the previous two. However, there seemed to be present in performance over a number of tasks a facility in visualization of solid objects as well as in two dimensional space that required such a factor.

4. *Memory.* Several different kinds of memory tasks were used in order to specify as completely as possible what kinds of memory factors might exist. Thurstone concludes from his evidence that an individual may have a good general memory without specification as to discrete things which he can remember well. This position seems somewhat antithetical to the position that there are a great many particular kinds of memories and not a general type of memory. For this reason, Thurstone cautioned that more experimental work needs to be done before the

general factor of memory is definitely accepted. Whether or not memory must be considered as general or particular in nature, Thurstone maintains that there is quite sufficient evidence to indicate that memory is a distinct mental ability of a primary nature.

5. *Perceptual speed.* This primary ability is displayed when the individual is asked to identify rapidly some material that is mixed in with distractors. Thurstone proposes that much further work is needed to define more precisely the character of this perceptual speed.

6. *Induction.* Thurstone thought that this might be the most interesting of the primary abilities which he found in his work with these college students. Essentially, it is found in those tasks where the individual has to discover a principle or rule governing material. This primary ability will coincide with the general intellectual faculty postulated by Spearman.

7. *Verbal reasoning.* In this ability, tasks which require performance on verbal analogies or the matching of proverbs are represented. Added to these are the kinds of numerical estimates which require deductive reasoning. Thurstone points to the fact that there are two distinct verbal abilities one of which he has called a word-fluency factor and the other of which is this verbal-reasoning factor.

Though the exact number of primary mental abilities was not known at that time, Thurstone made the point that there were some very practical results even in terms of the seven named here. It would no longer be necessary to describe an individual in terms of a single index of intelligence. Instead, one would have, using the information here, some seven indices indicating different kinds of intellectual performance. Performance on each set of tasks representing one of the abilities might then be plotted individually to yield a profile of performance by the individual in the primary mental abilities. The ups and downs which may occur in an individual's profile may be used for some kind of analysis, including vocational and educational guidance.

Further Applications

Further rationale, application, and description of the factors and how they were derived is contained in a monograph entitled *Primary Mental Abilities* published in 1938. One comment made by Thurstone in this publication was in reference to Spearman's concept of *g.* He points out that the work done to that time did not indicate the presence of a *g* and yet the methods used do not preclude it either. There was some commonality between tests that was unaccounted for by the common factors that had been disclosed by the factor analysis. Though the assumption might be made that any such commonality must reflect Spearman's *g,* Thurstone maintains that some alternate explanation may be possible. For example, it may be that this commonality among factors was some other factor whose variance was divided between the primary abilities disclosed.

Thurstone offers further support for factor analysis in the study of intellectual differences. This position was based on the premise that abilities exist differentially and may be disclosed in differential amounts among individuals. However, in the past only philosophical arguments had been offered as to what these may be and how they express themselves, and there were about as many different descriptions as there were philosophers. The factor method would overcome some of this disagreement existing among logical arguments by disclosing objectively what kinds of primary abilities exist and how they are expressed. Thurstone describes the assumptions and procedures followed in the factor-analytic technique. Procedurally, and in a very simple form, the objective performances of individuals are recorded on a large number of tasks. Using the performance on these tasks for statistical analysis, the fundamental abilities in terms of relations among but not between clusters must be isolated and described. It is necessary then to determine the factor loading of each ability in each of the tests which may be used. Given the factors derived, no matter what their number, and their loading in each test, it will be possible then to describe each individual in terms of the fundamental abilities which he possesses and the degree to which they are present. A more precise description of the factor-analytic technique is given both in this present citation (Thurstone, 1938a) and in *The Vectors of Mind* (Thurstone, 1935).

One of the problems which exists in factor-analytic techniques, and which serves as a basis for criticism by many competent statisticians, is the determination of what the factor may be labeled once it is identified. This problem Thurstone discusses pointing to the considerable psychological interest in determining what each primary ability is. The procedure followed by him, as by others, is to inspect the tests which contain the primary ability as well as those tests in which the primary ability is not present. On the basis of this inspection, the kind of content within which the ability occurs may be used to determine the label which will signify the factor. Where there is uncertainty about the exact nature of a factor or where alternative explanations are possible, further factorial methods may be used to experimentally determine the basis for labeling.

In this study of 1938 seven factors, plus two others not so clear, were extracted. The major factors were spatial relations (S), perception (P), number competence (N), verbal fluency (V), word fluency (W), memory (M), and induction (I). The two factors which were considered tentative were arithmetical reasoning (R) and deduction (D). As Thurstone points out, identification of any factor is unacceptable unless some psychological sense can be demonstrated for it. The interpretation that he made of the factors in his study had followed this requirement. The statistical procedure, factor analysis, discloses relationships which exist among performances. The psychologist must then assign meaning that should be attached to each factor.

One of the principal outcomes of the procedure and the derivation of the factors is to allow testing of each ability separately in the plotting of a mental profile for each subject who takes the test. Thurstone sees this procedure to be of considerable educational significance. Time limitations did not allow the use of all the tests which were used in the initial factor analysis and the resulting grouping of tests for labeling of factors. Some selection had to be made which would meet reasonable limitations of time and effort on the part of the individual being tested. One result of selecting a smaller number of tests to represent each factor is the reduction in reliability of subtest scores. Part of this problem may be overcome by inclusion of further subtests upon experimental use in educational settings. There are the further possibilities that subtest scores will be more precise and reliable because the saturation on each factor will be increased as purer and purer tests are employed. There is the further appealing possibility that such purity in test measures will no longer have to depend upon quite complex practical criteria to demonstrate sufficient validity as the composite test requires. Mental profiles will be usable not only in terms of educational programs but also in terms of occupational preferences and recommendations.

Extending the PMA to Other Groups

The first extension downward of the primary mental-abilities approach was with high-school seniors (Thurstone, 1940). The sample was administered thirty-six different tests, the factor loadings were computed, and the primary mental abilities were extracted. The results confirmed the factors discovered with the college sample. Still further downward extension of the procedure was published in 1941 (Thurstone and Thurstone, 1941). Eighth-grade children were used for the purpose of determining whether or not the primary mental abilities already identified were found in this group, or whether some other set of primary mental abilities might be present. In their discussion of the factors already disclosed among college and high-school students, the Thurstones make the valid point that one cannot assume that a given factor, though present in several age groups, has the same meaning for each age group. For this reason study of performance on kinds of tasks to determine primary mental ability saturation of the test is necessary for the several age levels.

From the work already done, the Thurstones present the view that there are six primary mental abilities which are clearly defined. These are *V*, *W*, *S*, *N*, *M*, and *I*. The last of these abilities, *I*, was also denoted as *R* (reasoning). Particularly for *V*, *W*, and *S*, test validities were very high. A strong case may be made for their presence in intellectual behavior. A common practice of grouping tests into three categories called verbal, numerical, and spatial had already been established. Of these three strongest factors, then, *V* and *W* would both enter the verbal category while *S* would be in the spatial category. The factors *N* and *M* also have sufficient validity to warrant their inclusion in a test battery, though not as strong evidence is available as for the first three. The last factor *I*, or *R*, may still be questionable, according to the Thurstones, and yet they include it because it seems to show the highest correlation with a general factor of a second-order nature which they believe related to the general intellective factor of Spearman.

Again they discuss the limitations that exist in any single score expression, and the consequent benefits that may be derived from a profile. At the same time that individual characteristics, at least as identified through the factor-analytic technique, may be examined and used for prediction from the profile, a general overall index can also be derived by averaging whatever abilities exist within the profile. They point out that there may be more than the six primary factors which they have identified and for which tests were then available. What other factors may be added in the future, however, would depend upon meeting the same criterion which they have used. A factor may not be called a primary mental ability unless ". . . it behaves as a functional unity that is strongly present in some test and almost completely absent in many others . . ." (Thurstone and Thurstone, 1941, p. 9). Even with the identification of primary mental abilities on such grounds, there is one further fact which must influence its acceptance or rejection. Any primary factor identified must meet the practical criterion of some social, vocational, or educational significance. If a case can be made for its importance and usefulness then it may be added to the data employed in social situations where it is applicable. In the presence of quite limited significance and usefulness, its theoretical and scientific interest and demonstration will not be sufficient for its inclusion in psychological examinations.

The most practical outcome of the analysis undertaken here with the eighth-grade children was the application in educational settings of profiles derived from performance on subtests. They selected three tasks to represent each of seven primary mental abilities (*P*, *M*, *V*, *W*, *S*, *N*, and *R*). In order to verify the factor analysis and to assure the proper selection of tests within each factor, a sample of 437 eighth-grade students was used. All subjects took all tests, and the data were used for a new factor analysis. The seven factors extracted from the prior work were again found to be present in performance with this new sample. In order to determine if the same second-order general factor was present as had been found before, the six primary factors which were most stable were used. For this purpose, then, factor *P* was excluded. As before, the evidence seemed to indicate some general factor which permeates each of the primary mental abilities. It is not a unique general factor separate from the abilities although it is consistently found throughout the battery. Thus, the Thurstones conclude that each of their primary factors should be regarded as some composite of an independent primary and general factor which it shares with the other primary factors. How to interpret the meaning of this general factor for its psychological significance is not so obvious to the Thurstones. For this reason they do not pursue the matter further.

In the same year, a summary of the work done with the eighth-grade children and the rationale for the selection of the subtests to include in the battery was presented (T. G. Thurstone, 1941). The point is made as well in this article that the use of the battery measuring the six primary mental abilities allows the psychologist to plot a profile of scores which are linearly independent. Because of their independence, a kind of information is available about a child and his intellectual functioning which could never be possible from a single measure such as the I.Q. The practical implications for such a procedure in school settings was also noted since the differential kinds of abilities probably have some direct applicability to performance in subject-matter areas in school. This kind of information was not possible with any test preceding the primary mental-abilities test published by the Thurstones. As a word of caution, however, it should be noted that many of the possibilities inherent in the procedure have not worked out as well as was hoped for. This is primarily due to the old problem of limited numbers of items within each subtest such that reliabilities are so low that predictive validity is greatly reduced. The concept remains an excellent one, the implementation is more difficult.

The success of the work to that time had led to its extension as well to children who were in kindergarten and first grade. Some fifty tasks were being used with these young children to determine again if the primary-ability structure found with older age groups may also be found there. If so, a battery of tests could be devised which could be used in educational and other social situations. Projected for the future was work with children in the intermediate grades, approximately at the fourth grade level.

By 1951, the factor structure pertinent to children of the various age levels had been determined and primary mental-abilities tests of a group nature were available for three different age levels ranging from five through seventeen. Publications of the work and its implications (e.g. Thurstone and Byrne, 1951) were presented in a manner to communicate easily to teachers and parents the meaning of intelligence as measured in terms of primary abilities. Applications and implications in school to problems of curriculum and with guidance counselors for purposes of decisions on such matters as occupation were included. Use of subtest scores as means of differential prediction, at least in the school setting, has been more limited than might be hoped for (see e.g. Edwards and Scannell, 1968, p. 89–91). It should be clear however that this is not a matter of any deficiency in the identification of factors by the Thurstones nor the inherent rationale for the procedures. The problem is almost exclusively one of ability to test sufficiently in depth to acquire reliable measures for each of the abilities in quite limited time intervals. Under ideal circumstances, regardless of whether the specific abilities denoted by the Thurstones are absolutely correct, the procedure might yield scores of great practical utility.

Further information about the utility of the approach was available by 1957 (T. G. Thurstone, 1957). As pointed out in this article, apparently the abilities of young children, even though they are relatively independent, may not be so clearly differentiated as is true with older children and with adults. Larger intercorrelations are found for first-grade children than they are for intermediate-grade or high-school students. As a result, either some common factor more heavily weights performances on the various primary mental abilities tested or the procedure used has not identified most clearly those primary mental abilities available to and used by very young children as compared with older ones.

Validity coefficients are also reported between the three levels of the test and selected criteria. Correlations of subtest scores and achievement in selected subject-matter areas tend to be moderate, a finding quite similar to most studies of relationships between intelligence and achievement. This would signify that some general measure which is nonspecific may do about as good a job of predicting the achievement in a specific subject-matter area as the primary mental ability which might seem to be most directly related to such achievement. When one departs from prediction in the school setting to later-life criteria, the tests seem to be little or no better than any other measure available. That the group tests have not been an overwhelming success, then, is apparent; the theory, the statistical implementation, and the implications from such an approach remain as a significant contribution by the Thurstones. Perhaps future work will yield practical outcomes which far exceed that of any other approach.

Summary

The work of Thurstone has had its greatest influence in the development of an increasing number of factorially "pure" tests. Thurstone believed that some general average, as yielded by most tests, did not offer sufficient precise information for individual prediction. By developing and applying factor-analytic techniques, a set of mental abilities was identified which he believed primary in nature. Tests for various age levels were then assembled, yielding six discrete scores as well as a weighted total.

The educational and psychological benefits hoped for by the Thurstones has not resulted from the procedures. Perhaps sufficiently reliable tests will be developed in the future to justify completely the anticipated gains. Even if this does not result, the statistical and measurement contributions of the Thurstones warrant major status in the testing movement.

References

Edwards, A. J., and Scannell, D. P., *Educational Psychology: The Teaching-Learning Process.* Scranton, Pa.: International Textbook, 1968.

Patterson, R. C., and Thurstone, L. L., *Motion Pictures and the Social Attitudes of Children.* New York: Macmillan, 1933.

Super, D. E., "Comments," *Personnel and Guidance Journal,* 1957, 35, 577–578.

Thurstone, L. L., "Mental Tests for Prospective Telegraphers, A Study of the Diagnostic Value of Mental Tests for Predicting Ability to Learn Telegraphy," *Journal of Applied Psychology,* 1919a, 3, 110–117.

———, "A Standardized Test for Office Clerks," *Journal of Applied Psychology,* 1919b, 3, 248–251.

———, "A Cycle-Omnibus Intelligence Test for College Students," *Journal of Educational Psychology,* 1921, 4, 265–278.

———, "Intelligence and Its Measurement: A Symposium," *Journal of Educational Psychology,* 1921, 12, 201–207.

———, "The Nature of General Intelligence and Ability," *British Journal of Psychology,* 1924a, 14, 243–247.

———, *The Nature of Intelligence.* New York: Harcourt, Brace, 1924b.

———, *The Fundamentals of Statistics.* New York: Macmillan, 1925.

———, "The Mental Age Concept," *Psychological Review,* 1926, 33, 268–278.

———, "Equally Often Notice Differences," *Journal of Educational Psychology,* 1927a, 18, 289–293.

———, "The Method of Paired Comparisons for Social Values," *Journal of Abnormal and Social Psychology,* 1927b, 4, 384–400.

———, *The Vectors of Mind.* Chicago: University of Chicago Press, 1935.

————, "A New Conception of Intelligence," *Educational Record,* 1936a, 17, 441–450.

————, "The Factorial Isolation of Primary Abilities," *Psychometrika,* 1936b, 1, 175–182.

————, *Primary Mental Abilities.* Chicago: University of Chicago Press, 1938a.

————, "A New Rotational Method in Factor Analysis," *Psychometrika,* 1938b, 3, 199–218.

————, "Experimental Studies of Simple Structures," *Psychometrika,* 1940, 5, 153–168.

————, "A Multiple Group Method of Factoring the Correlation Matrix," *Psychometrika,* 1945a, 10, 73–78.

————, "The Effects of Selection in Factor Analysis," *Psychometrika,* 1945b, 10, 165–198.

————, "The Prediction of Choice," *Psychometrika,* 1945c, 10, 237–253.

————, *Multiple-Factor Analysis; A Development and Expansion of the Vectors of Mind.* Chicago: University of Chicago Press, 1947.

————, "Psychological Implications of Factor Analysis," *American Psychologist,* 1948, 3, 402–408.

————, "Experimental Methods in Food Tasting," *Journal of Applied Psychology,* 1951, 35, 141–145.

————, "An Analytical Method for Simple Structure," *Psychometrika,* 1954a, 19, 173–182.

————, "The Measurement of Values," *Psychological Review,* 1954b, 61, 47–58.

————, *The Measurement of Values.* Chicago: University of Chicago Press, 1959.

————, and Ackerson, Luton, "The Mental Growth Curve for the Binet Tests," *Journal of Educational Psychology,* 1929, 20, 569–583.

————, and Chave, E. J., *The Measurement of Attitude,* Chicago: University of Chicago Press, 1929.

————, and Jones, L. V., "The Rational Origin for Measuring Subjective Values," *Journal of the American Statistical Association,* 1957, 52, 458–471.

————, and Thurstone, Thelma Gwinn, *Factorial Studies of Intelligence.* Psychometric Monographs No. 2 Chicago: University of Chicago Press, 1941.

Thurstone, Thelma Gwinn, "Primary Mental Abilities of Children," *Educational and Psychological Measurement,* 1941, 1, 105–116

————, "The Tests of Primary Abilities," *Personnel and Guidance Journal,* 1957, 35, 569–578.

————, and Byrne, Katherine Mann., *Mental Abilities of Children.* Chicago: Science Research Associates, 1951.

8

David Wechsler

Perhaps the most distinguished name in intelligence testing today is that of David Wechsler, primarily because the tests which he devised have been widely used and widely accepted. The first to publish an individual intelligence test for adults, Wechsler extended the concepts involved in building such a test downward to include children and has recently come out with a preschool scale. As is true with many other test constructors, Wechsler's theoretical notions about the nature of intelligence are not completely implemented in these tests. At the same time there is some parallel in the theory of Wechsler with the practical implementation in testing. As a result, an historical survey of Wechsler's publications will demonstrate the development of his philosophical orientation and reflect decisions about content of the scales.

Use of Tests Results

Because David Wechsler has spent a considerable portion of his life in a clinical setting, he has been much concerned about the behavioral implications of test results. Beginning with his earliest writings on intelligence and the testing of intelligence, he demonstrates the awareness of influences upon test scores and consequent utilization. One of his earliest papers dealt with the influence of education on Binet-Simon test scores (Wechsler, 1926). His purpose in the paper was to demonstrate the increase in variation in mental-age scores as corresponding increase in chronological age occurred. Such increases in variability should reflect the influence of education on intelligence as measured by this particular scale. Since some evidence was already available to the effect that educational level did influence score on the Binet-Simon test, Wechsler restricts himself in this article to demonstrating the degree to which education influences such scores and the consequent effects upon diagnosis.

Certain assumptions were made by Wechsler about influences which education might exert on intelligence-test measures. As a basic assumption, he reasons that if education does influence intelligence-test scores then variability should be modified in some fashion as individuals become more highly educated. If the educational process, further, tends to remove individual differences, that is, to make us more alike, variation should decrease with increasing age. However, if the educational process tends to make individuals less alike, variations should become greater as individuals become older. The only other alternative to these conditions is that variation would remain constant over the years. If this finding should result, the influence of education on test performance would be considered to be negligible.

The procedure employed by Wechsler was to use data available from Terman and from Burt as a means of determining means and standard deviations for mental ages at each chronological age level. Using data for years six through fourteen, he computed the coefficient of variability for each age level. These coefficients showed a tendency to become smaller with increasing chronological age. For the Terman data, ten of the thirty-six coefficients of variability were significant. By contrast, twenty-four of the thirty-six coefficients with the Burt data were significant. In both cases, significant differences were largely restricted to the years eleven through fourteen. These two sets of data represent revisions of the Binet Scale somewhat independent of each other, and used in different countries. The results differ enough from each other (differences in coefficients for the Terman data are largely restricted to age fourteen) that Wechsler needed to make a decision about which set of data appears to be the more reliable. He decided that the data from Burt were the more trustworthy, for these reasons: (1) the number of cases used at each year level by Burt was in every instance larger than the sample size in the Terman revision. (2) Variability differences in Burt's analysis were of such a nature that they appeared too clear-cut to be accounted for by chance factors. (3) Most important, the significant differences in the Burt data began to appear at the point at which they would be expected if education does in fact influence mental-age scores. Wechsler defends his position by saying that the first few years of formal education tend to emphasize training the sensory, perceptual, and conceptual powers of a child. Beginning about the fifth year of school, when the child is about eleven years of age, much more emphasis will be placed on acquisition of knowledge.

The content of history, literature, science, and so on, should influence facts and information available to the child that would bear greatest influence on performance on an individual test like the Stanford-Binet.

Since there is a decrease in variability beginning about year eleven and continuing through year fourteen, at least in the Burt data, Wechsler concludes that the assumption that education tends to reduce the variability in scores on Binet revisions is the acceptable assumption. Certainly such an assumption is somewhat suspect, since the study leaves much to be desired in terms of definitive data related to the problem investigated. That may be less important, however, than the implications that this early article had in developing the attitude of Wechsler toward the inadequacy of the Binet approach as a means of measuring intelligence for many common and practical situations. Wechsler found some limitations in the currently widely-used Binet scale which led him to seek other alternatives, both on theoretical and pragmatic grounds.

Early Differential Diagnosis

Some means of using test scores for determination of special abilities or disabilities was reflected in an article published by Wechsler in 1932 (Wechsler, 1932a). By this time, Wechsler was employed in the Psychiatric Division of Bellevue Hospital where certain kinds of differential diagnosis would be of great utility in the diagnosis and prospective treatment of individual cases. Though total score on a test will give a certain kind of information, it is insufficient for many kinds of problems encountered. Wechsler proposes in this article, then, the analyzation of an individual's performance on individual tests, in this case with the Army Alpha examination, as a means of determining special abilities and disabilities. As he points out, the Army Alpha is a superior instrument to the Stanford-Binet for this kind of analysis since equivalent kinds of material are involved in all levels of performance. The sub-tests which make up the Alpha reflect more nearly specific abilities than can be attributed to the kinds of items comprising the year levels of the Binet. In many instances, the Binet does not repeat a type of item at each year level so that grouping cannot occur even on this basis.

Certain measures of the Army Alpha Wechsler believes to be highly useful for the purpose at hand. He specifically speaks of the following subtests: Test 8 he believes measures range of information; Tests 2 and 6 measure arithmetical reasoning; Test 3 is a measure of comprehension of social relations; Test 4 correlates with language ability; Tests 5 and 7 measure what he believes to be abstract reasoning ability. Assuming that Wechsler's interpretation of the abilities reflected in subtest content are accurate, the next step becomes a statistical one. It is only necessary to determine the score that an individual must make on any of these individual tests in order to decide whether or not he may be rated as superior or inferior in respect to that particular ability. Wechsler includes a table in this article which reports median scores for the individual subtests and within given total score limits. He also reports evidence of the raw score deviation from this median necessary to be superior or inferior. Again, this article is perhaps less important for what it reports directly than it is for the implications in the future development of scales by Wechsler. Certainly, the possibilities inherent in differential diagnosis, or pattern analysis as it will later be called, are evident in this procedure advocated with the Army Alpha. The importance of the practical implications of such a procedure are self-evident. Needless to say, recognizing such importance and advocating the utility of such a procedure does not assure that stable results for predictive purposes are obtained.

Trait and Trait Variability

Implicitly, at least, Wechsler had adopted a belief in differential kinds of abilities expressed to differential degrees. Kinds of traits or capacities which exist in man may be demonstrated more readily anthropometrically than in any other form, though they are certainly not restricted to such physical measures. Whatever traits may be selected and demonstrated, the question of their range becomes important. Wechsler presented a formula for computing the range of human capacities (Wechsler, 1932b) and discussed the implications of finding about this range. He reports that in many instances, for any given measurable trait, the uppermost measure will maintain a ratio of about two and one-half to one over the lower measure. There are considerable exceptions to this figure, however, principally dealing with the simplicity of the trait measured. Thus where a trait may be measured in a fairly simple fashion, that is directly, the greater measure will frequently not exceed 1.3 times the size of the lower. An instance of this is in terms of height.

Even with what Wechsler titles a simple trait, he points to the fact that there is considerable complexity since more than one factor will influence its expression. As one moves from anthropometric traits into psychological ones, the complexity will increase. In order to determine the lowest limit of variability for any given trait, it would be necessary to have a trait which is determined by a single factor. Since this is not true even for the most directly anthropometric capacities, it cannot be expected with even more complex qualities. However, Wechsler believes that the true upper limits of variability for any given trait or function, no matter how complex, may be designated. The greater the number of variables influencing a trait, the smaller the absolute contribution of each to the variability obtained. Through mathematical derivation, Wechsler concluded that the limiting value expressing the range of variability in a trait is approximately 2.72 to 1. This position is extended, demonstrated, and somewhat modified in a book entitled *Range of Human Capacities* published in 1935, but updated and amended somewhat in an edition reprinted in 1952.

Diagnosis from Test Scores

Problems associated with intellectual deficiency were not new. In the school setting, they had led to the development of the original Binet-Simon Scales. Deficiency remained a problem not only in the educational setting, however, but also in other life situations and with adults. Retardation and its effects upon adult functioning, though recognized, had received but scant attention before Wechsler began some systematic definitional, performance, and prognostic work.

The problem of definition of mental deficiency was approached by Wechsler through consideration of deficiency, not as some kind of disease or psychological entity as it had been commonly considered, but in terms of its practical meaning. To Wechsler, mental deficiency is a label used to describe a class of individuals who are unable to cope with their environments (Wechsler, 1934). In the common-sense use of the term, the mental deficient is so labeled by the fact that he achieves a score significantly below the mean for his age group on a measure of ability. Though this is, to some degree, a usable definition, it is too restrictive to be inclusive. In the sense it is necessary perhaps but not sufficient. Wechsler maintains that mental deficiency cannot be defined in terms of mental age or intelligence quotient because these scores represent some measure of intellectual ability. Deficiency is not only a lack of such abilities but it is also an incapacity to apply whatever abilities the person possesses in a correct fashion to his environment. It is possible, then, for some individuals to be identified by test scores as mentally deficient when they are not so practically since they can deal effectively with the environment. On the other hand, in some instances the test will not so define the individual as deficient when in the practical situation he will be most deficient.

Aside from test scores, the medical concepts which define mental deficiency on the basis of some single criterion are equally inadequate. Wechsler believes this because there are several kinds of mental deficiency. His experience has led him to define at least two kinds of deficiency: one social, and the other intellectual. There is in addition probably a third form of deficiency which he labels emotional or moral defective. Though some degree of correlation would be found between each pair of these types of deficiency, the correlation coefficient is not sufficiently large to allow cross-identification from one kind of deficiency to the other. Thus, to some degree, each is independent of the others.

There are two interesting concepts included in this article. One of these deals with Wechsler's contention that the mental deficient represents a person who is unable to cope with his environment. This matter of effective dealing with his environment becomes an important aspect of the definition of intelligence which Wechsler later offers. There is the further matter that such scores as the mental age and intelligence quotient reflect intellectual abilities, a defined test score which is insufficient for a complete definition of intelligence. Test scores, whether the total or subtest, reflect such intellectual abilities. These are not synomyous with the mental energy which may be entitled intelligence.

Diagnosing Mental Deficiency

By 1939 the Wechsler-Bellevue Scale had been published and its utility for a number of practical problems could be more extensively investigated. Among the attempts to indicate its adequacy was a study comparing scores on the Wechsler-Bellevue with the Stanford-Binet Revision for diagnosing mental deficiency (Balinsky, Israel, and Wechsler, 1939). The Binet defines mental deficiency in terms of an obtained test score, demonstrated by a mental age sufficiently below the chronological age of the person to warrant assumption of developmental lack and prognosis of ineffective behavior. Without using mental ages as scores, the Wechsler-Bellevue may be used in the same fashion. As noted in the article cited above, Wechsler believed that scores in terms of intellectual abilities are not always sufficient for a diagnosis for mental deficiency.

The problem, then, becomes one of determining relative adequacy of the measure when psychometric results appear to be in opposition to clinical impressions. This is particularly true in those borderline cases so frequently demanding immediate practical solutions. The purpose of this study, then, was to determine the relative prognostic sufficiency of the Stanford-Binet and the Bellevue intelligence tests. This "relative prognostic efficiency" would be signified by the forecast efficiency of each test with ultimate psychiatric diagnosis and disposition of a given case.

The Stanford-Binet was used because of its wide popularity as a measure of individual intelligence and for the purpose of determining mental deficiency. At the same time, criticisms had been leveled against the Binet because of some restrictions in the scale. Wechsler proposes that the Bellevue test overcomes these restrictions and that as a result it should correlate better with practical criteria. For this reason, a direct comparison of predictions from the Binet and Bellevue Scales is both reasonable and desirable. The major differences that exist between the Binet and Bellevue are that the latter is a point not an age scale; it has been standardized on adults as well as adolescents, and it includes performance as well as verbal tests.

Wechsler believes the matter of including performance tests in a measure of intellectual abilities to be an important one. Discrepancies are sometimes found between scores on performance tests and those on a verbal test such as the Binet. Particularly is this true of borderline cases, those to whom some such label as "moron" is to be attached. Wechsler states that it was common practice among psychologists of the day to accept the Binet as the best measure of an individual's intellectual abilities and to disregard the performance-test score even if there was a high degree of disagreement. By contrast, he believes that a performance-scale has a great deal of information to offer in determining the correct labeling of an individual behaviorally.

The sample consisted of two groups of subjects, a substantial number of whom were tested both with the Binet and with the Bellevue Scales. The criterion used was the biserial correlation between I.Q. obtained on each of the two tests with the recommendation by a psychiatrist for institutionalization or noninstitutionalization. The results seem to confirm the superiority of the Bellevue Scale for the practical outcome of diagnosing mental deficiency in terms of ability to effectively cope with the environment. Effective coping with the environment, of course, is defined in terms of whether or not the psychiatrist commits or does not commit the individual. Balinsky, Israel, and Wechsler report that the forecasting efficiency is about forty percent as compared with only about five percent efficiency for the Stanford-Binet. Though the latter is obviously quite poor, the former is nothing to become excited about either. In any event, the authors conclude that the Bellevue Scale has a practical place in the clinical setting, at least for the kind of prediction here considered.

The articles and studies reviewed thus far indicate some departures by Wechsler from more conventional and traditional forms of testing. He sees a place for testing specific traits in order to deal more effectively with quite practical problems faced both clinically and scholastically. He maintains a utility in performance-scale scores that has never been utilized or realized before. His position opens opportunities to the measurement and prediction of intelligent behavior that had not been so systematically treated before.

Factors Influencing Intelligence-Test Scores

Though the idea that various nonintellective factors might influence intelligence-test scores was certainly not a new one, little more than lip service had been paid to the kinds of things which influence such test scores prior to some systematic description by Wechsler. To him, something more than ability as such was involved in intelligent behavior, including both test performance and responding in nontest situations. Clinical evidence was available from his observations that two individuals may measure the same on a test and yet not be able to cope with their environments equally effectively. Wechsler pointed out that statistical evidence was available in the fact that unaccounted-for variance among intercorrelations was the rule rather than the exception. In nearly all studies reporting correlation coefficients, some thirty to fifty percent of the variance between the two test scores was unaccounted for. This variance would reflect nonintellective factors, he believed, principally accounted for by drive, energy, impulsiveness, and the like (Wechsler, 1940).

Such factors should not be considered error variance and consequently something to be ignored or to be removed, if possible. Instead, Wechsler conceives of such features as drive and energy level as being themselves some kinds of basic capacities that enter the construct of general intelligence. As such, they are as important to the notion of general intelligence as are such factors as verbal ability or abstract reasoning ability, and should be considered as much a part of the construct of general intelligence as these. They are not to be equated with factors such as educability, health, or influences of the social setting of the individual, however. If, in point of fact, they are a part of the construct of general intelligence, then they should not be eliminated from the subject's test score. Probably they could not be completely eliminated even under the most ideal circumstances anyway. Wechsler advises that it is better to devise means of identifying such factors, measuring them as precisely as possible, and thus determining their weight in terms of the total score that is called general intelligence.

The ideas expressed about these nonintellective factors as they are a part of general intelligence were extended in a later article (Wechsler, 1943). In the ideal situation, intelligence test scores should be used to predict behavior of a more global nature. As such, the score should have meaning for the ability to deal effectively with a large variety of situations rather than only highly specific ones. When such a use of intelligence-test scores is proposed, limitations of the tests currently available become more apparent. This limitation is rather easily demonstrated by the fact that two persons of equivalent intelligence quotient, the score obtained on an intelligence test, may differ quite markedly from each other in terms of the ability to function globally in a practical sense. To Wechsler, the reason for this lies not in unreliability of the test nor in influences such as education, deprived environment, and the like. Instead, the problem lies in the fact that the test measures a restricted kind of behavior, a portion instead of all of the capacities that enter into intelligent behavior. The problem with intelligence tests, then, is not in terms of standardization, but in terms of lack of content.

Certainly the tests have been demonstrated to be effective measures either of some general factors, such as *g*, or specific ones, such as verbal ability, abstract reasoning, or other abilities. In this regard the tests and their expressions are both effective and meaningful. But there remains the matter of discrepancies between equivalent scores and differences in practical behavior. Wechsler believes such differences occur because the kinds of intellective factors measured by the test, whether general or specific, do not constitute all the factors which enter into test scores. Again, the evidence for this is in residual variance resulting from correlational analysis. Though a partial explanation may be supported that to some degree this is due to an insufficiency in the number of variables used in a matrix, this will not account for all the residual in Wechsler's viewpoint. From evidence already available from other studies, this residual variance is related to factors of temperament. In point of fact, Wechsler cites from studies of Alexander where the conclusion is drawn that the chief factor in educational achievement, at least in certain cases, is not one of ability but of temperament. Further, these temperament factors which enter into successful achievement are factors which intelligence tests do not measure. To Wechsler, these factors must be a part of the intelligence-test score, though a quantification of them is not yielded in the test performance. Such factors he calls nonintellective, though this does not diminish their importance in the intellective score.

How much of a contribution to the score these nonintellective factors make will vary from one test to another test. Wechsler states that most of the verbal tasks, particularly of the paper and pencil variety, would reflect only a small amount of residual due to these nonintellective factors. Performance tests, by contrast, contain effects of nonintellective factors to a much higher degree. In neither event, however, had there been any great attempt to specify these factors and to determine the quantifications and weight. As a result, the predictive efficiency of most tests is reduced to some minimum (but still significant) degree. In certain other instances, the tests appear to be very poor for their purposes simply because there is such a heavy weight of these nonintellective factors in the scale. The practical and clinical situations offer a number of instances where score differences are quite large between verbal and performance scales on the Bellevue. These differences have significance for social prognosis of the individual. Such differences, Wechsler states, cannot be accounted for solely on the basis of some differences in special abilities. They are probably much more closely related to the ability of the individual to cope with total situations in an effective manner. As an example, he points out that the "psychopath" who has only a modest I.Q. will frequently demonstrate an excellent ability to manipulate the environment even though this may be quite socially unsuitable. By contrast, neurotics, with higher I.Q.s, will not be able to manage their lives effectively so well. On the basis of I.Q. alone, these practical outcomes should not be found. In these cases, the individuals with the higher I.Q.s show less adaptive capacity: this, Wechsler believes, is the result of differences in nonintellective intelligence possessed by the two groups.

Wechsler defines these nonintellective factors in a general way. In effect, they include all affective and conative abilities which enter global behavior. It is necessary, then, to make a distinction between transient variables and stable ones. For example, if a child does poorly on an intelligence test because he is not interested or is emotionally upset at the moment, he may test better on a second trial. This second testing would not indicate the presence of these nonintellective factors in the test score. By contrast, the individual who is congenitally impulsive or emotionally unstable and who scores poorly at one time will continue to score poorly since this represents a more permanent mode of response for him. In this instance, then, nonintellective factors are operating.

Wechsler goes on to say that the basic question remaining is whether or not such conative and affective abilities should be equated with intellectual abilities in considering intelligence and its influences behaviorally. To him, the answer is an affirmative one and he feels this answer is supported by a number of studies which he cites. At that moment, he was unable to specify just which factors these were, what their influence on intelligence-test scores were, and how they should be determined. Indeed, he closes the article with the suggestion that psychologists need to construct scales which will reflect global intelligence in such a way that nonintellective factors will be specified and their influence on score determined. If and when this state of affairs is reached, Wechsler believes that the test will more nearly measure what is intelligent behavior in actual life. No longer will it be necessary to restrict predictions to such highly specific settings as who will be educationally most successful. The scores will do a better job as well in determining which individuals are going to succeed in life.

Further Refinements

The argument for the presence of conative and affective factors influencing intelligence-test scores as well as the cognitive ones was extended in 1950 with some additional refinements (Wechsler, 1950b). Wechsler now, says that general intelligence should not be equated with intellectual ability no matter how we define intellectual ability. General intelligence should be reserved as a label for some manifestation of the personality of the individual in a global sense. Too frequently, the attempts to measure intelligence have reflected some implicit belief that intelligence is restricted only to the intellectual elements or factors. For this reason, test content had been restricted to problems of reasoning, verbal behavior, spatial behavior, dealing with numbers, and the like. That most psychologists did not really accept this limited definition of intelligence Wechsler believes to be evidenced in the fact that definitions of the word are not restricted only to ability to learn or abstract but are extended to include the abilities of the individual to adjust and to achieve in life generally. The clinician particularly is aware of the fact that adjustment and achievement in life is much more than ability to deal with numbers or with words. Though such behaviors may be necessary, they must be accompanied also by certain nonintellective factors. These nonintellective factors reflect the temperament and personality of the individual. Wechsler feels that there must be a reorientation in the concept of general intelligence and he attempts to present some psychometric basis for measuring what is implicit within the definition of intelligence as adjustment and life achievement.

The intelligence test measures a sample of tasks which reflects some variety of mental abilities. When used by the psychometrician, the score obtained should reflect both the degree to which the individual has the abilities measured by the test and variation among the specified abilities. But rarely does the clinician restrict himself to any such report of score values. Instead, he tends to describe the individual in terms of much more comprehensive social interpretations than the test scores reflect. The score, however expressed, will be used for a number of purposes beyond that explicit to the test content. Wechsler states this idea as follows:

> An I.Q. is thus used, not only to determine comparative mental endowment, capacity to learn, presence of special abilities and disabilities, and evaluation of degree of mental deficiency, but also as a basis for school placement, for vocational guidance, for psychiatric diagnosis, and for the prediction of adjustment potentials in a variety of situations from infancy to old age, including such areas as child adoption, juvenile delinquency, fitness for military service, college success, and old-age counselling. (Wechsler, 1950b, p. 79)

Wechsler believes that intelligence tests are applicable in all of these situations, within some limits at least, so the question must be raised as to the nature of general intelligence. Restriction to some basic quality or even a number of intellectual abilities will not be sufficient. To Wechsler, the essential problem is not one of reliability as such but of validity. Again, he uses the example of two individuals obtaining the same I.Q. who differ greatly in terms of adaptation to the environment. That the question of such validity is not a new one he demonstrates through a review of literature on the subject. He refers to Thorndike's position that intelligence may be expressed on abstract, social, and concrete lines. He mentions the publication by Moss of a test designed to measure social intelligence, though the content itself did not do justice to the intent. The work of Doll in the development of the Vineland Social Maturity Scale is another example of the social implications of intellectual behavior. The use of performance tests as a measure of some kind of "practical intelligence" is also cited by Wechsler, though he points out that the results were more widely ignored than used. The development of his own test, the Bellevue Scale, attempted to combine performance and verbal tasks into some single measure of ability. He states that, unfortunately, the reason for the popularity of the Scales has not been that the combination yields a better estimate of the global rating of the individual, but because separate verbal and performance I.Q.s can be obtained with one test. The continued attempts by psychologists to break down test scores more and more rather than to get the maximum combination defeats one of the major purposes in testing, Wechsler believes.

Wechsler makes a strong point for the use of factor analysis to determine the concept of intelligence as a manifestation of the personality of the individual. Through the use of factor analysis, it should be possible to determine what traits the tests measure and the extent to which they measure each. Under conditions where factor-analytic techniques have been applied, some specific factors have been identified. Chief among these is a factor most generally labeled abstract reasoning. Wechsler points out that, whatever factors might be disclosed, it is essential that each represent some identifiable, relatively independent variable accounting for a certain portion of test variance. Under the test of conditions, there will remain a residual variation which is unaccounted for by the factors extracted. Usually this unaccounted for variance will amount to some forty to fifty percent of the total test variance. From the large number of studies done, and the consistent evidence of large amounts of residual variance, it is apparent that intelligence tests must measure some things other than those accounted for by the factors which are extracted. Attempts to break down this residual variance as some further definable and independent factors have not been very successful. This would seem to indicate that, whatever these other factors are which make up the residuals, they must occur in fairly small amounts.

Wechsler, in the preceding papers, had taken the position that these residuals might be considered nonintellective factors in intelligence. In terms of more recent data, he takes the position in this article that they are more realistically personality components of general intelligence. He cites evidence from studies to indicate support for his new position.

The results of such studies indicate that, among factors identified at least partially to that time, certain conative functions which he designates as drive, persistence, will, and perseveration are evident. In some instances, at least, temperament variables such as interest and achievement are also identifiable. The work has been slow primarily because psychologists have tended to separate personality from intelligence and to consider them separate entities. Though, by contrast, the clinician has operated as if he had evidence that personality components influence intelligence, he has tended to ignore factor-analytic work.

If intelligence is some function of the total personality of the individual, measures of intelligence should correlate to some degree with personality measures. Wechsler reports that data supports this position but that evaluation of results is difficult. One of the chief problems in this regard is the fact that paper-and-pencil personality measures tend to be unreliable, of uncertain validity, and unknown relevance. The answer lies not in this direction, then, but in developing tests which will not only measure cognitive factors but conative and nonintellective ones as well. Such tests would be much more applicable to the total personality functioning of the individual than any one of them alone.

Development into Maturity

One factor entering the measurement of intelligence concerns the rate at which intellectual abilities develop and the point at which they reach maturity. Using the then newly-published Wechsler Intelligence Scale for Children, this matter was considered for the various subtests found in the Scale (Wechsler, 1950a). Wechsler defines intellectual maturity as the point at which measures of performance no longer show significant increases with age. This is an operational definition, highly dependent upon the nature of the scale and the extent of the items used, but a very commonly accepted definition. But Wechsler goes further to consider what he calls substrate and behavioral evidence of maturity as well. In use of the term substrate, he means facets of mental functions which are independent, in their development, of special training and special education. He gives as examples of these such things as walking and talking. Such substrate abilities may be contrasted with behavioral abilities dependent upon training. Examples of such behavioral abilities he cites as riding a bicycle, and language ability. Though distinctions between substrate and behavioral performance may be made in the case of less complex functions, differentiation of very complex functions is not so simple. In this regard, he refers to the commonly-used arithmetical reasoning tests. The question becomes one of whether performance on arithmetical reasoning is some reflection of true native ability or the degree to which it is dependent upon training and instruction for expression.

An allied problem concerning the adequate evaluation of intellectual ability is the ineffectiveness of tests at younger age levels. The restrictions lie more in the kinds of tests that are used than in the degree of presence of the abilities, however, as may be illustrated by the use of a similarities and differences test to determine abstract reasoning ability. As Wechsler points out, children under six years of age or so might be assumed to lack abstract reasoning ability since they cannot perform very well on a test using similarities and differences. Yet, it is apparent that children under the age of six can do certain kinds of abstract reasoning, and it is certainly true that they generalize. The problem lies in devising a number of tasks which measure the presence of the function on a continuing scale.

With the inability to secure accurate measurement with very young children, it is difficult to determine the age at which given abilities appear and their developmental character. Though certain kinds of tests have been widely used as means of determining development in children, for example the Gesell test, these have reflected not so much maturation as they have behavioral aspects of maturation. The purpose in this particular article, then, is to use results from the WISC as a means of determining the development of intellectual functions over a fairly widespread span of a child's life. Results for all twelve subtests of the WISC, supposedly measuring somewhat different though overlapping intellectual abilities, comprise the data. Since the test was standardized in a fashion yielding equivalent age scores, Wechsler was in the position to present information bearing on the question of the point at which maturity is reached. As defined previously, this will be the point at which mean scores no longer increase. Again, the point must be made that the findings are influenced partly by the ceiling imposed in the subtests themselves.

Wechsler made the provisional assumption that mean scores for the subtests used in the WISC will no longer increase beyond the year fifteen. The growth curves computed by him, then, were determined by transmutations of raw scores on mean performance at each age and to weighted scores to year fifteen. The most generally found plot for the subtests was a rapid rise in score in the first years with a gradual slackening as age fifteen is approached. This is the rather classic curve reported for most mental abilities and physical abilities as well. There were one or two exceptions to this traditionally found curve, however. For example, performance on the memory-span test between the years five and fifteen did not show the usual ogive, reflecting instead a large number of plateaus, some of which were quite long. Wechsler speculates that the plateaus may be the result of problems in measurement, either because the units themselves are too large or because they are not sufficiently discrete. There is an alternative explanation, however, which he also presents. Contrary to currently accepted psychology, it may be that certain mental capacities are discontinuous functions in the sense that they may increase or decrease by specific amounts at any given time. If they are thus discontinuous, then many of the curves for mental functions which follow the ogive shape may be artifacts, external effects of training and education.

From the standpoint of the maturation of abilities, Wechsler feels that a more important finding concerned the differential rates of increases shown by the curves. Particularly is this true considering that most abilities show increases to age fifteen, though at progressively decreasing rates. For some of the abilities measured by the WISC, increases after age ten or so are so small as to be almost negligible. The most marked examples of this are those abilities which are not much influenced by teaching: this would include maze performance, picture completion, and digit span.

Wechsler discusses the implications of his findings primarily in terms of educational applications. First, he makes the point that he has substantiated prior findings that different kinds of abilities emerge and mature at different times in a child's life. If we assume that education to be effective will direct curricula to the maturational level of the child, then such findings should influence the educational program. Wechsler makes the point that this is an accepted principle in education but is very rarely practised. There are at least two reasons why the principle is not applied educationally. Perhaps the primary reason is that maturational ages of different kinds of intellectual functions simply have not been precisely enough defined to be utilized by educators. There is a second factor as well, according to Wechsler, reflecting some traditional misconceptions and biases. Certain subjects are placed in the curriculum, or are given to students, not on the basis of information as to applicability but in terms of their traditional placement. Perhaps the most common instance of this is in the introduction of reading instruction in the first grade.

Wechsler maintains that educators have tended to underestimate the abilities of children with the result that they have credited lack of achievement to lack of readiness or perhaps even lack of capacity to learn. He proposes that an alternative is inadequacy of teaching methods or presentation devices. He also mentions that this position is being reduced gradually, at least in progressive schools, by the introduction of more difficult subject matter earlier in the curricular life of the child. Such placement of subject matter may be defended if the data reported by Wechsler in this article concerning maturation of intellectual function are correct; that is, according to the data reported here, intellectual capacities have pretty well matured by the age of twelve, some of them a little before this, so that further development in the substrate abilities will not occur. Though certain kinds of social factors may still influence performance, say through socio-economic or cultural lack, changes which occur to the benefit of the child are possible because inhibiting factors are removed rather than because of any true change in the child's intellectual abilities. Wechsler makes the point: "This distinction is important because it points to the fact that the aim of education should not be to create abilities which it cannot, but to utilize them which it does not." (Wechsler, 1950a, p. 49).

After a brief discussion of problems in evaluating emotional maturity, Wechsler concludes by pointing to the cultural influences on decisions about development. In a society such as ours, there tends to be an undue prolongation of the period of infancy and childhood. Wechsler states that this is particularly detrimental when we consider that there is relatively early mental development, and probably emotional development as well, on the part of the child which is ignored by society. Instead, some artificial criteria of maturity are imposed upon the individual so that he is not permitted adult activities at the time at which he could first benefit from them. One outcome of this procedure is that there is some curtailment of the adult life of the individual through artificially imposed lack of participation in adult society, even though the individual could so participate.

Human Capacities and Their Range

In 1935 Wechsler had published a book extending the concept of limits of human variability proposed in an article published a little earlier (Wechsler, 1932b). This book, entitled *The Range of Human Capacities*, was reissued in 1952 in a somewhat amended form, updated with more current research (Wechsler, 1952). The book is most helpful in understanding a number of the theoretical and practical issues which Wechsler believes underlie intellectual performance and its measurement.

The problem concerned in this book is the limits of human variability and whether or not the limits found in one trait differ significantly from the limits found in other traits. Wechsler considers this not a scientific problem alone but a problem of human relationships as well, including ethics, education, industry, and politics. The scientific nature of the problem relates to determining fundamental characteristics of phenomena and the relationships which may exist between various phenomena. One outcome of this scientific procedure is to determine what are commonly called "natural constants." In the sciences, the number of natural constants is fairly small; in psychology, they are even smaller; in terms of human capacities, the existence of natural constants is almost totally unexplored. This is reflected in the fact that so many attempts have been made to demonstrate differences among individuals that likenesses among them have been largely neglected. Wechsler proceeds on the basis that human traits and abilities may be measured to the degree that they are expressed in terms of functions of basic units. Though the evidence is clear that all physical traits may be so measured and expressed, and that most physiological functions also meet the criterion, only the very simple intellectual traits and abilities can be so determined. This means that most of the abilities called "mental" do not yet qualify. Even so, Wechsler makes the point that he thinks it possible to show that human variability is quite limited, with the differences separating one human being from another on any trait or ability much smaller than is usually supposed.

The first step involved measurement, then, and measurement of capacity. Wechsler uses the term capacity in the practical sense of synonymity with ability. He takes the generally-accepted psychological position that the capacity of an individual is the degree to which that individual possesses a trait or defined ability. Some quantitative, or qualitative, judgment is made about the performance of the individual on that trait. From this performance, capacity is inferred. He cites as examples of such intellectual capacities, measures of memory, learning, and reasoning. These intellectual capacities may be compared with each other, as well as with other capacities of an affective, physical or other type, so long as measurement is possible.

Two assumptions must be made in order to pursue the topic further: first, whatever traits and abilities are to be compared must yield to some quantification, measurement; second, despite differences in measurement procedures, it must be possible to compare measures of one trait with the second trait. Meeting these assumptions will require that the measures be expressed in units of amounts rather than units of relative position or some other arbitrarily defined measure. In addition, qualitative factors must be taken into account, including the conditions under which measurements are made.

Differences among human beings, Wechsler states, are not so much in terms of kinds of abilities and traits possessed as they are in the degree to which the individual possesses them. For every capacity except those directly influenced by training, every individual may be expected to possess the trait to some degree. Differences in degree are expressed by increasing task difficulty. But such procedures yield gross measures of little scientific value in determining the actual range of human ability. To precisely reflect the range of variation in a human trait will require precise measurement of that trait in order to determine the distribution in the population, and a sufficiently large sample to allow adequate analysis of data. Meeting both of these requirements is difficult and had been little found in prior literature. To overcome problems in measurement, the most common procedure followed was to employ probability theory. The assumptions underlying probability theory, however, were not always met. These assumptions, according to Wechsler, include the independence of the individual factors and the absence of any unusual preponderant ones. By grouping on the one hand and by controlling certain conditions on the other, the difficulties associated with meeting these assumptions is partially overcome. In measuring human capacities, however, constancy of conditions is an extremely difficult criterion to meet. This is primarily due to the fact that we are sometimes ignorant of conditions which should be kept constant. Wechsler does mention several which reoccur so constantly that we can be sure some control may be exercised for them. One of these is age, still another is education, a third practice conditions. The most common source of distortion in probability distributions which must be controlled, however, is the selectivity of the group which is measured. Even if the sample used could be shown to be completely unbiased, there would still be sources of error not controlled simply because they have not yet been identified.

The identification and determination of such selective factors on the distribution of human capacities is not solved. Wechsler maintains, however, that he has chosen data in such a way as to consider other criteria than the usual one of numerical accuracy.

In reviewing the work done on the distribution of human traits, Wechsler concludes that the initial generalization that this distribution conforms to the normal law of error was both premature and incorrect. Instead, more commonly there will be found some degree of skewness or displacement or unlimited range rather than a true normal distribution. Indeed, Wechsler maintains that the distribution of most traits and abilities is asymmetrical. This fact is important, he says, because it makes the task of estimating limits of human capacities more difficult than it would be if the traits were indeed distributed in normal fashion.

Within such limitations, then, Wechsler discusses the computation of the range of human capacities of several types. This range, it will be remembered, is defined as the difference in magnitude of a trait between the highest and the lowest, the most efficient and the least efficient, in a normal population. For measures of intelligence, this term is specially used to refer to the differences between the highest and the lowest test scores achieved on a particular test. There are several problems with such a direct measurement. One of these represents the fact that the greatest and least measures in any sample probably do not represent the two extremes of the total population. Even so, and as a second objection, there is apt to be greater unreliability of extreme measures than of measures around the mean. Finally, there is the problem that extreme measures may represent operation of special factors and thereby increase error. For these reasons it has not been unusual for a semi-interquartile range or some other limited aspect of the sample to be used as the measure of best estimate of the variability on a trait. Wechsler attempts to overcome these problems by using a ratio of the extremes between the second and the nine hundred ninety-ninth individuals in every thousand observed in a sample. In such a procedure, the maximum score (that of the nine hundred ninety-ninth individual) is compared to the minimum score (that of the second individual) in the sample. Thus, in a sample of one thousand, if the nine hundred ninety-ninth individual had a "score" of 500, and the second individual in the sample had a "score" of 250, the ratio would be 500 to 250, or 2 to 1. Using this procedure, Wechsler computes the range ratios for a variety of human traits and abilities.

The inferences which Wechsler draws from the findings become the main conclusions of this book. These inferences are: "(1) The range of human capacities, when calculated in true units of amount, is exceedingly small. (2) There are calculable limits to human variability which are very probably biologically determined. (3) These limits partake of the characteristics of natural constants."*

These limits may be conceived as constant. While it is true that the range ratios of human capacities will be less fixed than those found in such a field as physics, the ratios for human capacities have central values of such a limited range that they may be considered relatively unvarying expressions of natural constants. The intellectual constants so found approximate the value of 2.5 to 1. Though this value is larger than is found for physical constants, the reason lies in the more precise measurement of physical traits and the fact that human capacities are more complicated by the intrusion of a large number of factors. This latter condition Wechsler titles a multiple-factor theory as an explanation for these findings. When all kinds of traits are considered, not just the intellectual ones, the range ratios are such that Wechsler can make the state-

---

*D. Wechsler. *The Range of Human Capacities.* Baltimore: Williams and Wilkins, 1952. p. 49. Reprinted, New York: Hafner Publishing Co., 1969.

ment that on the average the most efficient individual in any given task is able to do about twice as much as the least efficient member of his group.

One of the capacities discussed by Wechsler in terms of the changes which occur over the lifespan is that of intelligence. Using data from the Bellevue-Wechsler Scale administered to over two thousand individuals between the ages of seven and seventy, Wechsler reports that the growth curve of intelligence differs very little if any from typical growth curves of physical, physiological, and psychomotor abilities. The only differences appear to be in the fact that maximum achievement for intelligence will occur earlier in life than it will for other kinds of traits. Though some growth in intelligence continues after age fifteen, the growth is slowed down to about age twenty-five, where a definite decline begins and continues over the rest of the life span of the individual. His data agree with those found by Lehman and he concurs in Lehman's conclusion that much of man's original accomplishments will be completed probably before the age of thirty-five. Wechsler, however, makes it clear that he does not believe that individuals under age thirty should be put in all the responsible positions of society. Experience does play some role in the ability to assume leadership. At the same time, Wechsler believes that in many instances the importance of experience as such may be greatly exaggerated.

He would not advocate, at the same time, that the individual at age fifty is "over-the-hill" and should be scrapped. The individual of age fifty and above in all probability will not be as creative as he once was. He will not have the energy to do demanding jobs that he once had. But he will still be efficient. The upshot of this is:

> . . . These facts, namely the age curves presented in the preceding pages, supplemented by certain data derived from biographical studies of men of genius show: (1) that the native capacities of most men tend to attain their maximum between the ages of twenty-two and twenty-eight years, and in some cases even earlier; (2) beginning with about age twenty-five, there starts a steady decline in both physical and intellectual vigor which increases progressively with advancing age; (3) the decline between twenty-five and forty years is relatively small, but nevertheless perceptible, and does not justify the belief that there is even an approximate maintenance of vigor over any considerable number of years; (4) there is no evidence whatsoever for the belief that the average man maintains either his intellectual or physical vigor to the end of his natural life (three score and ten), even when spared from the ravages of disease; (5) the age curves of such mental abilities as have been measured indicate that intellectual capacity, contrary to current belief, begins to decline earlier rather than later than most physical capacities.*

*D. Wechsler. *The Range of Human Capacities.* Baltimore: Williams and Wilkins, 1952. p. 120. Reprinted, New York: Hafner Publishing Co., 1969.

Finally, Wechsler discusses extremes of intellectual competence; what he refers to as genius and efficiency. These terms are used not only in a quantitative but in a qualitative sense as well. Thus, not only would score values on a test of general intelligence help in making the assignment of a label to an individual, but his performance in environmental situations would also influence the use of this label.

The Definition of Intelligence

Wechsler, fairly early in his career, was able to formulate a definition of intelligence which he found usable and suitable to his purposes (see, for example, 1944). This definition tends to emphasize dynamic phases of intelligence and its expression. Because he is concerned about the ability of the individual to cope with his environment, and because personality must be a central concept in dealing with a construct like intelligence, his definition emphasizes the functioning of the total individual. Wechsler defines intelligence as: ". . . intelligence is the aggregate or global capacity of the individual to act purposefully, to think rationally and to deal effectively with his environment . . ." (Wechsler, 1958, p. 7). The "capacity" which Wechsler speaks of is conceived by him as a kind of mental energy, something equivalent to the g expressed by Spearman, which enters into all forms of behavior. For this reason this capacity or energy is global in its expression. Such global capacity we are unable to tap directly, but it has certain expressions, comprising the latter part of this definition, which we may more objectively determine. These include, then, purposeful action, rational thinking, effective dealing with the environment.

Whatever the global quality which the individual possesses as his intelligence, there are a variety of abilities which will be the expressions of that capacity. Such intellectual abilities we may be able to define and measure in a fairly rigorous and precise fashion. Whatever the number of these abilities which we may so define and measure, however, it is not possible to equate the sum of their expressions with the aggregate quality. Wechsler rejects a summation principle of intellectual abilities as the expression of a global capacity for three reasons. First, the product of intelligent behavior is dependent not only upon number or quality of abilities which the individual possesses but also in the way they combine. In combination, abilities assume a different pattern from that which is shown by each one singly or even if added together. This configurational quality, which might be closely related to the global capacity, escapes us in our attempt at measurement.

The second reason that Wechsler gives for rejecting a summation principle to explain the global capacity is that many other factors enter into and influence intellectual ability. These are the nonintellective and affective qualities discussed from prior work. Here, such things as drive and incentive, those qualities most often labeled motivational in nature, operate. These nonintellective factors are not a part of the global capacity itself, yet they do affect its expression. They are a part of the score which is achieved by the individual on a test. The problem lies in the fact that we do not know the degree to which they are present in the test and have no way to extract their values. Their unknown quantity in the score obtained by summing intellectual abilities removes us a step further from describing the aggregate or global capacity of the person.

The final reason given by Wechsler for rejecting the summation principle is that, given differential measurement, an excess in one trait will not tend to cancel out a deficiency in a second trait. The ability in which that excess occurs may add very little to the effectiveness of the total behavior of the individual, certainly not overcoming the effects of the deficiency in such coping behavior. Wechsler makes his point in this regard by using memory as an illustration. No one would question the need for memory as a requisite in intelligent action. But beyond a certain point, memory is not helpful in facing a great many situations in life. Probably the more specialized the ability, the more will this principle be true. What is needed for successful dealing with the environment is the appropriate combination of whatever abilities exist to make up the concept of general intelligence. This combination of abilities, of course, returns us to the idea of the configuration among abilities producing a pattern different from their sum.

We are faced, then, with a problem. Intelligence is not the sum of intellectual abilities. At the same time, the only possible way to evaluate quantitatively the nature of intelligence is to measure some aspects of the totality of each of these abilities. Wechsler sees no problem in this procedure so long as general intelligence is not equated with intellectual abilities. He makes the point that we do not know the nature of energy, and yet we use its effects for the good of society quite effectively. In just the same sense, we may not know the nature of general intelligence and yet be able to use its products expressed as intellectual abilities quite effectively. General intelligence allows us to do certain kinds of things: to make appropriate associations between events, to make correct inferences, to understand the literal and figurative meaning of words, to be able to solve problems of various kinds, and so on. Given these effects of general intelligence, we may make some inferences about the nature of general intelligence without getting directly to it.

A Defense of Intelligence Testing

In recent years, as stated in the first chapter of this text, intelligence testing has come increasingly under attack. In 1966, writing for the *New York Times Magazine,* Wechsler took a position in defense of the use of intelligence tests and the intelligence quotient in such social situations as the school (Wechsler, 1968). The article referred to here was written directly in terms of the abandonment of the I.Q. from pupil records in the New York City school system. The reason given for no longer recording I.Q.s was that such scores were unfair to culturally deprived individuals. In place of an intelligence-test score, achievement tests were used. Wechsler points out that at the same time some attempt was under way to develop more nonverbal scales to measure abilities so that language may be avoided. To him, neither of these substitutes will be adequate for replacing the I.Q.

Wechsler points out that a test is basically a device to elicit responses which may be evaluated as some fragments of behavior. Specifically, the intelligence test is a device used to evaluate behaviors that may be called intelligent. Any number of abilities might be used for the purpose at hand since there are so many ways in which the individual can demonstrate his competence. The essential criterion, then, becomes one of validity expressed as some correlation with designated criteria. As Wechsler points out, a test is considered an adequate measure of intelligence if it shows correlation coefficients of a moderate or high degree with such outcomes as ability to learn, ability to comprehend, ability to adjust, and so on. Of course, it is important to consider the population upon which the test is standardized. Validity must be considered in terms of such individuals, and if the standardization sample is of a select nature, the test should be applied only to representative individuals of that select group.

The major criticisms of intelligence tests have depended upon the use of item content heavily weighted in the verbal direction. An individual who comes from a deprived verbal background or who has a limited education will be penalized on such tests. There have been attempts to avoid problems of this nature by restricting the use of the term intelligence with such tests, or by devising so-called nonverbal items. Results of nonverbal, performance, and culture-fair tests have not been very satisfactory. The reason is that they do not correlate well with the specified criteria for which the test must be used. Though it may be true that for other kinds of outcomes they might be very suitable, they simply do not predict very well how the child will perform in school. As a result, the meaning of the scores is doubtful.

This returns us to the essential matter in intelligence testing, what Wechsler calls "the biggest bug-a-boo of intelligence testing"—the intelligence quotient. The attacks upon intelligence testing and the I.Q. since 1950 have become increasingly strong. Yet, as Wechsler points out, an I.Q. is most commonly used as a measure of relative brightness. As such it is only a means of ranking individuals in a group of known characteristics. It thus means no more or any less than a percentile rank or a z-score. Wechsler makes the excellent point that when a teacher assigns class grades on the basis of a normal curve or some kind of sliding scale, there tends to be an acceptance of this procedure with only a minimum of quarrel, yet this same procedure applied to an expression of a score on intelligence test rouses excited emotions. Of course, the problem is not in the derivation of the I.Q., but in the interpretation and utilization of the scales, as Wechsler states. The old concept of an invariant I.Q. from the moment a child is born still persists in some quarters, and if it is accepted and utilized in this fashion then it represents a matter for some concern. The trained psychometrist and psychologist, and the well-trained teacher would not make such a claim. It is true, particularly after the age of six years or so, that I.Q.s for groups tend to remain relatively stable. In the cases of individuals even within such groups, however, somewhat larger changes can and do occur. The quarrel is most frequently with the individual's I.Q. If there is a suspicion that his I.Q. is in error, Wechsler states that it would be better to retest him rather than to throw out the tests.

Over all, Wechsler concludes that there needs to be more testing done rather than less. Though critics would point as one argument against this the excessive cost, Wechsler negates this argument by pointing out that the cost of a school testing program is only an insignificant portion of the total cost of keeping a child in school yearly. Particularly would he increase the amount of testing done with individual-intelligence scales. He believes that it would stand the school and the child in good stead if the child were examined with an individual test as he entered school. Such a test in all probability need not then be administered for another three or four years.

One objective in testing is cited by Wechsler as being implicit in the aim of the test. Intelligence tests, to some degree, reflect the ability to learn and solve problems required in a particular environment. To criticize the use of tests with persons from disadvantaged backgrounds or from minority groups is unrealistic, Wechsler believes. If the tests are unfair it is because they record the unfairness of more general life situations. This unfairness will have its effects in the school setting as well. In concluding, Wechsler makes this telling point:

> The I.Q. has had a long life and will probably withstand the latest assaults on it. The most discouraging thing about them is not that they

are without merit, but that they are directed against the wrong target. It is true that the results of intelligence tests, and of others, too, are unfair to the disadvantaged, deprived and various minority groups but it is not the I.Q. that has made them so. The culprits are poor housing, broken homes, a lack of basic opportunities, etc., etc. . . . If the various pressure groups succeed in eliminating these problems the I.Q.'s of the disadvantaged will take care of themselves. (Wechsler, 1968, p. 306)

Summary

The scales constructed by Wechsler have received wide acceptance and use, both clinically and educationally. Though other contributions by him have been relatively overlooked in the dedication to the testing devices, there is the possibility that the scales may be less significant than theoretical matters. The emphasis ascribed to nonintellective factors in test scores, their role in determining scores of intellectual abilities, and their independence from intelligence offers possibilities, for example, not previously proposed. The distinction of intellectual abilities from intelligence is a significant theoretical contribution as well. Wechsler's influence on the testing movement has barely begun, and may offer alternatives and directions much superior to any test yet available, including the scales authored by him.

References

Balinsky, B., Israel, H., and Wechsler, D., "The Relative Effectiveness of the Stanford-Binet and the Bellevue Intelligence Scale in Diagnosing Mental Deficiency," *American Journal of Orthopsychiatry*, 1939, 9, 798–809.

Wechsler, D., "On the Influence of Education on Intelligence as Measured by the Binet-Simon Tests," *Journal of Educational Psychology*, 1926, 17, 248–257.

———, "Analytic Use of the Army Alpha Examination," *Journal of Applied Psychology*, 1932a, 16, 254–256.

———, "On the Limits of Human Variability," *Psychological Review*, 1932b, 39, 87–90.

———, "The Concept of Mental Deficiency in Theory and Practice," *Psychological Bulletin*, 1934, 31, 684.

———, "Nonintellective Factors in General Intelligence," *Psychological Bulletin*, 1940, 37, 444–445.

———, "Non-Intellective Factors in General Intelligence," *Journal of Abnormal Psychology*, 1943, 38, 101–103.

———, *The Measurement of Adult Intelligence.* Baltimore: Williams and Wilkins, 1944.

————, "Intellectual Development and Psychological Maturity," *Child Development*, 1950a, 21, 45–50

————, "Cognitive, Conative, and Non-Intellective Intelligence," *American Psychologist*, 1950b, 5, 78–83.

————, *The Range of Human Capacities.* Baltimore: Williams and Wilkins, 1952.

————, *The Measurement and Appraisal of Adult Intelligence.* Baltimore: Williams and Wilkins, 1958.

————, "The I.Q. Is an Intelligence Test," *New York Times Magazine,* June 26, 1966. Reprinted in R. K. Parker (ed.), *Readings in Educational Psychology.* Boston: Allyn and Bacon, 1968, pp. 299–306.

9

J. P. Guilford
and
Jean Piaget

I. Guilford

The promising leads for specific ways in which intelligence may express itself, first advocated by Spearman, and developed with the factor-analytic technique of the Thurstones, has had its most recent extensions in the work of Guilford. A distinguished contributor to theoretical and empirical measures of personality as well as to the field of statistics, Guilford's model or structure of intellect has become one of the most widely recognized expressions of intellectual traits ever offered in this country. Indeed, a strong case may be made for the fact that the model has received much greater acceptance and awareness than the outgrowth of the model: the measures of expressions of intellectual abilities of different types and degrees advocated and devised by Guilford and his colleagues.

Though the derivation and expression of the complex, three-dimensional structure of intellect is a work of fairly recent times, historical antecedents for the position taken by Guilford may be seen in earlier works (Guilford and Guilford, 1931). As a part of his work on personality, Guilford recognized the importance of creative expression in the behavior of the individual. He was among the first to begin to devise measures which might get at creative talent and its expression. In the article cited here, Guilford and Guilford make a distinction between artistic appreciation and production or performance. The tests devised in the late twenties had tended to emphasize appreciation rather than production. Though recognizing the importance of appreciation, the Guilfords maintain that such appreciation is hardly a sufficient condition for assuring that the individual entering an art course may eventually produce creative work. A test intended to assess the degree of artistic ability possessed by the individual should require some production by him. This production dimension, though not the only aspect of the model and not restricted to artistic performance only, is a present feature of Guilford's Structure of Intellect.

The Guilfords attempted to devise a task which would be as direct a reflection of artistic expression as possible, restricted very much to such expression, and therefore a highly specific measure rather than a general one. The task itself was almost classically simple: adjectives which may express feeling were spoken aloud and the subject drew simple lines to reflect his reaction to the adjective. Though the task was simple, the scoring procedures were quite complex. The Guilfords maintain that such a complex scoring system is necessary in order to achieve sufficient reliability and validity for the test. As an aside, any individual who has used some of the contemporary measures of divergent thinking can appreciate difficulties inherent in scoring. In any event, the theoretical principles underlying the procedure are of greater importance for our purposes here than the test itself. The subject was required to perform on a task fairly simple to administer and take, but difficult to score. The practical criterion of teacher ratings in a design course was the basis for validity. The Guilfords maintain that, though the task took only ten minutes to give, the creative ability of the students in the design course was rated as well as the teacher could estimate them after a semester's work. They also make the point, an important one in conjunction with Guilford's position in theoretical and empirical measures of intelligence, that the test did not measure, at least to any appreciable degree, the kind of ability that is measured by a test of general intelligence.

Further work in factor-analytic techniques applied to the measurement of personality yielded factors reflecting the intellectual nature of man's personality. For example, in a study reporting determination of such personality factors as social introversion, emotion, and some ascendence-submission factors, the Guilfords (Guilford and Guilford, 1936) report a factor which at the time they denoted as T. The content of the items which formed the cluster denoted by this factor seemed to them to reflect a thinking-introversion facet of personality or perhaps intellectual leadership. The evidence at the time was fairly limited and they pointed to a need for further study of the factor. The factor was more precisely defined and described by 1939 (Guilford and Guilford, 1939). Now the factor T seemed to them to reflect a behavior they referred to as habitual thinking of a meditative sort. In addition they also pointed to an LT factor, denoted by them as a liking for thinking of the problem-solving kind. In this study, in addition to other factors discussed, the T and LT factors appeared possibly to be of a primary nature. A further possible factor labeled *A* (alertness) was also a possibility from their data. These kinds of intellectual factors would seem to differ somewhat from the behaviors identified through conventional intelligence tests.

Along with such work as that cited above, Guilford was also interested in the constitution and use of currently available measures. He presented a revision of the Army Alpha, with factors denoted, and discussed the possible applications of such a test (Guilford, 1938). At the time, as he pointed out, greater emphasis was being placed on primary mental abilities in the measurement of intelligence as opposed to the conventional procedure of a single score as in tests like the Stanford-Binet. His revision of the Alpha was undertaken to derive some diagnostic measure for adults, particularly college students, utilizing items increasing with difficulty within each of the subtests. The procedure followed by him disclosed three variables or factors, each of which had potential application for determining individual strengths not denoted by the total score alone.

The primary factors found by Guilford were denoted by letters, since he felt that the precise nature of the factors was at that time not fully known. The general content of the items could be described in terms of these letters, however. Thus, the three factors were: *V*, some kind of verbal factor; *N*, some kind of numerical factor; and *R*, some kind of relations factor. Though with our current degree of sophistication, these factors may seem rather mundane and quite general, they were much less so at the time of publication. Guilford points out that the factor-analytic technique employed by him indicates that each of these was independent and fundamental to intellectual differences among individuals. The labels he has used, then, he sees as less important than the fact that the individual may be described with greater precision through employment of this revision of the Alpha. He anticipates some of the problems and needs of the precise and complete description of the individual's intellectual status with this statement:

> While the isolation of primary abilities is a problem that we can say has been solved with a certain degree of satisfaction, the scoring of individuals for those abilities separately has not yet been accomplished with the same success. The trouble is that no test is entirely pure, that is to say, dependent upon one primary ability and only one. So when we score a single homogeneous test, even this score is "contaminated" with more than the one factor that we are trying to gauge. The best hope is to find a pool of tests such that every test has in common the factor we wish to measure plus another factor or factors none of which the other tests in the pool hold with it in common. Summating the scores in the pool should, we hope, cancel out the effects of the other "foreign" factors, leaving the residual of truth concerning the factor in which we are interested. . . . (Guilford, 1938, p. 242–243)

Again, the importance of this work is not so much in the specific test employed or the factors derived, as in the direction to which the work points. From such an empirical background, a model and more precise measures are developed.

Human Abilities

The nature of abilities proposed theoretically and determined empirically soon received the attention of Guilford (Guilford, 1940). In his presidential address to the Midwestern Psychological Association, he surveyed the work of the 1930s and the measurement of mental abilities. His declared purpose was to survey the fundamental abilities which were accepted to the time, to see under what conditions these abilities were demonstrated by individuals, and to describe conditions applying to test construction and use particularly pertinent to such abilities. He pointed out that psychology, in its attempt to define and measure human abilities, had proceeded along a road from faculties to factors. Progress had often been slow and quite difficult, beginning with the work of Galton with his emphasis upon discrete functions and measures. This approach using discrete and discriminable functions, however, was abandoned for the method of tests proposed by the French psychologists, particularly Binet. Under this latter approach, complex mental faculties were proposed, and believed to be measured. Though such functions as memory, association, imagination, and so on, were described, they were not measured independently. Guilford points out that the implicit assumption must be that each of these functions correlates perfectly with every other function. Though correlational analysis did not bear out such a viewpoint, the implicit assumptions remained and still remain in many of the tests available today.

Out of this background came the construct intelligence. As Guilford aptly states, Binet was primarily responsible for the construct as it is most commonly used. He applied his procedures to a given, specific setting, particularly in attempts to discriminate the dull from the normal. Guilford describes the directive influence of such an approach by stating: "Had he never been given this assignment one wonders what direction the test movement might have taken . . ." (Guilford, 1940, p. 370). There is a further matter that the distinction between dull and normal and dull and bright signifies something about a unitary dimension of the mind. In this context, the single concept of intelligence was proposed, accepted, and implemented in the vast number of tests which soon followed. Problems of definition under this approach, though recognized, Guilford maintains were generally ignored or sloughed over.

A viable alternative to this state of affairs occurred with the proposal and implementation of factor-analytic theory and methods in the 1920s.

The complex statistical techniques employed in factor analysis led to the statement of a number of factors, some of which were considered of importance, others of which were not. At least two extremes had been expressed in the attitude toward the factor method and its importance for analyzing human abilities. At one extreme, according to Guilford, there were those who considered factors as nothing more than statistical artifacts. As such then they would lack meaning, being little more than restricted expressions of correlational techniques. Guilford, of course, rejects this viewpoint. At the other extreme, there were those who accepted factors as being some kind of real, basic unities. This idea was implied, for example, in the use of the term "primary mental abilities" as used by the Thurstones. The reality of the factors disclosed through the use of factor techniques must also be questioned, according to Guilford. Their primary nature is not known, with the result that the qualitative aspects implied by the terminology of the primary mental abilities are unknown. This does not belie the fact that some relatively independent factors are quantitatively demonstrated to exist. At that time, however, Guilford proposed that each factor that could be isolated and described served in a hypothetical function, subject to considerable further study.

Guilford firmly believes that the factorial approach is the one which assures greatest gains in understanding human abilities. With such an approach, causes of individual differences may be better described and significant social problems approached.

Criteria for Evaluating Tests

Given a series of psychological tests, of whatever type, we become concerned about the consistency with which the tests measure and the relevance of their scores to behavior. Though mechanical in some respects, the concepts of reliability and validity are essential to any test operation. What is meant by such terminology, and the stringency desirable in correlational values was the focus of an article appearing in 1946 (Guilford, 1946). Reliability and validity, however they may be defined, have traditionally determined the worth of any test. Such criteria he does not quarrel with, but he does suggest in this article some revisions in applications plus additional criteria for determining the worth of a test.

Among the assumptions that are made about reliability, Guilford specifically mentions beliefs concerning absolute reliability coefficients for any given test, the desirability of high reliability as such, the dependence of validity upon substantial reliability, and the presumed direct influence upon validity by increasing the reliability of the test. Among the commonly held opinions about validity, he refers specifically to beliefs that validity coefficients have some practical ceiling of about .60 for predictive validity, the rejection of tests whose validity coefficients are

below .20, the need for maximum correlation with some practical criterion for a given test, a decreasing increment to total validity by adding
more tests to a battery, and the need for some face validity.

Essentially, Guilford questions each of these beliefs in this article.
Each opinion is considered in turn, with conditions specified under which
the opinion is questionable. To Guilford, there can be no absolute standards either for reliability or for validity. All things remain relative. The
specific quality of each situation in which the test is used will determine
whether or not a high split-half reliability coefficient is needed or whether
one might settle for only a moderate reliability coefficient. In the same
way, the criterion which represents validity in the test may be more
situation-specific than it is test-specific. However, to Guilford, validity is
more important than reliability as such. Superior to either or both is the
factorial composition of the test. Where factorially independent subtests
with describable relationships to total score are available, a highly usable
battery results. Under such a set of circumstances, questions about reliability and validity are of less concern.

The Structure of Intellect

By the mid 1950s, work conducted by Guilford and his associates,
primarily for the Air Force, had crystallized into a form allowing an
expression of the structure of intellect. Elements entering into this structure had been described and discussed in a number of sources prior to
the first publication of the model itself (for example, see Guilford, 1953).
Particularly was Guilford interested in adult intellect and even more
particularly in the intellect shown by the superior human adult (Guilford,
1956). To him, psychologists had taken a much too restricted view of
human intelligence since the time of Binet. Particularly with the development of factor-analytic procedures, it was possible to extend considerably
the concept of human intelligence. As Guilford points out, however, the
results of factor-analytic techniques had greater effect on possible explanations of the nature of human intelligence than upon measurement as
such. Again, he stresses the fact that such tests as the Stanford-Binet and
the Wechsler Scales offer a single score or at best a limited number of
scores. Conceived of as measures of general intelligence, such scores are
limited to variance expressed in few factors but in a most complex fashion. Beginning with his work for the Air Force in the 1940s, Guilford
approached the problem of determining adult intelligence, particularly
for individuals of a high level. He began with the assumption that human
intelligence as a broad concept had not been explored by any method yet
available. Particularly had the thinking abilities been neglected, despite
their importance for intelligence, and most particularly the productive

thinking abilities. Initially, four kinds of thinking were arbitrarily designated and studied: reasoning, creativity, planning, and evaluation. The
factor-analytic technique was applied to the problem.

Guilford clearly designates the procedures that were followed in
building the structure. Each of the investigations undertaken by him
began with some hypothesis concerning unitary abilities that exist and
their measurable properties. Once the hypotheses were established, psychological tests were constructed or adapted for each of the presumed
factors so that a determination of presence or absence could be made.
Under statistical analysis, the presence or absence of the property could
be determined. In this procedure, the investigator had a fairly close
control over the central variable of concern: the psychological test. Additional variables such as testing conditions, sex, age, education, and moti-
vation, were held constant as much as possible. It is true that in most of
the studies done the sample had been constituted of men in the military
designated for officer training or some high-level position. Under such
conditions, it is possible that a number of other kinds of populations need
to be designated as well to determine the generalizability of the findings
with the specific samples used.

Results of the procedures followed led to a model positing two major
groups of intellectual factors (Guilford, 1956). One broad heading Guilford designates as thinking factors, the other as memory factors. There
are apparently a great many more factors which enter the thinking category than the memory category. The thinking factors are further subdivided into some three divisions, with one of these being further
subdivided. One set of factors relating to thinking is designated cognition. A second grouping is called production, and is further subdivided
into convergent-thinking abilities and divergent-thinking abilities. These
subcategories have been widely quoted and discussed for their implications for the expression of intellect. The final group of factors Guilford
designates as evaluation factors.

Guilford defines cognition factors as being those which are concerned with becoming aware of mental content or constructs of some
kind. The responses required in tests of cognition demand that something be comprehended, recognized, or discovered by the examinee. He
specifically notes that cognition tests represent functions on the receptor
end of behavior. The various kinds of cognitive abilities may be differentiated either in terms of material or content on the test, or in terms of
the kind of thing that must be dealt with or discovered, or both.

The production factors emphasize some end results. Guilford states
that after the individual has comprehended a situation he must do something about it, or to it. *What* he does about or to the situation would
represent production. This production may take one of two lines. The
first of these, referred to as convergent thinking, is reflected in the situa-

tion where a single conclusion or response is correct and/or required and the individual must determine this single response. Much of testing has emphasized such a type of production by the individual. In situations which require divergent thinking, however, there are apt to be many possible responses and the individual must search in a number of directions for possible conclusions. Any or all of these may be correct for the behavioral situation. This kind of thinking, sometimes expressed as creative, though perhaps loosely so, has generated much interest since Guilford's identification and exposition of it.

Finally, the evaluation factors are concerned with adequacy, suitability, and effectiveness of the products of thinking. After cognition and production have occurred, some decision must be made as to correctness, pragmatic utility, minimum or maximum adequacy. A judgment must be imposed, then.

For the battery of tests used and the factor-analytic results, all factors remaining seem reasonably to fall under the heading of memory factors. There are considerably fewer of these memory factors than of the thinking factors, but this does not negate their importance to overall behavior. The work indicates that there are a number of distinct memory abilities, as had been proposed by any number of theoreticians prior to Guilford and beginning with Binet. Recognition of many types of memory and provision for them in testing had been two quite different matters, however.

In this first presentation of the structure of intellect, Guilford points to the fact that about forty factors had been disclosed by study to that time, but he anticipated a great many more would be uncovered. Even with the somewhat limited number proposed in this article, he makes the point that any scientific need for parsimony seems indefensible. To him, attempts to achieve parsimony have been carried to extremes not justifiable, particularly in view of the problems introduced by the seeking for a single intellectual dimension.

He also makes the point that what constitutes a factor must be considered in two senses: one, the mathematical concept, and the other the psychological concept. The results reported to that date were in terms of mathematical factors. Whether each of these factors represents some single psychological factor or some combination of psychological factors could only be determined by additional experimental work and further interpretation through new factor analyses. Once a mathematical factor has been designated, there is the further matter of its origin. Whether factors are inherited or acquired in their basic nature cannot be determined by factor analysis alone. Again, experimental work will be needed to specifically determine answers to questions of heritability of factors.

One aspect of the origin of factors is the matter of point in the life of the individual at which each factor may develop. Again, at least in 1956, no very defensible answers were yet available and further research was urged. Guilford does make the assumption that the intellectual factors, when studied and determined, will be somewhat simpler for children than they are for adults. Apparently, then, the structure of intellect for children and adults will be the same, though complexity will differ. In the same way, superior adults will show greater complexity in the structure of intellect than will inferior adults.

The implications of the structure of intellect for psychological theory are particularly important to a greater understanding of the process of thinking. Guilford makes the point, as he had in prior writings, that the symbolic behavior that constitutes thinking has never been conceptualized in a comprehensive theory. One outcome of the structure of intellect, then, will be the designation of factors which reflect the kinds of symbols used by human beings in thinking. When the individual thinks, he employs factors that reflect cognition, production of one kind or the other, and evaluation, usually in that order. Where the thinking done by the individual is highly realistic, convergent thinking would be the more commonly found. Under situations where realism is not so important, where the individual is given some freedom in his mental behavior, divergent thinking is more apt to occur. These factors entering into thinking have particular implications, Guilford maintains, for problem-solving behavior. There is no single factor which may be designated as problem solving, and Guilford states this to be of some significance. The process of solving problems is highly complex. To attempt to determine a single function or process which will reflect problem solving is misguided. A better approach will be to determine the kinds of problems that are common to human behavior and attempt to specify as clearly as possible the abilities which influence a solution of each type of problem. The factors representing these abilities may then be designated, and tested through experimental and factor-analytic procedures.

In much the same way, the matter of creative thinking may be approached. As with problem solving, creativity is not a single or exclusive set of factors. What must be done in order to specify the nature of creative behavior is to determine the major aspects of creative production and to determine the factors which bring such production about.

Guilford believes he has sufficient evidence to reject any concept that "intelligence is the same as learning ability." If intelligence is not equated with learning ability, then the premises and uses of many current intelligence tests must be doubted. Indeed, Guilford points out that the term intelligence has not been defined in any very satisfactory manner. Factor analysis has never disclosed any central factor which might be designated by this label. Yet the term, he says, should be preserved since it does have utility. It is convenient to maintain such a concept even though it is "rather shifty" as a concept. Some gain would be made if we were to specify a number of different kinds of intelligences: intelligence *A*, intelligence *B*, and so on, describing specifically the content and the behavior outcomes of each of these. For this purpose, combinations of intellectual factors would be most helpful, particularly when the appropriate weights are assigned within the combinations. To some degree, of course, such combinations of weighted factors occur in the Binet and the Wechsler Scales. However, these have not been the basis for the building of the tests, with the result that the factors either are of a limited number, or are improperly selected, and therefore of limited utility. Guilford suggests that since intelligence tests will continue to be used for some time, two further steps be taken. The first improvement would be to specify the scores in terms of identified factors. This would allow extraction of the maximum amount of information available from the scores. The second improvement would be to emphasize in the content more of the productive-thinking factors or their social implications.

In his book entitled *Personality*, Guilford included a chapter on dimensions of aptitude (Guilford, 1959). This chapter added little to the structure itself but did devote more explicit discussion to the kinds of memory and thinking factors comprising the structure of intellect, proposed a three-dimensional model which would reflect the entire structure of intellect, and designated in some detail examples of tests and test items for each of the memory and thinking factors. A general plan was presented for the relationships among the major categories of intellectual abilities, composed of the factors discussed in the preceding article (See Figure 9-1).

The memory factors are still considered to be more limited than the

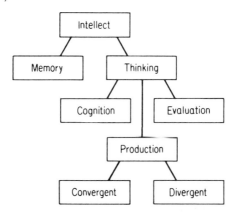

Fig. 9-1. General plan of intellect. (From *Personality*, J.P. Guilford, p. 360. Copyright 1959 by McGraw-Hill Book Company. Used with permission of McGraw-Hill Book Company.)

thinking factors. Guilford mentions specifically substance memory, reflected in tasks of visual memory, auditory memory, memory span, and memory for ideas; associative memory, as reflected in rote and meaningful memory tasks; and memory systems, as reflected in spatial position and temporal order.

The matrices reflecting each of the kinds of thinking factors, however, are much more extensive, though there are some significant gaps. As an example, the matrix of divergent-thinking factors is presented in Table 9.1. Within the matrix, it will be noted that eleven of the cells have factor labels entered, while eight of them do not. Thus, symbolic units will be presented by word fluency, semantic units by ideational fluency, but figural units at the time of the publication of this book had not been determined in terms of appropriate tests reflecting this factor.

Finally, in discussing his general theory of intellect, Guilford presents a three dimensional model which has been widely quoted and reviewed. The model is shown in Figure 9.2. There are the possibilities of 120 specific, measurable abilities or factors from this structure. As Guilford has pointed out, this is a model, not a definitive proposal at this stage, and much further research will be required to determine not only the adequacy of the model but the kinds of tests which reflect factors designated.

TABLE 9.1*
MATRIX OF DIVERGENT-THINKING FACTORS

Kind of Thinking Produced	Kind of Content		
	Figural	Symbolic	Semantic
Units		Word fluency	Ideational fluency
Classes	Figural spontaneous flexibility		Semantic spontaneous flexibility
Correlates			Associational fluency
Systems		Expressional fluency	
Transformations	Figural adaptive flexibility	Symbolic adaptive flexibility	Originality
Implications	Elaboration +		Elaboration +

+ Now appears to be one factor but it may be a confounding of two, a figural and a semantic factor.

* From *Personality* by J. P. Guilford. Copyright 1959, McGraw-Hill Book Company. Used with permission of McGraw-Hill Book Company, p. 382.

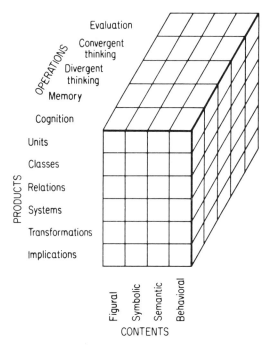

Fig. 9-2. The structure of intellect. (From *Personality*,
J.P. Guilford, p. 397. Copyright 1959 by McGraw-Hill
Book Company. Used with permission of McGraw-Hill
Book Company.)

An Updating of the Model

With further research, Guilford was able to fill in some of the cells
which were blank in the Structure of Intellect as proposed in 1959. The
model remains unchanged, but it is more complete (Guilford, 1966). One
of the significant areas of development in this 1965 model is the designation of some abilities for dealing with behavioral information. Guilford
refers to this as the area that E. L. Thorndike had called social intelligence
in his work. Now, tests are available which yield some information about
those factors necessary for creative dealing with other persons. There
is some limited discussion as well of such topics as differentiation of
abilities with increasing age, and the implication of the structure of
intellect for psychological theory. Among the comments by Guilford
concerning theoretical importance is the congruence he sees between
certain aspects of the model and proposals of Piaget.

But the newness of the model revolves essentially around problem
solving. Guilford proposes a problem-solving model which employs concepts of the structure of intellect. The traditional approach to problem

solving has been a series of steps beginning with recognition of the problem, then analyzing elements of the problem, proposing some solutions, and judging the adequacy of the solutions. In view of current work, this traditional model appears too simple. In the Guilford proposal, with initial input from either an environmental or semantic source, there will be the employment of cognition, production, and evaluation. Though he conceives this model to be general rather than specific, the basic operations needed to solve problems are included. The specific operations employed will depend upon the nature of the problem encountered.

The Nature of Human Intelligence

The most recent work published by Guilford and dealing directly with the structure of intellect is a book entitled *The Nature of Human Intelligence* (Guilford, 1967a). The book represents very little change, but a considerable amount of designation and extension. Because of its contemporary nature, this is probably the single best source for the student to become acquainted with Guilford's proposals. Despite the considerable detail, or perhaps because of it, only a few matters will be considered in the present discussion.

For one thing, Guilford returns to the matter of the psychological nature of factors disclosed through mathematical procedures. Something more is needed than a collection of ability tests that work. Yet, as Guilford points out, the psychometrician too often settles for the pragmatic outcome of workable tests, sufficient to his purposes. By such an individual, theory is frequently ignored, perhaps even despised. Yet theory does add some degree of meaning and significance to the pragmatic outcomes utilized by the psychometrician. There must be concern, then, for the underlying bases, both theoretical and primary, of test scores.

The psychological nature of a factor becomes the important question, then. Guilford makes the point that more and more individuals are questioning the nature of psychological factors, and he feels this to be an encouraging development. At the present tiime there is no answer which can be unquestionably accepted, though the extensive and diversified work to this time has offered some reasonable suggestions. He points out that, as a factor is disclosed through mathematical techniques, it is reasonable to assume some variable or trait underlies this factor along which individuals will differ on a continuum from low to high. There are, then, test observations with their scores for a sample of persons, and these are manifest variables. The underlying factors and factor scales along which individuals differ cannot be directly observed, but they may be estimated. Test scores indicate to us the performance level of the individual. Factor scores indicate the quantity of a given trait which the individual has. The question becomes, what is the attribute? Guilford believes that when correlations are available for a given factor test with other tests, it becomes possible to determine measurement psychologically. He demonstrates this through the example of three kinds of performance correlated with each other but relatively independent of other forms of performance. The content of the tests will differ. When a significantly high correlation among performances on these tasks is found, their common nature may be postulated.

In his final chapter, Guilford touches on several issues which have been a concern of intelligence testing over the past fifty years or so. One of these matters concerns the effects of environment upon intellectual status of the individual. There are a number of problems concerned with determining effects of environmental conditions on intellectual functioning because of problems both in describing environment and in measuring intelligence. Despite these problems Guilford believes that a poor environment, one which offers little stimulation with regard to learning, will be detrimental to intellectual development of the individual. Evidence about the effects of enriched environments on those who are already normal or superior are not so clear cut. As for sex differences, using tasks fitted to the structure-of-intellect categories, some small differences have been disclosed. Guilford points out that only very limited research in this area has been done until this time. Similarly, limited research has been done with the effects of drugs on intellectual functioning, but he states that the more discrete designation of abilities possible with the structure of intellect should make such a kind of investigation reasonable for determining specific effects on given factors.

A second matter dealt with by Guilford of concern to the testing movement is that of mental growth and decline. Results from studies on variability as disclosed by the structure of intellect indicate that former beliefs about the maximum age of mental development must be greatly revised. Over all, Guilford states that the age of maximum functioning is much higher than had been conceived before. In certain instances, maximum growth may not be achieved until well after the age of thirty, particularly in such areas as divergent thinking. Of course, individuals show differences in terms of their own growth curves. Of possibly even greater significance, Guilford points out that there are differential growth curves for the various kinds of intellectual abilities within the individual. As for mental decline, there are also large differences for the age at which decline sets in and for the rate of decline in intellectual functioning generally, as well as in the specific abilities. Guilford believes that most of the measures used to determine the degree of mental deterioration are subject to objection based upon data using factor tests.

The educational process and its psychological foundations needs to be questioned as well, Guilford believes. The predominant theory in educational work, that of stimulus-response connectionism, is much too limited for helping teachers to determine the nature of mental functioning of pupils and their intellectual development. The traditional approaches emphasize only one of some six products of information. Considerable expansion needs to be conducted educationally into other kind of products in order to benefit the child educationally to a maximum. The nature of the intellectual factors disclosed to this date also require some reconsideration of the old formal discipline issue. Some evidence on transfer indicates that perhaps the position that all learning is highly specific is not so defensible as it appeared to be from earlier research. There may be some justification at least to underlying principles of the old "formal discipline" viewpoint. Children should be given the opportunity for practicing various kinds of intellectual skills in order to develop to their maximum the underlying intellectual abilities. By extension, the structure of intellect should have its influence upon the curriculum, particuarly the curriculum designed for the individual child, and upon teaching methods and techniques. Examination approaches must also reflect the kinds of intellectual abilities desired and desirable.

Some Comments on Creativity

Guilford has given some attention not only to creativity in the sense of artistic work, but in terms of human interaction as well. In discussing certain factors that may aid or hinder creativity (Guilford, 1962), the creative individual is defined as one who would think with greater fluency, more flexibility, and greater originality. These kinds of mental behaviors would be found in all kinds of situations, not just those of direct creative production in the arts. Tasks, from the structure of intellect, have been available to measure fluency, flexibility, and originality. Particularly have measures of originality been missing in conventional attempts to measure intelligence (Guilford, 1967b). In a quite recent article (Guilford, Hendricks, and Hoepner, 1968), the structure of intellect has been used to try to identify individuals who may be able to solve social problems in a creative fashion. The initial work in this area indicates that several divergent production factors seem to be found most often in individuals who are successful in dealing with social problems. This extension of the meaning of "creativity" may offer opportunities for effective change largely lacking in the past because of lack of control. Certainly, the recognition of social problems is increasing year by year. Unfortunately, precise and fairly rigorous recognition of factors necessary to their amelioration has not so increased. In so far as the intellectual factors identified in the structure of intellect contribute to solutions, Guilford's work will have assumed an importance far beyond that of any prior attempts to describe and measure intelligence.

II. Piaget

The model and methods of Piaget have centered around developmental characteristics of children. Within such characteristics, of course, lies the dimension of intelligence. Piaget considers intelligence in terms of its place within the scheme of development so that there is an interrelatedness in his writings on intelligence to other aspects of his theory. Yet he has discussed the role of intelligence in discrete forms in at least two major works: the first of these is *The Psychology of Intelligence* (1960), based upon a series of lectures given in 1942 in France and later published in 1947, with a translation in 1960; the second is the better-known *The Origins of Intelligence in Children* published in this country in 1952.

The Psychology of Intelligence deals more specifically with the nature or model of intelligence proposed by Piaget, while *The Origins of Intelligence in Children* describes observable outcomes in measures. For purposes of this text, the former will be emphasized more heavily than the latter.

In his preface to *The Psychology of Intelligence,* Piaget outlines the contents of the text. He begins by defining intelligence and how it particularly is related to the various adaptive processes of the individual in various situations. He then moves into the psychology of thinking and demonstrates the relationship of the intelligent act to the procedure of "grouping," given definitive structures. With intelligence conceived of as a form of equilibrium toward which every cognitive process evolves, he next discusses problems of perception and habit. He closes with some discussion of the development and socialization of intelligence.

To Piaget, intelligence must be considered in terms of some duality; it has both a biological and a logical nature. Rather than being antithetical, Piaget proposes that in unity these two offer the greatest possible explanation of intelligence with our present stage of knowledge. Despite expressed concern about the biological nature of intelligence, however, it seems fair to state that Piaget's major attempts are in the direction of logic.

Every response, whether internally or externally determined, constitutes an adaptation or, what Piaget feels is a better statement, a readaptation of the individual. When there is some need on the part of the individual, equilibrium is upset. The purpose of behavior, then, is to restore this equilibrium between the individual and his environment. Behavior is a reflection of such a functional relationship and contains two essential but highly related facets: the affective component and the cognitive component. Affect, to Piaget, is more than emotion; it represents some energetic form, the energy of the functioning organism. Cognition is also defined in a broader sense than usual: the cognitive nature of behavior is considered to be essentially one of structure. In behavioral situations, then, where equilibrium is disturbed, the organism attempts by means both of an energy system and an imposition of structure to reestablish its equilibrium.

More specifically, Piaget describes any act of intelligence as consisting, first, of some internal energy regulation. This will be influenced by interest, effort, ease, and the like, of the individual. Further regulation comes from external sources as exemplified in values of whatever solutions are being sought and values of objects that are available to the subject. Each of these internal and external controls represents affect. What are usually considered as unrelated expressions called "feelings" and "intelligence" are merely expressions of the same general type but reflecting an internal or external regulatory source.

Nor should the term intelligence be restricted to some discrete and highly differentiated class of cognitive processes. It is not a means of structure divorced from other means. Intelligence represents a form of equilibrium utilizing structure from all sources available to the organism. Its cognitive nature is structure, but perceptions, habits, all kinds of elementary motor mechanisms will be used. To Piaget, intelligence becomes a kind of generic term that reflects a superior type of equilibrium in cognitive structures. This means that intelligence has a most central role in all life of the organism and it must display considerable plasticity to achieve the kind of durable structural equilibrium which is necessary to successful living by the organism. Essentially, the role of intelligence is adaptation.

Adaptation, as it applies to intelligence, must be defined. Essentially, it is the equilibrium existing between the responses of the individual and the environment. For the action of the individual on the environment, Piaget uses the term assimilation. Past experience with the same kinds of objects will lead to the individual imposing structure on the objects encountered. For the effects of the environment on the individual, Piaget uses the term accommodation. In this condition, the individual must accommodate himself to the exigencies of the environment. The major term adaptation, then, represents the equilibrium between assimilation and accommodation, or the interaction between the individual and environment. This equilibrium represents Piaget's definition of intelligence. Such a definition is operational, in Piaget's viewpoint. In intelligent behavior, intellectual operations reflect actions by the individual since they contain both something produced by him and a possible experiment on reality. To understand intelligence, then, requires a description of operations arising from actions of the individual and the laws of equilibrium which govern this derivation.

To study intelligence requires some reversal of mental actions so that what is internal, the operation, can be described. For this purpose, Piaget believes that mathematical expression represents the most direct means of determining the nature of intelligence. The symbols used in mathematics reflect mental actions or operations of thought. In the same way, logical thought may be considered both in terms of logical analysis and psychological analysis. To Piaget, logical thought is operational since it extends the area of action by internalization. Piaget cautions that this viewpoint may be overly simplified, however, since every operation cannot be reduced to a single action. Thus, to realize psychological reality will require the viewpoint that mentality consists of complex operational systems, not of isolated operations which act as predecessor and derivative elements of the system. These operations do become organized into systems. Again, the problem in understanding intelligence is to determine the manner in which equilibrium of systems is established. To accomplish this task, Piaget suggests the use of groups in much the same sense in which they are used mathematically to describe series of numbers. Psychologically, and thus in the sense of intelligence, grouping applies to the form of equilibrium in operations. A grouping must be a well-defined structure, capable of distinction at successive levels.

Piaget describes the behavior of children of varous ages on tasks which allow for description of the structure of grouping. He also describes the action of the mind in approaching problems. For example, the child will ask a series of questions when encountering a concrete problem, ranging from such a question as "What is it?" to questions about purpose and quantity and the like. Whatever questions are asked are dependent upon some previous grouping or individual group since all of us use various schemes of classifying in order to delineate the problem. The groupings available to us are developed throughout life, beginning in infancy and being modified with succeeding experience. Like the child, as adults we have certain anticipatory schemes which we apply; the scheme is dependent upon the structure of groupings already available to the individual.

> Every problem, whether it concerns the anticipatory hypothesis regarding the solution or its detailed checking, is thus no more than a particular system of operations to be put into effect within the corresponding complex grouping. In order to find our way, we do not have to reconstruct the whole of space, but simply to complete its filling out in a given sector. In order to foresee an event, repair a bicycle, make out a budget, or decide on a program of action, there is no need to build up the whole

of causality in time, to review all accepted values, etc.; the solution to be found is attained simply by extending and completing the relationships already grouped except for correcting the groupings when there are errors of detail, and, above all, subdividing and differentiating it, but not by rebuilding it in its entirety. As for verification this is possible only in accordance with the rules of the grouping itself, by the fitting of the new relations into the previously existent system. (Piaget, 1960, p. 39)

Through experience, then, we continue to assimilate aspects of reality to intelligence, by which is meant establishing equilibrium on the basis of the grouping of the assimilative framework. While thoughts are being formed, they tend to be in some degree of dis-equilibrium or at least a state of unstable equilibrium. As we acquire experience, each new acquisition has its effects on already acquired ideas. Either this will tend in the direction of verification or express some degree of contradiction with groupings already held. In terms of the operation, new elements are added positively and easily, leading to greater coherence of the already present grouping.

Under certain conditions, equilibrium may be described in such a manner as to explain the mechanism of intelligence. These conditions reduce to:

1. Co-ordination of operations as a psychological condition.

2. The possibility of reversibility in action. Piaget believes this possibility of reversibility to be the most clearly defined characteristic of intelligence. By "reversibility," he means the plausibility of a converse operation for every original operation in the group. In intelligence, not only must this possibility exist but at times it must be exercised by the individual in order for the intelligence to express itself.

3. Operations must combine in an associative sense. By this, Piaget means that thought is not restricted only to certain channels once begun, but may deviate in any one of a number of directions at any given time. Yet the outcome of thought may be similar regardless of the mental route followed. Such deviation in thought is peculiar to intelligence, Piaget believes.

4. For a given operation, when combined with its converse, annulment occurs. In this condition, the individual must then return to the mental starting point. Piaget points out that one distinction between the adult and the child is the fact that the child does not return to his original position under such conditions of annulment. Having made an original hypothesis, even though rejecting it, the child has some distortion in the thought processes.

5. Restricted to quantitative matters only, where the above four are qualitative as well, there is a need to express combinativity. The unit added to itself gives a new number, mathematically. In the qualitative

sense, however, repetition of an event does not change the event itself.

In summary, Piaget makes it clear that much of the terminology discussed so far is descriptive, not definitive. Thus, "groupings" is a term used to signify that at a given level thought reaches equilibrium. In the same context, equilibrium allows structure of operations to be conserved while new elements may be assimilated. To some degree such equilibrium will be permanent but at the same time it must also be mobile, since mobility is necessary to acceptance of the concept of reversibility. But Piaget says: "Yet neither pointing out this state of equilibrium nor even stating its necessary conditions constitutes an explanation" (Piaget, 1960, p. 48). The remainder of this little book then attempts to take the next necessary step, tracing the development of intelligence in psychology and relating this development to equilibrium. In doing so, Piaget believes that the resulting explanation of intelligence will demonstrate the relationship of higher mental operations with all development. Development itself, then, involves some evolving states which are governed by the necessity of equilibrium as he describes the term.

Intelligence and Perception

First attention is given to the relationship between intelligence and perception. Piaget defines perception as the knowledge which each of us has of objects or the movements of objects through direct contact. A question may be raised which involves whether or not perceptual structures may be used to explain thought and intelligence. In his discussion, Piaget concludes that intelligence and perception are quite separate. First of all, the five conditions leading to grouping, earlier described, are not realized in terms of perceptual structures which are developed. There is, then, almost an opposition between perceptual and intellectual mechanisms. He raises the question as to whether or not the essential difference between intelligence and perception may not lie in the matter of complexity. Perhaps perception reflects some process, which he describes as being essentially statistical in nature, confined to a certain stage of development. Intelligence, on the other hand, will require a nature where complex relations are dealt with at a high level. In this sense, perception demonstrates structures which are irreversible and intransitive. The laws of grouping cannot be applied to perceptual phenomena. Since true grouping cannot be obtained at the perceptual level, perceptual constancy does not possess the reversibility and mobility of intelligence. However, perceptual activity is a predecessor of certain intellectual traits.

Essentially, as perception develops, there is increasing decentralization mentally, certain spatial and temporal transportations, a large number of comparisons derived, transpositions, anticpations, and analysis which will be increasingly mobile and will allow increasingly for reversibility. These kinds of activities increase with age and the relative degree of their presence accounts for the fact that young children perceive more syncretistically than older ones.

Habit and Sensory-Motor Intelligence

Before language is developed, it is difficult to determine about the presence and formation of intelligence. Yet, as Piaget points out, it is crucial to determine something about development of intelligence in the young child if we are to understand intelligence at other times in the life of the individual. One means of approaching this problem is to determine the kinds of habits developed by the individual in infancy and to determine the relationship of these habits to intelligence. The question becomes one, then, of whether or not habits developed in infancy are the basis of intelligence; or are they some unrelated behaviors. Piaget concludes from a logical analysis that there is some unity between sensorimotor processes leading to perceptual activity, habits which are formed, and intelligence of a preverbal nature. Intelligence does not suddently arrive, then, but becomes an extension of the perceptions and habits developed by the child. The order proposed by Piaget is somewhat as follows: Present and immediate contact with the world leads to perception, followed by automatic connections which develop between perceptions and responses which become habit. As perception and habits develop and operate at greater distances both spatially and temporally and in more complex directions, then mobility and reversibility will begin to develop. As these latter elements occur, intelligence begins. What constitutes the nature of early intelligence is the kind of mobile equilibrium which the processes of perception and habit tend toward. Insufficient as an explanation of intelligence, nevertheless, perception and habit may be necessary prerequisites to the development of intelligence.

The Development of Thought

Thinking is reflected in operations which achieve equilibrium through groupings, or what might be called reversibility and combinativity. Though having its beginnings in sensory-motor intelligence as described above, some further explanation is needed to determine the nature and direction of thought. Piaget says there are three conditions which are necessary for the individual to make the transition from sensory-motor intelligence to reflection. The first of these conditions requires an increase in speed such that the individual is so aware of successive phases in any action that it becomes essentially a simultaneous whole. Second, it is necessary that there be an awareness on the part of the individual both of desired results of action and of the mechanisms involved so that he will be able to search for a solution conscious of the nature of that solution. Third, there must be some increase of "distance" so that symbolic action enters into behavior well beyond the present status of space and time. Under these circumstances, Piaget maintains that thought is neither translation nor mere continuation of sensory-motor processes in some symbolic form. Some new plane is now necessary to explain this matter of thinking and symbolism.

Certain stages may be identified and described in the development of thought. Piaget describes four principal periods which he believes have been demonstrated.

1. When the child is able to use language as a symbolic function, beginning about age one and a half and continuing to about age four, development of symbolic and preconceptual thought begins and continues.

2. Beginning with age four and continuing to about age eight, there is a continuation of symbolic and preconceptual thought into an intuitive stage. As progressions occur in intuitive thought, the threshold of the operation of thinking is reached.

3. From age seven or eight up to about age twelve, the frequently cited concrete operations begin and develop. These concrete operations represent operational groupings of thought related to actual objects which may be manipulated or may be realized through the senses.

4. Beginning about age twelve and continuing during adolescence, formal thought is perfected. With the groupings which characterize formal thought, we have reflective intelligence. Each of these stages is discussed by Piaget, but in considerably more detail in *The Origins of Intelligence in Children* (Piaget, 1952).

Symbolic and Preconceptual Thought

As language begins to develop, it is necessary to distinguish between significants and significates. While the child develops verbal signs which are significates, the use of a system of such verbal signs depends on a more general symbolic function which may be called a significant. The young child, then, must discover signs and invent symbols. Though one may argue that there is already a system which may be used by the child, Piaget maintains that the system already available is not adequate to the youngster since it is in part unacceptable at very young age levels and is difficult to master. Under these circumstances, the child will continue an egocentric assimilation of reality in his actions and must utilize symbolic play (or imaginative play) to meet such needs. Concepts have not yet developed, and for this reason the period is referred to as preconceptual in nature.

The preconcepts developed by the child are really notions which he attaches to his verbal signs as he uses them. These notions are as apt to be restricted to the individuality of elements as they are to the generality of the concept. Piaget uses the example that a child of two years of age or so will be just as apt to say "the moon" as he will "the moons." There is little distinction on his part as to whether the observed reflection represents a single case at different times or a class of distinct individual cases. The very young child with developing language simply cannot deal with general classes since he does not distinguish between all and some. This level of preconceptual thought operates at some point between sensorimotor schema and the actual concept in terms of the way in which it is assimilated.

Intuitive Thought

Though preconceptual thought is distinguishable only in observation, by age four the young child has sufficient language to converse and therefore allow thought to be experimentally manipulated. The child may now deal with experimental objects, respond in a stable and communicable fashion, and according to Piaget, this admits of a new structuring. Conceptual behavior increases in the years from four to seven, even though it is still prelogical rather than logical. During this time in his life, the child uses intuitive reason and regulation, much analogous in a representative sense to the perceptual adjustments that he makes while on the sensory-motor plane in younger years.

To illustrate this stage of intellectual development, Piaget uses the example of lack of conservation of quantity in a child of this age. Two receptacles of identical size and shape are filled with an equal number of beads. The child recognizes that the containers have the same number of beads, and he observes as one of the containers is emptied into a different shape container. Under questioning the child then reports that the quantity of beads has changed. The reason for this error Piaget explains on the basis that the child is still operating at a prelogical level. At the same time, such intuitive thought represents a positive change in the thought level of the child. It is a significant development over preconceptual thought. There is now regulation of a type, though operations are not yet possible.

This matter of intuition versus operations is illustrated further in another example. Piaget says that if the child is given two glasses each of a different shape and asked to place a bead simultaneously in each glass, one bead with the left hand and another with the right hand, the child can maintain equivalence in the two receptacles if small numbers are used. But if the shapes of the receptacles change radically, even though the child places a bead simultaneously in each receptacle, he soon begins to lose the concept of equality. Once again, then, intuition has assumed expression of operation, and this is a reflection of the intellectual thought at this stage of a child's life.

This stage is further differentiated from later stages of intellectual development by the fact that the ability to express reversibility in thought is lacking. Through demonstration and tests, Piaget makes the point that the child between the ages of four and seven cannot mentally anticipate that half a turn will change a given order (abc) into its opposite (cba). Even when allowed to directly manipulate the materials, and thus determine that the half turn does operate in this fashion, the child cannot employ this knowledge in further relationships. When asked, for example, the effect of three half turns, he is unable to make an accurate prediction. The concept of position and effects of change, the matter of invariance in the middle position, and so on, are not possible until the child has reached a stage where some general grouping of the relations involved is mentally possible. This usually occurs around the age of seven.

As with its predecessor, preconceptual thought, Piaget maintains that intuitive thought comes directly from sensory-motor intelligence and is an extension of the first level.

> Just as the latter assimilates objects to response schemata, so intuition is always in the first place a kind of action carried out in thought; pouring from one vessel to another, establishing a correspondence, joining, serializing, displacing, etc., are still response schemata to which representation assimilates reality. But the accommodation of these schemata to objects, instead of remaining practical, provides imitation or imaginal significants which enable the same assimilation to occur in thought. So in the second place, intuition is an imaginal thought, more refined than that of the previous period, since it concerns complex configurations and not merely simple syncretic collections symbolized by type-individuals; but it still uses representative symbolism and therefore constantly exhibits some of the limitations that are inherent in this (Piaget, 1960, p. 137-138).

Despite the gains in intellectual level, there is still in intuitive thought the absence of transitive, reversible, and associative combinativity. Intuitive thought is largely phenomenological and egocentric. But during this period, there is a gradual movement in the direction of some articulated intuitions, which are leading toward the possibility of reversibility and the development of operations.

Concrete Operations

At some point in the life of the child, then, articulated intuitions become operational systems. The determination of the presence of a systematic mode of thought is always rapid and sometimes quite sudden, according to Piaget. Its determination cannot be based on prior definitions. But the sudden nature should not be overstressed, as Piaget makes clear by speaking of operations as being ". . . formed by a kind of thawing out of intuitive structures . . ." (p. 139). The problem is to determine the internal process which brings a transition from some level of intuitive thought to the kind of mobile equilibrium which represents operations.

The answer is reflected in the appearance of the principle of conservation of quantity. The principle of grouping is now available to the child and is used by him. For example, in the problem cited previously of two glasses containing beads with one glass poured into a glass of a different size, when the child reaches the stage of concrete operations, he now knows that the quantity remains unchanged despite the change in receptacles. Now, then, intuitive relations have been combined so that transformations of reversibility, combinativity and identity are possible. "Grouping" has occurred. The psychological nature of the grouping is dependent upon what Piaget refers to as "complete decentralization" of "complete conversion of thought." Before this stage of intellectual development, the child has always centered on some particular state of the object viewed and some point of view that is peculiar to him as an individual. In the level of operations, thinking no longer is related only to particular states of the object but now allows certain kinds of detours and reversals. Different kinds of viewpoints may be realized and combined in an objective fashion. There is now an equilibrium between the object and the accommodation of the individual to subjective aspects of objects.

Despite the fact that, with concrete operations, different logical, arithmetical, and spatio-temporal groupings are possible, formal logical groupings which may be applied to all ideas and reasoning is not yet present in the child. Piaget feels that this is an essential point when considering educational applications of his theory of intelligence. If teaching is to be adapted to the developmental stage of the child rather than to the logical bias of the traditional approaches in curriculum setting, this fact must be appreciated and employed. The child may reach the operational level where he can manipulate objects yet fail with even very simple verbal compositions. This is the reason for calling this level "concrete." The operations are not yet formal; they remain closely related to action. There is, of course, a logical structure employing the speech that is necessary to expression. This however, does not mean that the child can carry on a logical discourse independent of action.

This matter is further complicated by the fact that the child may employ conservation, transitivity, and equivalence, with one kind of material or kind of idea, and yet be unable to employ the same principles with other systems of ideas. This stresses all the more the lack of formal logic in the child of this age level up to about twelve. The groupings which he has, then, are still closely related to kinds of concrete ideas which have been structured prior to the age of eight.

Formal Operations

Around age twelve formal thought begins and reaches its maximum during adolescence, according to Piaget. An adolescent differs from the child in that he can think beyond the present and is capable of formulating theories about events and ideas. There is an increasing ability to reason in a hypothetic-deductive manner from age twelve onward.

There is a new mode of reasoning which has not been possible to the individual before. In this level of formal thought, the individual reflects on operations, with the result that he is now operating on operations or the results of operations. Piaget believes that the same operational content is involved at this stage, so that there is still the matter of classing, serializing, enumerating, and so on. But such classification, serialization and the like are not what is now grouped in the formal operation procedure. What the individual does now is to group propositions that will express such operations. "Formal operations, therefore, consist essentially of 'implications' (in the narrow sense of the word) and 'contradictions' established between propositions which themselves express classifications, seriations, etc." (page 149).

Formal logic, as a final stage, does not describe all thought. Indeed, the formal operations of adolescents are a structure representing the final equilibrium evolving from the prior stage of concrete operations, which in turn have evolved from lower levels of intellectual process. There is, thus, a hierarchy of developmental stages in intellectual growth which may be identified and specifically dealt with, according to Piaget.

Social Influences on Intellectual Development

Society plays an important part in the development of the individual by the fact that it provides him with certain signs which influence his thought as well as compelling him to recognize certain facts. In this particular, Piaget maintains that society has a greater influence on the structures of the individual than even the physical environment. There is, then, the matter of socialization of the intelligence of the individual.

During the period of sensorimotor intelligence, social influences are strongly exerted on the infant. The child receives from other persons the greatest pleasures that he knows: from the provision for physical needs to the development and provision for psychological needs. Both positive and negative reinforcers may be employed, but for some time they reflect only kinds of signals rather than rules for the child. Since the child is incapable of thought, he reacts to signs only as signals. There is, then, very little extensive gratification of intellectual structures as a result of the social life in early infancy.

As language is acquired, however, social relationships exert a more profound influence on the thought of the individual. There are three matters which Piaget feels should be understood about the social influences of developing language. First, in initial stages of language development, the individual symbol is still of greater influence on the child than the collective sign. Second, language does give the child a prepared system of ideas, classifications, etc. He uses from the collection only those which he wishes, ignoring all that is beyond his mental level. What is assimilated is dependent upon the intellectual structure of the individual. Third, the acquisition of language and the modes of thought associated with language are subject to different influences. The former of these is influenced by social relations, which guide the child to accept certain intellectual values and a large number of ready-made ideas and behavioral norms. Still, at least to about the age of seven, egocentrism will exert its influence on what is accepted by the child. As a result, the structures that are associated with preoperational levels of thought preclude forming of cooperative social functions which will lead to logic.

With the appearance of concrete operations, the possibility of social cooperation increases. With such cooperation, logic may begin to develop. Logic, then, represents some complex of awareness, intellectual feelings, responses, all of which are influenced to some degree by social interrelationships. To Piaget, logic requires some norms because it reflects a morality of thinking that is bestowed and accepted by other individuals. The individual avoids self-contradiction not only because it is necessary to operational stability, but also because it is a kind of moral imperative necessary to intellectual interaction in cooperation. Words and ideas must show a certain amount of constancy and meaning, again, not only for conditions of operational thought but also as a social obligation.

Cause and effect are explainable from two different viewpoints. When the question is raised as to whether or not grouping is cause or effect of cooperation, Piaget maintains that there are two distinct and complementary answers. First of all, if there were not some interchange of thought in cooperation with other persons, an individual could never group operations into some coherent whole. From this viewpoint, social life must be the basis upon which operational grouping occurs. Conversely, any exchange of thought from one individual to another presupposes some law of equilibrium that will allow operational groupings. In this viewpoint, the equilibrating nature of grouping is autonomous for social life to have any effect.

Testing Intelligence

Phillips (1969), in a discussion of the meaning of Piaget's theory of intelligence, describes a test currently being developed to measure intelligence from the Piagetian viewpoint. As Phillips points out, Piaget's observational methods differ radically from the traditional means of testing mental ability. However, the kind of system employed by Piaget should allow testing, though this will be novel in the sense of most conventionally accepted tests. The test is being developed by Pinard and his colleagues at the University of Montreal. According to Phillips, it is an attempt to employ Piaget's methods of fairness and flexibility in questioning with more traditional psychometric methods emphasizing standardization in the administration of the test.

Traditionally, in the development of scales based upon Binet's approach, a percentage-passing technique has been employed in the placement of items. By contrast, the test being developed at Montreal employs the developmental approach such that the child's performance will reflect a stage of development evolved from observation and theory. Test items, then, will not be located according to percentage passing but in terms of significant aspects of stages of development.

Another distinction lies in the administration of the test. In traditional testing of the Binet type, a highly structured interview technique is used in the sense that no variance in questioning or scoring is allowed. Items are scored plus or minus with no feedback to the individual and no attempt to determine reasons for wrong answers. In an approach employing the Piaget model, a wrong answer may give more information about the intellectual development of the child than a right answer. Particularly is this true if the reason for a wrong response can be determined for the particular child. This is so since the questions are chosen in such a way that the child may demonstrate the quality of his thinking. Each successive item, rather than being determined strictly by a standardized, structured procedure, will be determined by the content of the response made to the preceding item in the Piaget approach. There is much less structure, then, in this new intelligence test than has been usually found in conventional testing.

In the quantification of the Binet scales, each item has the same value, regardless of difficulty. For this reason, a mental age determined from a Stanford-Binet does not reflect a genetic stage of development for the individual child. Instead, the score achieved on a Stanford-Binet is a sum of items passed in a series of gradually increased level of difficulty over one or more age levels. By contrast, the approach taken with the new Piaget-type scale developed in Montreal emphasizes qualitative analysis of performance for scoring purposes. This qualitative analysis will disclose the child's level of intellectual development.

As Phillips points out, a highly trained specialist will be necessary in the administration of a test of this type. Since the format is unstructured, the psychometrist of the conventional type will be ill-equipped to administer and interpret such a test. Whoever administers the test must have a thorough understanding of Piaget's theory in order to determine what questions to ask next. One problem may lie in the testing time required. Phillips reports that in standardizing the test, the average individual testing time was about ten hours. Though, in the development of the instrument, some reduction may be expected in time needed for testing with precision, the test may be administered over a period of several days rather than in a single sitting.

But, as Phillips points out, the Piaget-type scale could very well bring information on a number of questions not previously investigated due to limitations in the scales available to us. We may be able to attain a more precise notion of intellectual development in given children, and thus be able to determine appropriate curricula objectively and accurately.

References

I. J. P. Guilford

Guilford, J. P., "A New Revision of the Army Alpha Examination and a Weighted Scoring for Three Primary Factors," *Journal of Applied Psychology,* 1938, 22, 239–246.

———, "Human Abilities," *Psychological Review,* 1940, 47, 367–394.

———, "New Standards for Test Evaluation," *Educational and Psychological Measurement,* 1946, 6, 427, 438.

———, "Some Recent Findings on Thinking Abilities and Their Implications," *Journal of Communications,* 1953, 3, 49–58.

————, "The Structure of Intellect," *Psychological Bulletin,* 1956, 53, 267–293.

————, *Personality.* New York: McGraw-Hill 1959.

————, "Factors That Aid and Hinder Creativity," *Teachers College Record,* 1962, 63, 380–392.

————, "Intelligence; 1965 Model," *American Psychologist,* 1966, 21, 20–26.

————, *The Nature of Human Intelligence.* New York: McGraw-Hill, 1967a.

————, "Creativity: Yesterday, Today, and Tomorrow," *Journal of Creative Behavior,* 1967b, 1, 3–14.

————, and Guilford, Ruth B., "A Prognostic Test for Students in Design," *Journal of Applied Psychology,* 1931, 15, 335–345.

————, and Guilford, Ruth B., "Personality Factors *X, S, E,* and *M,* and Their Measurement," *Journal of Psychology,* 1936, 2, 109–127.

————, and Guilford, Ruth B., "Personality Factors *D, R, T,* and *A." Journal of Abnormal and Social Psychology,* 1939, 34, 21–36.

————, Hendricks, Moana, and Hoepner, R., "Solving Social Problems Creatively," *Journal of Creative Behavior,* 1968, 2, 155–164.

II. Jean Piaget

Phillips, J. L., Jr., *The Origins of Intellect: Piaget's Theory.* San Francisco: W. H. Freeman, 1969.

Piaget, J., *The Psychology of Intelligence.* Translated by M. Piercy and D. E. Berlyne. Paterson, N.J.: Littlefield, Adams, 1960.

————, *The Origins of Intelligence in Children.* Translated by Margaret Cook. New York: International Universities Press, 1952.

10

Epilog: A Summary and Evaluation

In 1896, Binet and Henri proposed that the behaviors emanating from intelligence may be expressed in two directions. There is, first, the possibility of a variety of mental functions, each of which is of significance in its own right. They paid tribute to such a notion by speaking of abilities such as judgment, reasoning, memory, and so on. Such abilities, in so far as they exist and are measured, should be reflected in the items included in the scales devised by him and Simon. At the same time, Binet made it clear that his major interest and emphasis was not in the direction of identifying what the mental traits might be nor even specifically how to measure them. Instead, his interest was in determining the combination of whatever abilities exist and in expressing these in a general score. This combination of abilities in a general mode of functioning represents the second direction.

In the efforts immediately following the work of Binet, primarily in this country, the notion of general ability expressed as some sum of performances on a variety of types of items was paramount. Most tests developed, beginning with Terman, were devised to measure "general" ability. Even scales with specific subtests provided a total score, a tacit acceptance of the importance of "general intelligence." Particularly with the work of Spearman, however, and its extrapolation in this country by the Thurstones and Guilford, more intense efforts to identify the traits which might be specific and which might be measured independently began and continued. In more recent years, it is fair to say that much more effort is being expended toward identifying specific types of abilities than in developing precise and rigorous measures of general ability. One major change since the publication of the 1905 Binet-Simon Scale is this movement from some arbitrary general score to a set of specific scores.

Implications of General and Specific Approaches

The course of development, then, has reflected two schools of thought about the measurement of intelligence. The Binet approach, found in his test and followed by his adherents, has tended to reflect a generalist position. Here, some sampling of a number of types of abilities, usually without designating specifically what these abilities may be, is combined into a total score which is thought to be representative of the general intellectual functioning of the individual. Items may reflect more than one faculty simultaneously. If the sample of items and their combination are representative, the score should be usable for prediction to a number of general-behavior situations. For example, the child who performs well on a Binet-type scale and achieves a high score, should perform, generally, quite well in academic work. One could not predict from his score how he would perform specifically in such areas as mathematics, science, history, and so on. There may be differences in the level of performance from one area to another; the child should perform above the norms in all areas, however, if the general measure is adequate.

There are rather obvious limitations to such an approach, limitations which have been recognized and debated since Binet began his work. Perhaps the most pertinent one is that items are most often selected and included in the test on the basis of capacity to discriminate between two groups of known characteristics. The "general" measure predicts school achievement well because it is built to do so. Whether several factors of intelligence are measured, what they may be, and what their combination is in general ability, are questions left unanswered. A case in point is the 1937 Stanford-Binet, and the factor analysis undertaken by McNemar (1942, pp. 99–138). The possibility of "general" intelligence and its measurement, either theoretically or practically, is not disproved by the norming procedure. One may debate, however, whether any test actually measures general ability in the strict sense.

Measures of specific abilities, commonly determined by factor analysis, should, then, be superior in demonstrating designated behaviors. If the traits which are identified are independent of each other and yet correlated with ability, it should be possible to make prediction of a specific type for individuals. Such prediction should not be restricted just to school settings but to specific aspects of life as well. Particularly should it be possible to deal with prediction for the individual since the behavior pattern on the subtest may be correlated with specific behaviors in other settings. This goal has seemed as unattainable, practically, as the effects of general intelligence. Reasons for this fact will be presented in later discussion.

Considerations in Test Selection

Both types of tests have remained popular to the present time. Perhaps in given settings one test will preponderate over the other; but in most settings the examiner will choose the instrument appropriate to the kind of prediction he wishes to make. Indeed, decisions about testing based upon whether the test itself is of a general or specific type are simplistic. Either approach contains the possibility of error so that the psychometrist must exercise care in the selection of the test. There is, first of all, the implicit assumption whenever we use a test that the test setting itself is representative of the situation to which prediction is to be made. It does not take much experience for the psychometrist to become aware of the fact that the test setting is atypical rather that typical. In the use of individual instruments, for example, a child or adult is isolated in a room with another adult, perhaps totally a stranger to the individual, and asked a series of questions about which, in the majority of instances, he has not had instruction.

The setting and procedure under which individual testing is done, then, cannot be defensible for the types of predictions which are desired. Whenever we assume that the test setting itself is representative of other behavioral situations, the probability of error is increased. The content of the test, the care with which it has been built and normed, and the degree to which demonstrable predictive situations have been identified, all assume the burden for demonstrating utility of the score obtained with the instrument. It is not possible to overemphasize the necessity for the psychometrist to be more than a mere mechanic. Proficiency in administration of the WISC, the Stanford-Binet, or any other test is hardly sufficient, however necessary such skill may be. A psychometrist, to be truly proficient, must be familiar with the content of a variety of tests, each of which at one time or another may be used by him for the specific purposes for which referrals are made. There is added to the burden of test content, therefore, the burden for the psychometrist of being totally informed.

Using Individual Tests

Individual tests were devised for purposes of making decisions and predictions about the individual. Only a superficial acquaintance with individual tests, however, indicates that data relevant to test scores is based upon groups. The possibility of an error in prediction about the individual will consequently be greater than will be the prediction for groups. For this reason some psychometrists will tend to use the more general measure simply because it will not put them in the position of making highly specific statements about the individual. In so far as such statements are pertinent to the referral problem, no contention can be made with this issue. But for many other situations, such general statements will not be so worthwhile. As a result, those tests which have tended to adopt a specific approach to the measurement of ability will find increasing acceptance and use. On the face of the matter, it would seem that such specific tests should be usable for more accurate individual prediction. Unfortunately, such is not the case. One reason for this is the fact that tests which measure in specific areas are devised primarily on a statistical basis, and therefore less on the basis of human performance. From a large pool of items, those items for which group performance is interrelated, but which are independent of other clusters, will be selected as specific abilities. If measures of "general ability" suffer from lack of demonstration of traits composing the general ability, measures of specific ability suffer from lack of demonstration of behavioral importance. Though factorially "pure" the utility of the measures is undisclosed.

One major area for tests with specific sub-parts is the demonstration of validity for behavioral situations. This particularly becomes an issue as more and more specific traits are identified. For example, the structure of intellect proposed by Guilford has lacked much utility even though factorially pure tests were available to fit within that structure. For the question of the purpose to which such tests might be put, there was little or no answer. Meeker's (1969) application of tests from the structure of intellect in the school setting for specific problems of prediction is necessary and heartening. Continuation of such efforts will demonstrate limitations and consequent strengths in such specific measures so that utility may be expanded in the future. In the meantime, the psychometrist must not accept on face value the subtests and their titles. This is particularly true in such instruments as the Wechsler Scales. Not only are these not factorially pure tests, but the basis for their inclusion in the test in the first place is not always clear. In brief, the promise of the specific instrument has not yet been assured, though the future may indeed fulfil such promise.

Issues of Reliability and Validity

There is another point of some concern in the use of all tests, but one which is especially relevant to specific measures that yield individual subtest scores. As the test is subdivided, score expressions become more error-prone as a consequence of reduced reliability. It is not unusual to find that subtests have lower reliabilities than total test scores, and consequently have higher standard errors of measurement. Any prediction about subtest performance must be influenced by this fact. Particularly if subtest differences are to be used, error must be considered. Thorndike and Hagen (1955) have demonstrated that difference scores are subject to increased error, whether between total tests or between subtests. As a result, difference scores will contain greater error than either subtest alone. Statistical means for determining the amount of error under these circumstances are available and the psychometrist should be familiar with and use them. Essentially, the procedure followed in difference scores removes common factors but leaves error from both sources. The role of error is consequently increased. If some "pattern" of differences among subtests is used, the error increases by the amount of error in each subtest; hence, differences in scores become less reliable and more susceptible to predictive error.

The development of specific tests has caused measurement experts to re-examine concepts of reliability and validity. Traditionally, validity has been considered only in relation to reliability. Certain of the more specific, factorially pure tests, exhibit very low reliability. Several writers in the field of ability measurement, including Guilford, have pointed to the need to reappraise this traditional approach in terms of newer kinds of testing. Such a reappraisal seems reasonable and necessary as more factorially pure tests are developed. There is a possibility under such circumstances that validity may be obtained with very little reliability. As astounding as this statement would be to many test experts of past generations, it is one which must be increasingly accepted for validation today. It does seem plausible that a test of "originality" may have low reliability but very high validity for specific forms of behavior and outcomes. This may be true less because of the trait than because of the method of measurement, where many responses to a relatively restricted item may be acceptable. This issue will become an increasingly important one in testing of all sorts, including intelligence testing, in the future.

A Note on the Future of Testing

Significant strides have been made since the early publications of Binet in the matter of defining and measuring intellectual ability. Indeed, it seems reasonable to state that we know more about the psychological trait of ability than we do about any other single psychological trait. This includes both limitations and strengths of our measures and predictions.

A subsidiary issue has become increasingly prominent in recent years. The whole matter of testing for ability, the meaning of the measure, and the fairness of predictions made from the measures will be increasingly exploited apparently in the next decade or two. Faults must be corrected, bias inimical to individual development and functioning removed, and error increasingly stabilized and controlled for. Substituting ignorance for experience will not do this job. For this reason, the testing movement should continue and should benefit from its critics, so long as the ultimate outcome is not destruction. Perhaps it will be necessary to change types of scores used; certainly, it will be necessary to expand our viewpoint of intelligence and its expressions and measurement. This latter point is already under way to a considerable degree. In any event, current threats are not a part of the problem of measurement and expression of intelligence as such. Wechsler (1968) has discussed this issue lucidly and thoroughly. Hopefully, such arguments as he presents will be heard and adhered to by school personnel, clinicians, and others in a decision-making capacity.

One of the interesting outcomes of a survey of the type conducted in this book is the point that no theory or model has become the basis of developing a test, except possibly the work of Guilford. One might almost consider the matter of intelligence from two viewpoints: one philosophical and the other pragmatic. It would be possible, and indeed intellectually stimulating, to study the philosophy of intelligence in its own right. Under such a heading might be included the various theories that have been proposed from the time of Binet to the present. Independently, then, the matter of measurement and utilization of these outcomes could be studied. Certainly the psychometrist who is exposed to both kinds of knowledge and uses them in his work should be superior to that psychometrist who is little more than a mechanic.

References

Binet, A., and Henri, V., "La Psychologie Individuelle," *L'Année Psychologique*, 1896, 2, 411–465.

McNemar, Q., *The Revision of the Stanford-Binet Scale: An Analysis of the Standardization Data.* Boston: Houghton Mifflin, 1942.

Meeker, Mary Nacol, *The Structure of Intellect: Its Interpretation and Uses.* Columbus, Ohio: Charles E. Merrill, 1969.

Thorndike, R. L., and Hagen, Elizabeth, *Measurement and Evaluation in Psychology and Education.* New York: Wiley, 1955. Pp. 190–194.

Wechsler, D., "The I.Q. Is An Intelligence Test," New York Times Magazine, June 26, 1966. Reprinted in R. K. Parker (ed.), *Readings in Educational Psychology.* Boston: Allyn and Bacon, 1968. Pp. 299–306.

Subject Index

Author Index